P9-ASE-958

PRACTICAL
META-ANALYSIS

Applied Social Research Methods Series
Volume 49

APPLIED SOCIAL RESEARCH METHODS SERIES

Series Editors
LEONARD BICKMAN, Peabody College, Vanderbilt University, Nashville
DEBRA J. ROG, Vanderbilt University, Washington, DC

Other volumes in this series are listed at the end of the book

PRACTICAL META-ANALYSIS

Mark W. Lipsey
David B. Wilson

Applied Social Research Methods Series
Volume 49

SAGE Publications
International Educational and Professional Publisher
Thousand Oaks London New Delhi

Copyright © 2001 by Sage Publications, Inc.

All rights reserved. No part of this book may be reproduced or utilized in any form or by any means, electronic or mechanical, including photocopying, recording, or by any information storage and retrieval system, without permission in writing from the publisher.

For information address:

SAGE Publications, Inc.
2455 Teller Road
Thousand Oaks, California 91320
e-mail: order@sagepub.com

SAGE Publications Ltd.
6 Bonhill Street
London EC2A 4PU
United Kingdom

SAGE Publications India Pvt. Ltd.
M-32 Market
Greater Kailash I
New Delhi 110 048 India

Printed in the United States of America

Library of Congress Cataloging-in-Publication Data

Lipsey, Mark W.
  Practical meta-analysis / by Mark W. Lipsey & David B. Wilson.
    p. cm. — (Applied social research methods series ; v. 49)
  Includes bibliographical references and index.
  ISBN 978-0-7619-2167-7 (alk. paper). — ISBN 978-0-7619-2168-4 (pbk. : alk. paper)
    1. Meta-analysis. 2. Social sciences—Statistical methods. I. Wilson, David B., 1961– II.
  Title. III Series.

  HA29 .L83153 2000
  300'.7'2—dc21

                                                                    00-035379

This book is printed on acid-free paper.

09   10   9

Acquiring Editor: C. Deborah Laughton
Editorial Assistant: Eileen Carr
Sage Production Editor: Sanford Robinson
Typesetter: Technical Typesetting Inc.

Contents

Acknowledgments

We thank Steve Leff and his colleagues at HSRI for stimulating the initial meta-analysis "toolkit" that has evolved into this volume and for helping improve the final product. Our appreciation also goes to Sandra Jo Wilson for generously sharing the juvenile delinquency challenge meta-analysis used as a running example throughout this book, to Will Shadish for his valuable suggestions and encouragement as the manuscript progressed, to Jim Derzon for his spirited partnership in the many meta-analysis projects that sharpened our understanding of the craft, and to Laurie Samuels for her assiduous work on the index. Finally, to the many students who labored through draft versions in our workshops and seminars, we offer a special thanks for your patience and tactful editorial assistance.

To Bill Garvey, who painted the big picture in his seminar room
as in his studio. MWL

To Sue for all of her love and support. DBW

1

Introduction

In 1952, Hans Eysenck started a raging debate in clinical psychology by arguing that psychotherapy had no beneficial effects on patients (Eysenck, 1952). By the mid-1970s, hundreds of studies of psychotherapy had produced a dizzying array of positive, null, and negative results, and reviews of those studies had failed to resolve the debate. To assess Eysenck's claim, Gene V. Glass statistically standardized and averaged treatment-control differences for 375 psychotherapy studies, calling his method "meta-analysis." He and his colleague, Mary Lee Smith, published their results in a now classic paper, concluding that psychotherapy was indeed effective (Smith & Glass, 1977). Eysenck was unconvinced and attempted to discredit the method by calling it "an exercise in mega-silliness" (1978). Despite the criticisms of Eysenck and other scholars, meta-analysis is now widely accepted as a method of summarizing the results of empirical studies within the behavioral, social, and health sciences.

At about the same time that Glass was developing his method of meta-analysis, similar statistical approaches to research synthesis were being crafted by Rosenthal and Rubin (1978) in the area of interpersonal expectancy effects and by Schmidt and Hunter (1977) in the area of validity generalization of employment tests. The term *meta-analysis* has come to encompass all of the methods and techniques of quantitative research synthesis developed by these and other researchers. Since the pioneering work in the 1970s, literally thousands of meta-analyses have been conducted and great improvements have been made in meta-analysis methodology.

SITUATIONS TO WHICH META-ANALYSIS IS APPLICABLE

Meta-analysis can be understood as a form of survey research in which research reports, rather than people, are surveyed. A coding form (survey protocol) is developed, a sample or population of research reports is gathered, and each research study is "interviewed" by a coder who reads it carefully and codes the appropriate information about its characteristics and quantitative findings. The resulting data are then analyzed using special adaptations of conventional statistical techniques to investigate and describe the pattern of findings in the selected set of studies.

Meta-analysis is only one of many ways to summarize, integrate, and interpret selected sets of scholarly works in the various disciplines and it has an important, but somewhat circumscribed domain of applicability. First, meta-analysis applies only to empirical research studies; it cannot be used to summarize theoretical papers, conventional research reviews, policy proposals, and the like. Second, it applies only to research studies that produce quantitative findings, that is, studies using quantitative measurement of variables and reporting descriptive or inferential statistics to summarize the resulting data. This rules out qualitative forms of research such as case studies, ethnography, and "naturalistic" inquiry. Third, meta-analysis is a technique for encoding and analyzing the statistics that summarize research findings as they are typically presented in research reports. If the full data sets for the studies of interest are available, it will generally be more appropriate and informative to analyze them directly using conventional procedures rather than meta-analyze summary statistics.

In addition, because meta-analysis focuses on the aggregation and comparison of the findings of different research studies, it is necessary that those findings be of a sort that can be meaningfully compared. This means that the findings must (a) be conceptually comparable, that is, deal with the same constructs and relationships and (b) be configured in similar statistical forms. For instance, a set of studies of the effectiveness of treatment for depression could be meta-analyzed if the various treatments were judged to be appropriate for comparison with each other and if treatment findings were in the same basic form, e.g., measures of depression contrasted for a treatment and control group of respondents. It would not generally be appropriate to include studies of distinctly different topics in the same meta-analysis, e.g., studies of treatment for depression and studies of gender differences in spatial visualization. This is often referred to as the "apples and oranges" problem in meta-analysis—attempting to summarize or integrate over studies that do not really deal with the same constructs and relationships.

Similarly, it is not generally appropriate to combine study findings derived from different research designs and appearing in different statistical forms, even if they deal with the same topic. For instance, experimental studies of treatment for depression using treatment versus control group comparisons generally would not be combined with observational studies in which level of depression was correlated with level of service received. Though both types of study deal in some fashion with the relationship between treatment and depression, the differences in the research designs, the nature of the quantitative relationships constituting the findings, and the meaning of those findings are so great that they would be difficult to incorporate in the same meta-analysis. Of course, one might separately meta-analyze the experimental findings and correlational findings, using appropriate procedures for each, and then draw some conclusions across both meta-analyses.

The set of findings included in a meta-analysis must result from comparable research designs for practical reasons as well as conceptual ones. Meta-analysis represents each study's findings in the form of *effect sizes*. An effect size is a statistic that encodes the critical quantitative information from each relevant study finding. Different types of study findings generally require different effect size statistics. Studies that produce bivariate correlations, for instance, are typically meta-analyzed using a different effect size statistic than studies that compare groups of subjects on the mean values of dependent variables. Similarly, findings that report pre–post mean differences for a single subject sample use a still different effect size statistic, and there are others even more specialized.

Given comparable statistical forms, the definition of what study findings are conceptually comparable for purposes of meta-analysis is often fixed only in the eye of the beholder. Findings that appear categorically different to one analyst may seem similar to another. Glass's meta-analysis of the effectiveness of psychotherapy (Smith & Glass, 1977), for instance, was criticized for combining findings from distinctly different therapies, e.g., cognitive behavioral, psychodynamic, gestalt, etc. Glass claimed that his interest was in the overall effectiveness of the whole broad class of psychotherapies and in comparisons between the different types, hence all had to be represented in the meta-analysis. Another analyst might have a narrower interest and meta-analyze only study findings on, say, desensitization therapy for snake phobias. In either case, however, it is essential that the analyst have a definition of the domain of interest and a rationale for the inclusion and exclusion of studies from the meta-analysis. Others may criticize that definition and rationale but, as long as they are explicit, each reviewer can judge for him or herself whether they are meaningful.

THE KEY CONCEPT
OF EFFECT SIZE

Given a set of quantitative research findings judged to deal with the same topic and involve comparable research designs, a significant problem still remains for anyone who wants to encode those results into a database that can be meaningfully analyzed. With rare exceptions, such studies will not use the same operationalizations (measurement procedures) for their key variables. Say, for instance, we select comparison group studies of the effectiveness of treatment for depression. Some studies may use Beck's depression inventory as the outcome variable, some may use the Hamilton rating scale for depression, some may use therapists' ratings of depression, and some may have other idiosyncratic but reasonable measures of this construct. With these quite different measures yielding different numerical values that are meaningful only in relation to the specific operationalizations and scales used, how can their quantitative findings be encoded in a way that allows them to be statistically combined and compared?

The answer relates to an essential feature of meta-analysis, indeed, the feature that makes meta-analysis possible and provides the hub around which the entire process revolves. The various effect size statistics used to code different forms of quantitative study findings in meta-analysis are based on the concept of *standardization*. The effect size statistic produces a statistical standardization of the study findings such that the resulting numerical values are interpretable in a consistent fashion across all the variables and measures involved. Standardization in this context has much the same meaning it does when we speak of standardized scores in testing and measurement. For instance, we might convert mathematics achievement test scores to percentiles, or z-scores standardized on the standard deviation of a sample of scores, and thus be able to compare them meaningfully with a different variable, e.g., reading achievement scores. Johnny may be at the 85th percentile on math but only at the 60th percentile on reading.

In similar fashion, the most common effect size statistics in meta-analysis standardize on the variation in the sample distributions of scores for the measures of interest. Thus the mean difference between a treatment and a control group on the Beck's depression inventory can be represented in terms of standard deviation units, as can the mean ratings of therapists, and all such other quantitative measures of depression. In the metric of standard deviation units, one can combine and compare results across different measures and operationalizations. A study using Beck's depression inventory may show a difference of .30 standard deviations between treatment and control group while a study using therapists' ratings may show a difference of .42 standard deviations. Assuming the same underlying population from which the respective samples are drawn, we can compare these numbers, use them in statistical analysis to compute means, variances, correlations, and the like, and generally treat them as meaningful indicators of the same thing—in this case, differences between the amount of depression experienced by respondents in the treatment group and those in the control group relative to the estimated population variability on depression.

The key to meta-analysis, therefore, is defining an effect size statistic capable of representing the quantitative findings of a set of research studies in a standardized form that permits meaningful numerical comparison and analysis across the studies. There are many possibilities. The dichotomous categorization of study findings into those that are statistically significant and those that are not is a rudimentary form of effect size. A slightly more differentiated version is the *p*-value (e.g., $p = .03$, $p = .50$) for each statistical significance test (Becker, 1994). These, however, are not very good effect size statistics. The more desirable forms index both the *magnitude* and the *direction* of a relationship, not merely its statistical significance. In addition, they are defined so that there is relatively little confounding with other issues, such as sample size, which figures prominently in significance test results.

The meta-analyst should use an effect size statistic that provides appropriate standardization for the particular research design, form of quantitative finding, variables, and operationalizations presented in the set of studies under investigation. There are many effect size statistics that are workable for one circumstance or another but, in practice, only a few are widely used. Most empirical findings fall into one of several generic categories for which specific effect size statistics and related statistical procedures are developed and are widely recognized. A range of useful effect size statistics is defined in Chapter 3 along with the research situations to which they are most applicable.

THE STRENGTHS OF META-ANALYSIS

Why should one consider using meta-analysis to summarize and analyze a body of research studies rather than conventional research reviewing techniques? There are basically four reasons that constitute the primary advantages of meta-analysis.

First, meta-analysis procedures impose a useful discipline on the process of summarizing research findings. Good meta-analysis is conducted as a structured research technique in its own right and hence requires that each step be documented and open to scrutiny. It involves specification of the criteria that define the population of study findings at issue, organized search strategies to identify and retrieve eligible studies, formal coding of study characteristics and findings, and data analysis to support the conclusions that are drawn. By making the research summarizing process explicit and systematic, the consumer can assess the author's assumptions, procedures, evidence, and conclusions rather than take on faith that the conclusions are valid.

Second, meta-analysis represents key study findings in a manner that is more differentiated and sophisticated than conventional review procedures that rely on qualitative summaries or "vote-counting" on statistical significance. By encoding the magnitude and direction of each relevant statistical relationship in a collection of studies, meta-analysis effect sizes constitute a variable sensitive to findings of different strength across studies. By contrast, using statistical significance to differentiate studies that find effects from those that do not is potentially quite misleading. Statistical significance reflects both the magnitude of the estimated effect and the sampling error around that estimate, the latter almost entirely a function of sample size. Thus, studies with small samples may find effects or relationships of meaningful magnitude that are not statistically significant because of low statistical power (Lipsey, 1990; Schmidt, 1992, 1996).

Third, meta-analysis is capable of finding effects or relationships that are obscured in other approaches to summarizing research. Qualitative, narrative summaries of findings, while informative, do not lend themselves to detailed scrutiny of the differences between studies and associated differences in their findings. The systematic coding of study characteristics typical in meta-analysis, on the other hand, permits an analytically precise examination of the relationships between study findings and such study features as respondent characteristics, nature of treatment, research design, and measurement procedures. Furthermore, by estimating the size of the effect in each study and pooling those estimates across studies (giving greater weight to larger studies), meta-analysis produces synthesized effect estimates with considerably more statistical power than individual studies. Thus, meaningful effects and relationships upon which studies agree, and differential effects related to study differences, are both more likely to be discovered by meta-analysis than by less systematic and analytic approaches.

Fourth, meta-analysis provides an organized way of handling information from a large number of study findings under review. When the number of studies or amount of information extracted from each study passes a fairly low threshold, note-taking or coding on index cards cannot effectively keep track of all the details. The systematic coding procedures of meta-analysis and the construction of a computerized database to record the resulting information, by contrast, have almost unlimited capability for detailing information from each study and covering large numbers of studies. A meta-analysis conducted by one of the authors of this volume, for instance, resulted in a database of more than 150 items of information for each of nearly 500 studies (Lipsey, 1992). We hasten to add, however, that meta-analysis does not require large numbers of studies and, in some circumstances, can be usefully applied to as few as two or three study findings.

THE WEAKNESSES OF META-ANALYSIS

Meta-analysis is not without disadvantages and it is the subject of harsh criticism from some quarters (Sharpe, 1997). One disadvantage of meta-analysis is simply the amount of effort and expertise it takes. Properly done, a meta-analysis with more than a handful of study findings is labor intensive and takes considerably more time than a conventional qualitative research review. Additionally, many aspects of meta-analysis require specialized knowledge, especially the selection and computation of appropriate effect sizes and the application of statistical analysis to them. The major objective of this book, of course, is to make that specialized knowledge available at a practical level to interested persons who wish to conduct, or understand, meta-analysis.

Another concern about meta-analysis relates to its structured and somewhat mechanical procedures, which, in other regard, can be viewed as strengths. For some applications (and some critics say for all applications), the relatively objective coding of data elements and effect sizes from research studies, and the type of analysis to which such data lend themselves, may not be sensitive to important issues, e.g., the social context of the study, theoretical influences and implications, methodological quality, more subtle or complex aspects of design, procedure, or results, and the like. To draw on the survey research analogy used earlier, meta-analysis is a structured, closed-ended questionnaire approach to summarizing research findings. Some survey applications require a more open-ended approach, e.g., unstructured interviews or focus groups, to deal with the complexity or subtlety of certain topics. It may well be that some research issues also require a more qualitative assessment and summary than meta-analysis can provide. Of course, there is no reason in principle why both meta-analytic and qualitative reviews cannot be done on the same body of research findings, with overall conclusions drawn from both. One approach to meta-analysis, what Slavin (1986, 1995) calls *best evidence synthesis*, attempts to do just that, combining qualitative and quantitative reviewing techniques in the same research review.

Perhaps the most persistent criticism of meta-analysis has to do with the mix of studies included (the apples and oranges issue mentioned earlier). Critics argue, with some justification, that mean effect sizes and other such summary statistics produced by meta-analysis are not meaningful if they are aggregated over incommensurable study findings. There would be little sense, for instance, in constructing the distribution of effect sizes for a mix of study findings on methadone maintenance for drug abusers, gender differences in social skills, and effects of unionization on employee morale. On the other hand, few would object to a meta-analysis of findings from virtual replications of the same study. Most of the criticism on this point, however, has been well short of such obvious extremes. The gray area in between becomes controversial when a meta-analyst includes study findings that are clearly not replications, but are claimed to relate to a broader theme. As noted earlier, Smith and Glass (1977) included a wide range of studies of psychotherapy in their pioneering meta-analysis on the grounds that the issue of interest to them was the overall effectiveness of psychotherapy. However, they were stridently criticized by researchers who saw vast differences between the different therapies and different outcome variables and felt it was misleading to report average effectiveness over such distinct approaches as behavioral therapy, psychodynamic therapy, and gestalt therapy and such diverse outcomes as fear and anxiety, self-esteem, global adjustment, emotional-somatic problems, and work and school functioning.

The problem comes in, of course, when the different types of study findings are averaged together in a grand mean effect size. Meta-analysts who wish to deal with broad topics are increasingly approaching their task as one of comparison rather than aggregation. Where distinctly different subcategories of study findings are represented in a meta-analysis, they can be broken out separately and the distribution of effect sizes and related statistics can be reported for each, permitting comparison among them. Additionally, technical advances in meta-analysis have made it possible to statistically test for homogeneity to determine if a grouping of effect sizes from different studies shows more variation than would be expected from sampling error alone. This provides an empirical test for whether studies show such disparate results that it may not be plausible to presume that they are comparable. Put differently, contemporary meta-analysis is increasingly attending to the variance of effect size distributions rather than the means of those distributions. That is, the primary question of interest often has to do with identifying the sources of differences in study findings, rather than aggregating results together into a grand average. This emphasis provides a more careful handling of distinctly different subgroups of study findings and runs less risk of vexing critics who are concerned about such differences.

A related and more troublesome issue is the mixing of study findings of different methodological quality in the same meta-analysis. Some critics argue that a research synthesis should be based only on findings from the highest quality studies and should not be degraded by inclusion of those from methodologically flawed studies. Indeed, some approaches to meta-analysis set very strict methodological criteria for inclusion, e.g., the best evidence synthesis method mentioned earlier (Slavin, 1986). What makes this point controversial is that there are problematic trade-offs and judgment calls whichever way the meta-analyst goes. One difficulty is that, aside from a few simple canons, there is relatively little agreement among researchers on what constitutes methodological quality. Moreover, few research areas provide studies that all reviewers would agree are methodologically impeccable in sufficient numbers to make a meaningful meta-analysis. Many areas of research, especially those that deal with applied topics, provide virtually no perfect studies and the ones closest to textbook standards may be conducted in circumstances that are unrepresentative of those in which the meta-analyst is most interested. For instance, methodologically rigorous studies of psychotherapy are more likely in demonstration projects and university clinics than in routine mental health practice (Weisz, Donenberg, Han, & Weiss, 1995; Weisz, Weiss, & Donenberg, 1992). Thus, much of the knowledge we have on some issues resides in studies that are methodologically imperfect and potentially misleading. The meta-analyst must decide how far to go with inclusion of findings from studies that are judged interpretable but flawed, knowing that relaxed methodological standards may result in a derisive reproach of "garbage in, garbage out," while stringent standards are likely to exclude much, or most, of the available evidence on a topic.

Two approaches have emerged on this issue. One is to keep the methodological criteria strict and accept the consequences in regard to the limitations thus imposed on the proportion of available and relevant study findings that may be included. In this instance, the meta-analyst has assurance that the synthesis is based on only the "best" evidence but its results may summarize only a narrow research domain and have little generality. The other approach is to treat methodological variation among studies as an empirical matter to be investigated as part of the meta-analysis (Greenland, 1994). In this case, less stringent methodological criteria are imposed, but the meta-analyst carefully codes methodological characteristics that may influence the study findings. One phase of statistical analysis then investigates the extent to which various methodological features are related to study findings (e.g., random vs. nonrandom assignment in treatment studies). If a questionable methodological practice has no demonstrable relationship to study findings, the corresponding findings are included in the final analysis, which thus gains the benefit of the evidence they contain. If, however, studies with the questionable practice show results significantly different from those without that problem, they can then be excluded from the final results or used only with statistical adjustments to correct for their bias.

RECENT HISTORY AND CONTEMPORARY USAGE OF META-ANALYSIS

Published examples of the quantitative synthesis of findings from different studies can be found as far back as 1904 when Karl Pearson averaged the correlations between inoculation for typhoid fever and mortality for five separate samples (Cooper & Hedges, 1994). As mentioned at the beginning of this chapter, however, the modern era of meta-analysis began with the work of Glass on psychotherapy (Glass, 1976; Smith & Glass, 1977; Smith, Glass, & Miller, 1980), Schmidt and Hunter (1977) on validity coefficients for employment tests, and Rosenthal and Rubin (1978) on interpersonal expectancy effects.

Stimulated in large part by these intriguing applications, the next phase of development focused primarily on the methodological and statistical underpinnings of meta-analysis. This period, in the early 1980s, was marked by the publication of a number of book-length expositions of the concepts, methods, and statistical theory of various versions of meta-analysis (Glass, McGaw, & Smith, 1981; Hedges & Olkin, 1985; Hunter, Schmidt, & Jackson, 1982; Light & Pillemer, 1984; Rosenthal, 1984; Wolf, 1986). The practical and methodological guidance provided by these volumes, combined with the interest generated by the pioneering work, ignited a virtual explosion of meta-analytic applications and commentary upon those applications. Meta-analysis spread rapidly in the social sciences, especially education and psychology, and caught on with especial vigor in the health sciences where it has been virtually institutionalized as the preferred approach to integrating the findings of clinical trials research (Chalmers, et al., 1987; Olkin, 1992; Sacks, et al., 1987).

Meanwhile, another generation of more sophisticated methodological and statistical work has expanded and strengthened the foundations of meta-analysis (e.g., Cook et al., 1992; Cooper, 1989; Hunter & Schmidt, 1990b; Rosenthal, 1991). The pinnacle of these efforts was the publication of the *Handbook of Research Synthesis* (Cooper & Hedges, 1994) under the sponsorship of the Russell Sage Foundation, a compendium of 32 chapters covering virtually every aspect of meta-analysis and authored by an array of preeminent contributors to the field. Against this background, it is the task of the present volume to integrate and translate the most current methodological and statistical work into a practical guide for conducting state-of-the-art meta-analysis of empirical research findings in the social and behavioral sciences.

OVERVIEW OF BOOK

In Chapters 2 through 8 we provide a step-by-step guide to conducting a meta-analysis through the analysis and interpretation of effect size data. Chapter 2 discusses how to formulate a topic, identify relevant research studies, and retrieve reports of those studies. Chapters 3 through 7 deal with coding the studies and organizing and analyzing the resulting data. To illustrate various points along the way, we constructed an example using ten studies on the effectiveness of "challenge" programs to treat juvenile delinquency.[1] Challenge programs use some physical challenge, such as rock climbing or wilderness survival training, as a vehicle for changing attitudes and behaviors (more about this later).

This book is intended to be a concise introduction to meta-analysis. Our target audience is graduate students and professionals within the behavioral and health sciences wishing to become proficient at conducting a meta-analysis. Much of the currently available writing on meta-analysis is either highly technical or out-of-date. We strive to present the state-of-the-art in meta-analytic practice at a level accessible to anyone with a basic understanding of statistics and research methods. Readers interested in a more technical discussion of the underlying statistical theory and ongoing debates are referred to Cooper and Hedges (1994) and Wang and Bushman (1998). In addition, we have tried to present practical guidance on all aspects of the synthesis process, something that is not well developed in most other treatments of this subject.

NOTE

1. This meta-analysis was developed by Sandra Jo Wilson and we appreciate her willingness to let us use it as an example.

2

Problem Specification and Study Retrieval

Like any research, meta-analysis should begin with a careful statement of the topic to be investigated or the question to be answered. This statement will guide the selection of research studies, the coding of information from those studies, and the analysis of the resulting data. The problem statement needs to be straightforward and complete but, at this stage of the process, need not be highly detailed (that will come when eligibility criteria are developed, as discussed later). The problem statement applicable to the studies of challenge programs that we will use as an example is as follows:

> How effective are challenge programs in reducing the subsequent antisocial behavior of juveniles with behavioral problems? What are the characteristics of the most and least effective programs? Do these programs have favorable effects on other outcomes such as relations with peers, locus-of-control, and self-esteem?

Note that this problem statement yields a preliminary specification of the research literature at issue (studies of the effects of challenge programs on juveniles with behavioral problems), the major category of independent variables that is of interest (program characteristics), and the key dependent variables at issue (antisocial behavior, interpersonal relationships, locus-of-control, and self-esteem).

IDENTIFYING THE FORM OF THE RESEARCH FINDINGS TO BE META-ANALYZED

Quantitative research findings take many different forms. Those of interest to the meta-analyst may appear as differences between group means, correlations between variables, proportion of observations in a particular category, and so forth. The findings pertinent to the topic or question a meta-analysis addresses must eventually be coded using some effect size statistic. To be comparable with each other and, therefore, meaningful to analyze, the *same* effect size statistic must be used for coding *all* the findings in a given meta-analysis. The meta-analyst, therefore, must identify the form(s) of research findings relevant to the topic of the meta-analysis and ensure that they can be represented with a common effect size statistic. If not, the research findings of interest should be sorted to distinguish those that require different effect size statistics and each of the resulting categories should be meta-analyzed separately.

Chapter 3 of this volume describes the various effect size statistics a meta-analyst might use. For now we focus only on the general forms of research findings that may be germane to the topic or question the meta-analyst wishes to investigate. While some forms of research findings can be represented with well-known effect size statistics that are widely used in meta-analysis (e.g., the standardized mean difference, the correlation coefficient, and the odds-ratio), others require specialized effect size statistics that may need to be developed ad hoc and, indeed, may be impossible to develop given the current state of the art. With this in mind, we provide a brief listing of some of the forms of research findings that can usually be represented with "off-the-shelf" effect size statistics already developed and described by meta-analysts for general application.

Central Tendency Description. A research finding of this type describes a characteristic of interest measured on a single sample of respondents. The distribution of values on that variable is summarized with some statistic representing its central tendency such as a mean, median, mode, or proportion. For instance, a survey study might report the proportion of women in a given sample who experience migraine headaches. If various studies provide such findings for a number of samples, meta-analysis techniques could be applied to summarize the distribution of those findings across the samples and analyze their relationships with various study and sample characteristics. Most of the common statistics for describing central tendency in such research can be configured as effect size statistics usable for meta-analysis *if the operationalization of the variable of interest is the same for all findings.* That is, all of the studies need to have used the same measure, such as a collection of studies measuring the mean level of depression with the Beck depression inventory in samples of adolescent drug users.

Pre–Post Contrasts. Another form of research finding from a single sample compares the central tendency (e.g., mean or proportion) on a variable measured at one time with the central tendency on the same variable measured at a later time. This is often done to examine change, e.g., how much better the reading scores for a sample of children are at the end of the school year than at the beginning. The descriptive statistics used to represent this finding are generally either the direct difference between the two central tendency values, or the central tendency of the gain or difference scores defined as the difference between the Time 1 and Time 2 values for each respondent. An effect size statistic for pre–post contrasts represented as standardized differences between means was developed for general meta-analysis applications by Becker (1988) and other, more specialized versions can be readily configured.

Group Contrasts. This type of research finding involves one or more variables measured on two or more groups of respondents and then compared across groups. The descriptive statistics typically reported are the central tendency values, e.g., a mean or proportion, upon which the groups can be compared. There are two forms of group contrast research that are often of interest to meta-analysts:

(a) *Experimental or clinical trials research.* In this case, the respondent groups being compared represent the conditions in an experiment or quasi-experiment, e.g., a group receiving treatment and a control group. The contrast between the experimental and control group on the values of an outcome variable is interpreted as the effect of treatment. For instance, the research studies in our challenge example compare the outcome status of a group participating in a challenge program with that of a control group not participating.

(b) *Group differences research.* In this instance, the respondent groups being contrasted are identified on some basis other than assignment to experimental conditions. The characteristics that distinguish the groups may occur naturally or may be defined by the researcher or some other social agent. Research on gender differences, for instance, compares males and females on selected variables. Similarly, research might compare other demographic groups, different diagnostic categories of patients, and the like. Research investigating the difference in reading ability between learning disabled students and low-achieving, but not learning disabled students would present findings of this sort.

Whether from experimental research or group differences research, appropriate effect size statistics for research findings involving the comparison of two groups are available and widely used in meta-analysis (Rosenthal, 1994). Indeed, the most frequent application of meta-analysis is to research findings of this sort, especially experimental research that assesses the effects of treatment or intervention. Where comparison among three or more groups is at issue, the groups can be examined two by two but no general techniques are available for comparing three or more groups simultaneously.

Association Between Variables. This type of research finding represents the covariation over respondents of two variables to determine if there is an association between them. For instance, such research might examine the correlation between family socioeconomic status and students' mathematics grades in elementary school. A finding of this sort might be reported as a correlation coefficient or as some index of association derived from a cross-tabulation of the variables, e.g., a chi-square coefficient, odds-ratio, lambda, or the like. In this general category of research there are also two rather distinct varieties that are often of interest to meta-analysts:

(a) *Measurement research.* In this instance the associations at issue concern the characteristics of measurement instruments. For instance, a test–retest reliability coefficient represents such a correlation. Another common instance is the study of predictive validity, as when the correlation between scores on the SAT test and later college grades is obtained to assess the validity of the SAT for selecting students likely to do well in college.

(b) *Individual differences research.* This more general category of correlational research examines the covariation between selected characteristics or experiences of individuals. For instance, such research might examine the relationship between number of siblings and IQ, the relationship between alcohol use and domestic violence, or the relationship between the amount of time spent on homework and students' high school grades.

Meta-analysis of research findings on the association or correlation between two variables of interest is common and there are several effect size statistics applicable to such situations (Hunter & Schmidt, 1990b; Rosenthal, 1994). Indeed, the product-moment correlation coefficient itself can be configured as an effect size statistic in many such applications.

Each of the preceding forms of research findings can usually be meta-analyzed in a straightforward way using one of the established effect size statistics that is discussed in the next chapter. On the other hand, forms of research findings other than those described above may be difficult to meta-analyze. In some cases, the primary findings may not be easily represented by any of the common effect size statistics but other data may be reported that can be used. For instance, multiple regression results cannot generally be represented in an effect size statistic but a study may report the correlation matrix upon which the multiple regression is based.

Selected bivariate correlations from that matrix could then be used as effect sizes; they constitute research findings in the form of associations between variables, as described earlier. In some cases, a proficient meta-analyst may be able to develop a workable effect size statistic that can be applied to the form of the research finding of interest. However, since fully usable effect size statistics must be accompanied by sufficient statistical theory to specify their standard errors, such ad hoc development will generally require a high level of technical skill.

While there are some forms of research findings that cannot readily be meta-analyzed using established effect size statistics, a wide range of the extant social science research yields findings in the forms listed above. The major exceptions are findings generated by multivariate analysis, e.g., multiple regression, discriminant analysis, factor analysis, structural equation modeling, and the like. Meta-analysts have not yet developed effect size statistics that adequately represent this form of research finding and, indeed, their complexity and the diversity across studies with regard to the selection of variables involved may make this impossible. This text, therefore, will concentrate on meta-analysis of the forms of research findings identified above and leave all others for more specialized treatment elsewhere.

STUDY ELIGIBILITY CRITERIA

With a topic specified that can be addressed by meta-analysis and a clear idea of the type of research finding that is relevant to that topic, the prospective meta-analyst can turn to the task of identifying the research studies appropriate to include in the meta-analysis. One characteristic of a good meta-analysis is that the researcher is very explicit about the population of research studies whose findings are to be examined and summarized. This makes it easy to communicate the research domain of interest to consumers of the meta-analysis and, most important, provides essential guidance to the process of selecting or rejecting studies for inclusion in the meta-analysis.

With these purposes in mind, we strongly recommend that prospective meta-analysts draw up a detailed written specification of the criteria a research study must meet if its findings are to be included in the meta-analysis. The particulars of the eligibility criteria will depend upon the topic of the meta-analysis but there are certain general categories that should be considered for most applications: (a) the distinguishing features of a qualifying study, (b) research respondents, (c) key variables,

(d) research designs, (e) cultural and linguistic range, (f) time frame, and (g) the publication type. The particulars of each category will vary greatly from one meta-analysis to the next, depending on the focus and purpose of the synthesis, and may be either relatively restrictive or inclusive. Each of these categories is discussed below.

Distinguishing Features. What are the distinguishing features of a study that make it pertinent to the meta-analysis topic? If the meta-analysis addresses questions of the effectiveness of intervention, for instance, a critical feature would be the nature of the intervention. Thus, the eligibility criteria might specify the characteristics an intervention must have to be relevant, provide whatever definitions are needed, and, perhaps, even give examples of what is included and excluded. If the meta-analysis deals with group comparisons (e.g., gender differences), the criteria would specify the nature of the groups and comparisons at issue. If the meta-analysis topic deals with the association between two constructs, the criteria would define those constructs and indicate how their operationalizations can be recognized.

Research Respondents. What are the pertinent characteristics of the research respondents (subject sample) who provide the data in a study appropriate for the meta-analysis? Relevant studies, for instance, may include only those with juveniles as subjects, in which case a definition should be provided about what is meant by a juvenile (under the age of 18 or 21? what about samples that mix juveniles and adults?). Similarly, the meta-analyst may wish to restrict eligible studies to those using subjects with certain other demographic characteristics, those found in certain settings (e.g., elementary schools), those with or without certain symptoms, those of certain cultures (e.g., only English-speaking), certain regions, and the like. Alternatively, the interests of a meta-analyst may require a very inclusive explication of pertinent characteristics of research respondents.

Key Variables. What are the key variables that must be represented in the study for it to be appropriate for the meta-analysis? With intervention or treatment studies, for instance, this criterion might refer to specific outcome variables needed to address the target questions. With group comparison studies, it might refer to certain essential variables on which the groups are contrasted. In correlational studies there may be certain covariates or control variables that are desired as well as particular constructs to be represented in the key correlation(s) defined in the distinguishing features of the study, discussed earlier. In addition, since meta-analysis revolves around the coding of effect size statistics to represent study findings, one necessary criterion in this category is that sufficient statistical information be reported in a study to permit calculation or estimation of an appropriate effect size statistic or other desired summary information for effects or relationships involving the key variables.

Research Methods. What research designs and methodological features qualify a study for the meta-analysis and which disqualify it? A primary criterion, of course, is that which specifies the form of the research findings that are relevant, as discussed in the previous section of this chapter. In intervention studies, for instance, this criterion would necessarily deal with experimental design and would indicate whether only random assignment control group studies were eligible, quasi-experiments of various sorts, and the like. Also, assorted other methodological or procedural features are likely to be important in any given research area. For instance, the meta-analyst may want to include only double-blind studies, or those with placebo controls, or only prospective studies, or those using a specified set of measures known to be valid and reliable, and so forth. At this point, it may be worth reviewing the discussion in Chapter 1 on the trade-offs the meta-analyst faces when setting criteria on method quality. Further consideration of this issue is presented at the end of this section. Restrictive criteria allow the meta-analysis to be based on the best studies, but may limit the number and range of eligible studies. More relaxed criteria may make fuller use of the available research, but may also introduce errors or bias into the meta-analysis.

Cultural and Linguistic Range. What is the cultural and linguistic range of the studies to be included? Research is produced in many countries and languages. The meta-analyst should indicate which are pertinent to the research question to be addressed and justify any restrictions that do not follow from that research question. It is not uncommon, for instance, for meta-analysts to exclude studies that are not reported in English simply because of the practical difficulties of translation. If the relative cultural homogeneity resulting from this restriction is appropriate to the research question, the associated selection criteria should be defined. If cultural or linguistic restrictiveness is not necessary for pursuit of the research question, the biases and limitations inherent in any such restriction should be considered and addressed as part of the meta-analysis.

Time Frame. What is the time frame within which eligible studies must be conducted, if any? The meta-analyst may be interested in only the most recent studies, e.g., dating from the point that a certain controversy surfaced or a certain method or instrument became available. Or, there may be a certain time period that is most appropriate to the particular research of interest, e.g., attitude studies during the "sexual revolution" of the 1960s. As with the cultural and linguistic criteria described above, the meta-analyst should carefully consider the issue of what time frame is appropriate and develop criteria for which there is more than arbitrary justification.

Publication Type. What types of research reports are appropriate for the meta-analysis? The range of possible report types may be quite broad and include published journal articles, books, dissertations, technical reports, unpublished manuscripts, conference presentations, and the like. If there are to be any restrictions on the types of research reports to be included in the meta-analysis, they should be specified and justified. As with the English-language issue mentioned earlier, meta-analysts often make a decision of convenience on this matter, e.g., using only formally published material since it is the easiest to locate. Sometimes this restriction is defended on the grounds that, since published material is refereed, it represents higher quality research and thus this criterion is a proxy for methodological quality. This rationale is generally not very convincing. In many research areas, unpublished material may be as good as the published and, in any event, the decision is better made on the basis of explicit methodological criteria than by using publication status as a proxy. Even more important, it is known that the effects reported in published studies are generally larger than those reported in unpublished ones (Begg, 1994; Lipsey & Wilson, 1993; Smith, 1980). Decisions ranging from the author's consideration of whether to write up a study for publication to the editor's judgment on whether to publish it are influenced by the magnitude of study effects and the associated degree of statistical significance (Bozarth & Roberts, 1972). This means that the meta-analyst who excludes unpublished studies is quite likely to introduce an upward bias into the size of effects that will be found. Eligibility criteria that restrict studies according to publication source, therefore, should be considered very carefully and be well justified.

A statement of eligibility criteria for our example of the effects of challenge programs on juvenile delinquency is provided in Exhibit 2.1. It illustrates the issues that must be considered and suggests the level of detail needed to effectively guide the selection of appropriate studies. We should caution, however, that only rarely does the version of the eligibility criteria that is first drafted serve well without revision. Typically, once the search for eligible studies is underway, certain studies are found whose eligibility is ambiguous under the criteria or which challenge the criteria in ways that require reconsideration. The eligibility criteria thus are iterative; they evolve with the cumulative experience of applying them to specific candidate studies. Of course, as changes are made in those criteria, they must be applied retroactively to any studies examined prior to that change.

Methodological Quality Revisited

Because of the controversy often associated with the meta-analyst's methodological criteria for study selection, and the difficulty of determining appropriate criteria, additional discussion is needed. We offer the following points for consideration. First, as mentioned earlier, there are only hard choices in deciding how inclusive of methodological variation a meta-analysis should be. More inclusive approaches have the benefits of larger numbers of studies to work with, fuller representation of available research on a topic, and the opportunity to empirically examine the relationship between method characteristics and study findings. Inevitably,

---

(a) *Distinguishing Features.* Eligible studies must involve the use of challenge programs to reduce, prevent or treat delinquency or antisocial behavior similar to delinquency. Challenge programs are those that employ experiential learning on *both* of two interrelated dimensions: the challenge dimension (physically challenging activities or events) and the social dimension (prosocial or therapeutic interactions with peers and/or program staff). Boot camps, nonwilderness, and nonresidential programs are eligible if the report demonstrates both the challenge and social dimensions. Recreational programs (e.g., midnight basketball, cycling clubs, other sports programs) are not eligible unless they specifically incorporate both the challenge and social dimensions. Challenge programs targeted exclusively on substance abuse without any other components of antisocial behavior or delinquency are *not* eligible. [The delineation of the distinctive features of studies eligible for this meta-analysis was based on an examination of literature reviews and a sample of studies of challenge programs.]

(b) *Research Respondents.* Eligible studies must involve antisocial or delinquent youth (ages 12 to 21) as treatment and comparison participants. Studies in which the program participants are not specifically identified as delinquent or antisocial, but the outcome measures include measures of delinquency, antisocial behavior, or closely related factors (e.g., anger control) are eligible for this study. [The focus of this meta-analysis is on antisocial adolescents. Twelve years of age is generally recognized as the start of adolescence and 21 years of age is the legal age of majority in most states, marking the end of adolescence.]

Exhibit 2.1. Eligibility criteria for a meta-analysis of challenge programs for juvenile delinquency.

(c) *Key Variables.* Studies must report at least one quantitative outcome measure of antisocial behavior or delinquency. The measure must be behavioral, rather than relying on the emotional or attitudinal state of the adolescent. Only studies from which an effect size can be computed are eligible. [The purpose of this meta-analysis is to examine the effects of challenge programs on antisocial and delinquent behaviors, therefore, only those studies that report results on such a measure are to be included.]

(d) *Research Methods.* Studies must use a control or comparison group design. The control condition can be "treatment as usual," placebo, wait-list, or no treatment. The key is that the control condition should not represent a concentrated effort to produce change. A treatment versus treatment comparison is eligible only if one treatment is clearly intended as a control for the other, e.g., "treatment as usual" versus an innovative treatment. Nonequivalent comparison designs in which groups were not randomly assigned to conditions are eligible only if there are pretest measures on a delinquency or antisocial behavior variable or a variable highly correlated with delinquency (e.g., gender, age, prior delinquency history). One group pretest–posttest designs are not eligible. [This criterion allows for the inclusion of studies of high methodological quality (i.e., randomized designs) and studies with sufficient data to assess the similarity of the groups being compared. Excluded are studies of dubious methodological quality (i.e., nonrandomized studies lacking a pretest or a comparison group).]

(e) *Cultural and Linguistic Range.* Studies must be conducted in an English-speaking country and be reported in English. [The concepts of delinquency and antisocial behavior are culturally embedded. Therefore, the inclusion of delinquency studies from different cultures seems inappropriate.]

(f) *Time Frame.* Only studies conducted since 1950, inclusively, are eligible. [This restricts the meta-analysis to "modern" studies, defined as those conducted after World War II. Studies prior to 1950 are expected to differ in important ways because of the different historical context and research paradigms of the time.]

(g) *Publication Types.* Published and unpublished studies are eligible, including refereed journals, nonrefereed journals, dissertations, government reports, technical reports, etc. [Given the purpose of this meta-analysis to summarize the empirical evidence on the effects of challenge programs and the potential upward bias of published studies, all eligible studies, regardless of publication form, are deemed eligible.]

Exhibit 2.1. *Cont.*

however, broader methodological criteria will include studies that some critics will find unacceptable and that, indeed, may yield erroneous results if not handled carefully. Less inclusive approaches, on the other hand, have the advantage of yielding results based on the most credible studies. The costs of stricter criteria are smaller samples of studies, the loss of data from excluded, potentially useful studies, and the possibility that the more methodologically rigorous studies are conducted in unrepresentative circumstances and produce findings of limited generalizability.

Second, research findings do not appear to be generally robust to methodological differences among studies. The relatively few meta-analyses that have examined a wide range of methodological characteristics in relationship to study findings have typically found that there is a strong connection (e.g., Lipsey, 1992; Schulz et al., 1995; Sellers et al., 1997; Shadish, 1992; Weiss & Weisz, 1990; Wilson, 1995). What is more problematic is that the method characteristics that make the most difference are not necessarily those the meta-analysts assume will be most influential. The methodological criteria a meta-analyst develops, therefore, are likely to be important but it will be difficult to know in advance which method issues will be most important.

Third, the quality of methodological reporting in the social and behavioral science research literature is poor. Reports are often silent or ambiguous on important methodological and procedural matters making it difficult for the analyst to determine what was done. The meta-analyst who develops elaborate and detailed methodological criteria for study selection, therefore, will most likely find that study reports do not provide sufficient information for those criteria to be confidently applied.

Fourth, methodological quality is something that seems to exist largely in the eye of the beholder (McGuire et al., 1985). Other than a few agreed upon methodological canons (valid measures, random assignment, etc.) researchers do not generally agree on what methods and procedures are superior in a given area of study, and they do not agree on how serious it is if they are compromised.

Fifth, a few researchers and meta-analysts have developed schemes for assessing methodological quality. Despite some lack of agreement among them, they provide many potentially valuable suggestions about method features that may be important. Some of these suggestions are included in later discussion about coding studies for meta-analysis (Chapter 4). The source material can be consulted for further information (e.g., Bangert-Drowns et al., 1997; Chalmers, et al., 1981; Gibbs, 1989; Sindhu et al., 1997; Wortman, 1994).

Sixth, where methodological features of studies are concerned, there should be a reciprocal relationship between the restrictiveness of the eligibility criteria and the extent of coding after studies are selected. The more methodological variation permitted in the meta-analysis by the eligibility criteria, the more important it is to code a wide range of methodological and procedural features. That coding gives the analyst the opportunity to examine the extent to which studies with different methods yield different findings and make whatever adjustments may be needed to improve the validity of the conclusions.

Finally, though most meta-analyses focus on substantive aspects of the studies they summarize, meta-analysis can be equally valuable for studying method as an issue in its own right (e.g., Heinsman & Shadish, 1996; Wilson, 1995). With meta-analysis we can examine the relationships that appear between the methods used in studies and the findings of those studies. Thus, meta-analysis provides an opportunity to discover which methodological features are important to study design and which are not. The prospective meta-analyst, therefore, should view methodological issues as something to be considered for investigation and not only in relation to eligibility criteria.

IDENTIFYING, LOCATING, AND RETRIEVING RESEARCH REPORTS

A careful and complete statement of the eligibility criteria for studies appropriate for a meta-analysis defines the population of studies that should be included in the meta-analysis. It is unlikely that such a population contains so many studies that appreciable efficiency is gained from drawing a representative sample. In addition, the meta-analyst often wants to break down the studies into various categories with sufficient studies in each to permit analysis and comparison. Typically, therefore, meta-analysts attempt to identify and retrieve every study in the defined population rather than sample from that population.

The first step in organizing a search for eligible studies is to develop a meticulous accounting system to record progress in identifying candidate reports, the status of the search for each report, and an indication of the outcome of completed searches. While this can be done on index cards, there are considerable advantages to using a computer database program such as *FileMaker® Pro, dBASE® IV*, or *Microsoft Access®*. This system should be set up as a bibliography with fields for information about the search status for each item. A new entry is made in this bibliography whenever a reference is obtained to a study judged to be possibly eligible for the meta-analysis on the basis of the information available at the time it is identified. Some meta-analysts also enter the full abstract if it is available, or file a photocopy separately in a cross-linked manual file. Each distinct bibliographic entry should be given its own separate identification number for ease of cross-referencing to the various other data files that will be created during the meta-analysis.

Additional fields in this bibliographic file might encode useful descriptive information if it is available, e.g., the source of the citation, type of report (journal article, technical report, dissertation, etc.). The fields included to record progress on the search for each report might use codes such as "search pending," "available in library X," "not found or not available in local library," "requested through interlibrary loan," "requested from author," "ordered from vendor X," and so forth, each with an associated field showing the date of the last update in its status. The final code in this series would indicate that the report was retrieved on a particular date or that the search was abandoned and why (e.g., the study was determined to be ineligible or no source was found from which the report could be obtained). Careful maintenance of an accounting system like this not only helps the meta-analyst organize a thorough search, but provides a record of the candidate studies considered, the proportion found, and which were dropped or abandoned and for what reasons.

Another set of fields should be created in this bibliographic database to monitor the processing of those reports retrieved and deemed eligible for the meta-analysis. Such fields might, for instance, encode the form in which the report was retrieved (e.g., microfiche, photocopy, technical report, book, etc.), who screened it for eligibility (e.g., initials) and on what date, whether it has been coded yet and, if so, on what date and by whom. This data allows a subset of the overall bibliographic file to double as a monitoring mechanism to ensure that all retrieved reports are screened and, if eligible, coded. It also permits tracking of when critical actions were taken and by whom so that there is a trail that will help the meta-analyst resolve any problems that arise.

Finding References

We turn now to the search process itself, consisting of two parts: (a) finding bibliographic references to potentially eligible studies and, (b) obtaining copies of those studies to screen and, if eligible, to code for inclusion in the meta-analysis. The more challenging of these two steps is to develop an adequate bibliography of candidate studies. The best bibliography at this stage is one that is inclusive, but relatively focused. That is, the meta-analyst should include every reference that has a reasonable prospect of being eligible, but should exercise restraint in adding low probability prospects. The latter can require a great deal of labor to track down that is wasted if they then prove ineligible.

In searching for relevant citations, the most effective strategy is to use multiple sources since, for all but the most narrowly focused study areas, no one source will identify all the potentially eligible study reports. The sources that should be employed in a comprehensive search include (a) review articles, (b) references in studies, (c) computerized bibliographic databases, (d) bibliographic reference volumes, (e) relevant journals, (f) conference programs and proceedings, (g) authors or experts in the area of interest, and (h) government agencies. Each of these sources is discussed below.

Review Articles. Good sources to begin with are the references in any existing review articles (or prior meta-analyses) overlapping the relevant topic. Even if there is not sufficient discussion of each cited study to permit an eligibility determination, their inclusion in a pertinent review makes them reasonable prospects. For this reason, the search should usually pursue review articles as vigorously as candidate studies.

References in Studies. Another good source consists of the references in those eligible (and near eligible) studies that are retrieved since it is common for a study of a particular topic to cite other similar studies on the same topic. This tactic should be used throughout the meta-analysis search. That is, as each candidate research report is retrieved and screened, its references should also be examined to determine if they identify any candidate studies not already known.

In thorough literature searches for meta-analysis it is often found that only part of the eligible research is covered in conventional research reviews and cross-citations among research studies. This is especially true of unpublished studies, but applies to a surprising extent to published work as well, particularly in applied areas where researchers from different disciplines may be working on similar problems. It is imperative, therefore, that the meta-analyst attempting to retrieve as much as possible of a defined population of research studies use search strategies that go beyond the network of existing review articles and the cross-citations among the studies referenced in those articles. The following sources provide a means of doing that, though it is at the cost of a larger proportion of irrelevancies and false positives.

Computerized Bibliographic Databases. An important method of obtaining references is keyword searches of selected bibliographic databases. Many such databases are available, including such standbys as *Psychological Abstracts* (PsycINFO and PsycLit are the computerized forms), *Sociological Abstracts, ERIC* (Educational Resources Information Center), and *MEDLINE* (searchable for free through the National Library of Medicine). Other useful, but less familiar, sources are also available such as the *Library of Congress* book index (LC MARC), the *National Technical Information Service* of government documents (NTIS), the *National Criminal Justice Reference Service* (NCJRS), *Ageline, Economic Literature Index,* and *Family Resources.* Additional computer databases and access information are provided in Appendix A.

Most university libraries provide access to these databases on CD-ROM disks (though these are being phased out by many universities) or through Internet web-based services, such as EBSCO, FirstSearch, Institute for Scientific Information, and SilverPlatter. Although a small, focused meta-analysis can be well served by these web-based search tools, our experience is that they do not generally allow for complex searches (such as that illustrated later in Exhibit 2.2) that are common to large scale meta-analyses. Searches of this type are possible through telnet-based search tools, such as those available from Dialog Corporation or Ovid Technologies, although these services can be costly for individual researchers.

A meta-analyst may be tempted to search only one computerized database, assuming it is the most relevant and covers everything that any more peripheral database would cover. If interest is in an education topic, for instance, ERIC may seem sufficient. We would caution, however, that meta-analysts who have compared results from searching different databases (e.g., Glass, McGaw, & Smith, 1981) have found surprisingly little overlap. Thus, a comprehensive search will generally require multiple databases.

There is an art to conducting effective computer keyword searches that is mastered largely through experience. Perhaps the most important general advice concerns preparation of the keywords that will be used for each search. Typical computer searches examine the title, the abstract, and a set of standardized descriptors (usually drawn from a designated thesaurus) associated with each entry. To effectively locate a high proportion of candidate studies for a meta-analysis, the search must be based on a set of keywords that broadly cover the relevant domain. This means (a) identifying all those standardized descriptors in a given database that may be associated with studies of interest and (b) identifying the range of terms that different researchers might include in their study titles or abstracts that give a clue that the study might deal with the topic of interest. Careful perusal of review articles and those research reports found early will give some guidance regarding the appropriate keywords. If a thesaurus for standardized descriptors is available for a given database, this should also be examined. If not, the descriptors associated with the most relevant items that emerge from a preliminary computer search should be used in a refined search.

A useful feature of most computerized bibliographic search programs is the "wildcard" symbol, usually "*" or "?." This feature allows the search of a single word to incorporate multiple variations of that word. For example, searching for the keyword "delinquen*" would return all titles and abstracts with the words delinquent, delinquents, or delinquency. This feature greatly expands the capabilities of the search and simplifies the set of keywords that must be searched. A new feature of some computerized bibliographic databases is the automatic "explosion" of search terms to related terms through the use of a built-in thesaurus.

Inevitably, any computer keyword search will yield only a small proportion of "hits" on true candidate studies and many items that are irrelevant, some bizarrely so. These must be separated manually by a knowledgeable researcher who can read the title and abstract of each report identified in a computer search and determine what follow up is needed, e.g., retrieval and further screening or clearly ineligible with no need to be screened further. Skillful searching, however, can reduce the proportion of dross that must be filtered out manually. The most important procedure is to make effective use of keyword combinations and conjunctive and disjunctive commands in the computer search. For instance, a meta-analyst may be searching on a topic for which there are both human and animal studies, but be interested only in the human studies. Most search programs have a NOT option so that one can specify certain keywords that remove a citation from a search. In one search on the relationship between alcohol and aggression, for instance, we had to specify "not fish" to exclude the surprisingly large number of studies that administered alcohol to fish and observed territorial fighting behavior.

Trying to narrow the scope of the search by including keywords that identify the type of subject samples of interest and the type of research can also be helpful. This must be done with great care, however, because if those keywords are themselves too restrictive, eligible studies will be missed. If the meta-analyst is interested in studies of the effectiveness of treatment for juvenile delinquents, for example, keywords may be included for both juveniles as a subject type and treatment effectiveness studies as a research type, along with those that identify delinquency as the key topic. In simplified form, this search would ask for studies that conjoined keywords identifying crime or delinquency with keywords identifying youthful samples and keywords identifying treatment effectiveness research. In this case, however, the youth-related and treatment-study-related key-

Type of Sample
juvenile(s), adolescent(s), adolescence, youth, boys, girls, teenage(r), delinquent, predelinquent, child, children, high school, elementary school, behavior(al) problem, antisocial, troubled, behavior disorder, or aggressive

Type of Intervention
challenge, wilderness, outward bound, outdoor, ropes, rock climbing, survival training, or forestry

Type of Research
outcome(s), evaluation, evaluate(d), effectiveness, effects, experiment, experimental, controlled, control group, random(ized), clinical trial(s), impact, or assessment

Exhibit 2.2. Example of keywords used in various combinations to search for studies of the effects of challenge programs on juvenile delinquency.

words must be developed with as much care as the delinquency keywords. Juvenile samples, for instance, may be identified as "youth," "children," boys," "girls," "adolescents," and so forth. Developing a set of keywords that reliably identify treatment effectiveness studies is even more difficult. Exhibit 2.2 presents a set of keywords we used to search for studies on the effects of challenge programs for juvenile delinquents that shows the range of possibilities that must be considered to conduct an effective search. These keywords were combined with a combination of "or" and "and" statements into a single search of each relevant database.

A couple of distinctive computerized databases merit special mention. *The Social Science Citation Index* (SSCI) supports searches for subsequent reports that have referenced a given report with which the search is initiated. With SSCI, then, the meta-analyst can take a set of eligible studies and identify any subsequent study that cited any from that set. Some of those will themselves usually be studies on the same topic. This database is especially useful for finding the most recent material on a topic and identifying work in other disciplines (if there is a cross-citation) that may otherwise be missed.

Another distinctive source is *Dissertation Abstracts Online* (the electronic version of *Dissertation Abstracts International*) which provides abstracts of most of the doctoral dissertations completed in the United States, and some proportion of those done in Canada. Dissertation studies are often very relevant to a meta-analysis, especially one attempting to identify and retrieve research that has not been formally published. *Dissertations Abstracts Online* is a virtually unique source for access to this research base.

As useful and convenient as computer bibliography searches are, they still may miss important, eligible studies. This can happen because of vagaries of keywording, limitations of search strategies, idiosyncratic author titles and abstracts, and the like. A comprehensive search, therefore, would add other sources that might correct for some of these deficiencies, such as the following.

Bibliographic Reference Volumes. Many of the abstracting services and bibliographic databases are available in a hard-copy form for manual searching, e.g., the annual volumes of *Psychological Abstracts, Sociological Abstracts*, and ERIC. Even though they contain the same material as the computerized versions, it can still be productive to supplement computer searches with manual searches through these volumes. The abstracts in these volumes are typically organized into distinct sections under broad headings for different subfields. Scanning through the abstracts in those sections most relevant to the topic of interest will often turn up eligible studies missed in the computer search because of the absence of the particular keywords on which that search was based. This technique is also a good way to develop a list of keywords for the computer search. When promising abstracts are found, note can be taken of the descriptive words they employ that might serve as a guide to other pertinent material.

Relevant Journals. As the bibliography of candidate studies for a meta-analysis grows, it will become apparent that certain journals have contributed multiple entries. Given that those publications clearly carry the type of study that is of interest, it is possible that they contain others that have not yet been identified. A useful technique, therefore, is to scan through the table of contents and check potentially relevant articles in all the volumes of that journal falling within the time lines of the eligibility criteria. This of course generally requires that the run of journal volumes be on the shelf in an accessible library. If the volumes are not physically available, it may be that the journal in question is covered in *Current Contents in the Social Sciences*, a referencing service that reproduces the table of contents pages from a wide selection of academic journals in the social and behavioral sciences. Promising titles that appear there can be pursued in manual or computerized bibliographic databases to locate further information useful for determining if attempts should be made to retrieve the full study. Also useful are computerized tables of contents, such as *Carl UnCover* available through the Internet at URL address http://uncweb.carl.org/.

Conference Programs and Proceedings. Some bibliographic services cover informal publications such as conference papers (notably ERIC in education), but it is atypical. Many professional organizations, however, publish programs or proceedings of their conferences that give information about the papers presented and, sometimes, author addresses. A useful approach, therefore, is to identify the research-oriented professional associations pertinent to the topic of interest and, by writing to their offices or appropriate officers, to obtain copies of program and proceeding material. This will often be available for recent years, but not always for many years prior. With this material, the meta-analyst can write to authors and request copies of specific papers (and related material the author might have). Additionally, the names of authors who reported on relevant studies can be looked up in the appropriate bibliographic database to identify published papers or other pertinent material.

Authors and Experts. For a fully comprehensive search, it is advisable to write to those authors who have published research in the area of interest, or experts familiar with that area, and enlist their assistance in identifying studies not yet found. This inquiry might simply ask for identification of any papers of their own or others they think may be relevant. A better approach, perhaps, is to send a copy of the bibliography of eligible studies identified to date and ask if the author–expert can suggest additional studies that should be considered. Other relevant authors may be identified through Internet LISTSERVs and news groups.

Government Agencies. A source that should not be overlooked is research-oriented government agencies, especially those that fund or commission research. In the health area, for instance, the relevant units of the National Institutes of Health (NIH) may have published monographs, proceedings, research summaries, and the like that will be useful to the meta-analyst. They will also have records on funded research projects that may identify relevant researchers or research in process. The bureaucratic structure of such organizations can make it difficult to find the right office and personnel to provide information on a given topic, but with persistence it can be done. A useful tool is the phone book of the agency, or the overall phone book for U.S. government agencies, often available from sponsored research offices at universities. There are also useful computerized databases that can yield important information, e.g., *the National Technical Information Service* (NTIS), the *Smithsonian Science Information Exchange* (SSIE), *Current Research*, and the indices from the *Government Publication Office* (GPO), e.g., *GPO Monthly Catalog* and *GPO Publications Reference File*. The resources of pertinent state and local agencies should not be overlooked either, though finding appropriate offices and personnel are often difficult at this level.

Retrieving Research Reports

As the bibliography of candidate studies is developed, the meta-analyst will begin retrieving copies of the identified studies. When the full text of each report is examined, a more definitive determination of its eligibility can be made. Those deemed eligible are then moved forward to the coding phase.

Once bibliographic information is obtained on a study, retrieval is generally rather straightforward. Journal articles and books can usually be located in university libraries. In addition, most university libraries participate in interlibrary loan services that enable them to borrow or obtain copies of material held in other libraries if it is not in their own collection. Researchers who are not based at a university or an organization with comparable library facilities will need to gain access to a suitable library to conduct a thorough meta-analysis. Fortunately, most university libraries have procedures that permit use by researchers who are not associated with the university. In other cases, the nonuniversity meta-analyst may be able to collaborate with a university researcher and gain access to an academic library in that way.

While a university library is the central resource for obtaining copies of study reports for meta-analysis, there are other avenues that must generally be used as well. Doctoral dissertations, for instance, can sometimes be obtained through interlibrary loan or by writing to the author or faculty chairperson, but these approaches are not usually sufficient to retrieve all the dissertations of interest. Most of the dissertations listed in *Dissertation Abstracts International*, however, are available for purchase from University Microfilms Inc. (UMI) in paper copy or microfiche. The reference desk of most university libraries will have the UMI order forms, along with the order forms for ERIC and other document depositories.

As with the identification of studies, the meta-analyst should be prepared to write letters to appropriate persons or institutions to retrieve study reports. Copies of journal articles, conference papers, technical reports, and even books can often be obtained directly from the author, if the author can be located. We have found it useful to collect membership directories from professional organizations as an aid to finding authors and obtaining mailing addresses (e.g., American Psychological Association, American Psychological Society, American Educational Research Association, American Evaluation Association, American Sociological Association, and the like). These materials, and other useful directories, are often available in university libraries as well (e.g., *The National Faculty Directory, The Faculty White Pages, The AMA Directory of Physicians, Who's Who in America*, etc.).

Letters may also be written to agencies and institutions that have published or sponsored the research of interest. Journal and book publishers, of course, can be contacted for purchase of the materials they have published. Many state and local agencies will share copies of technical reports they have commissioned if those reports are still available. Similarly, many federal agencies make available copies of research reports and related materials prepared under their auspices. The vast resources of the Government Printing Office should not be overlooked either (Appendix A identifies computerized databases that index the GPO publications).

Inevitably, it will prove difficult or impossible to retrieve some reports identified as likely prospects for the meta-analysis. A vigorous attempt should be made to retrieve everything feasible, however, to come as close as possible to obtaining the full population of studies defined by the eligibility criteria. Any omissions potentially create a selection bias—the studies not retrieved may yield different results, on average, than those retrieved, making the latter at least somewhat unrepresentative of the full population of research findings. The fewer omitted reports, the less chance there is for a significant bias in the resulting meta-analysis. For those reports that are impossible to retrieve, it is important to maintain careful accounting sufficient to indicate what can be determined about their nature (e.g., publication type, date) and how many there are. With this information, the meta-analyst can document the approximate proportion of studies missing from the population defined by the eligibility criteria and the extent to which their general characteristics differ from those of the studies retrieved.

Finally, we recommend that copies of the reports for all eligible studies be obtained and kept on file as part of the archives for the meta-analysis. It may be tempting to reduce costs by coding studies in the library or using borrowed materials that are then returned. Very often, however, meta-analysts find that questions arise at later stages of the meta-analysis that require consulting the original study material to resolve. If that original material is not on file, it is much more difficult, and sometimes impossible, to recheck or augment the initial coding. In addition, there is always the possibility that a meta-analysis will engender some controversy that attracts other researchers who wish to replicate it or stimulates the author to revisit the original studies to address some issue or criticism that has been raised. These situations are most easily dealt with when copies of the original study reports are kept on hand.

3

Selecting, Computing, and Coding the Effect Size Statistic

A critical step in meta-analysis is to encode or "measure" selected research findings on a numerical scale, such that the resulting values can be meaningfully compared with each other and analyzed much like any set of values on a variable. Most commonly, the research findings of interest are relationships of a particular form between two specified constructs. For instance, the findings of interest may be the differences between experimental conditions measured on a dependent variable representing a certain outcome construct. The numerical value assigned to each such research finding for purposes of meta-analysis indicates the strength of the relationship observed in a particular study, e.g., the size of the treatment effect found or the correlation between two constructs.

As mentioned earlier, the index used to represent study findings in meta-analysis is an *effect size statistic*. Once a set of quantitative research findings representing a specified relationship is identified, those findings are encoded into values of an appropriate effect size statistic and carried forward for analysis. Which effect size statistic is appropriate depends upon the nature of the research findings, the statistical forms in which they are reported, and the hypotheses being tested by the meta-analysis. General forms of research findings for which appropriate effect size statistics are readily available were described in the previous chapter. In this chapter various useful effect size statistics are described in detail. First, however, it is instructive to examine the nature of effect size statistics and the information that must be obtained to compute and use them.

EFFECT SIZE STATISTICS AND THEIR VARIANCES

The effect size statistics used in meta-analysis embody information about either the direction or the magnitude of quantitative research findings, or both. In this volume we discuss only those that indicate both direction and magnitude. Not included, therefore, are such indexes as simple direction of effects (e.g., dichotomous coding of whether treatment groups outperform control groups in experimental studies) and p-values from statistical significance testing, which confound effect magnitude with sample size. The methods for combining p-values test only whether findings from multiple studies are statistically significant when taken groupwise. They yield no information about the overall magnitude of effect or the consistency of effects across studies (Becker, 1994; Rosenthal, 1991).

For purposes of meta-analysis, a single *research finding* is a statistical representation of one empirical relationship involving the variable(s) of interest to the meta-analyst measured on a single subject sample. For instance, the numerical value of a correlation coefficient reported for a given sample is a research finding. Similarly, the difference between the means on an outcome variable for two conditions in an experiment is a research finding. Note that one research study may present more than one research finding. These may involve different variables, as when several variables are intercorrelated in a correlation matrix or used as multiple outcome variables in an experiment; different samples, as when experimental results are reported separately for males and females; or different times of measurement, as when the difference between treatment and control group means is reported for the period immediately after intervention and for some later time. The meta-analyst may be interested in all these different findings or only some designated subset of them.

Each of the research findings must be encoded as a value on the same effect size statistic if they are to be analyzed together. That is, the type of effect size statistic must be the same across studies to allow for meaningful analysis. In addition, the effect size statistic chosen must be appropriate to the nature of the relationship described in the selected research findings and to the statistical forms in which those findings are reported. The actual coding of a research finding is a matter of computing a value from the quantitative information provided in the research report that conforms to the chosen effect size type. If the reported information is insufficient to compute an exact effect size value (which is distressingly common), it still may be possible to estimate the effect size value from what is reported. Formulas and procedures for estimating effect size values from quantitative information that is incomplete or presented in forms different from that required for direct computation are a necessary and important part of effect size coding in meta-analysis.

In addition to the effect size, there is another statistic that must be coded to represent a research finding in meta-analysis. As previously noted, each research finding is based on a single subject sample, though the subjects may be divided into subsamples that are compared in some research designs, e.g., experiments. The number of subjects in the sample almost always varies from study to study so that different effect size values will be based on different sample sizes. From a statistical perspective, effect size values based on larger samples are more precise estimates of the corresponding population value than those based on smaller samples. That is, the sampling error is smaller for effect sizes estimated from large samples than for those estimated from small samples.

This feature of effect size values complicates statistical analysis, even a simple analysis such as computing a mean effect size. The problem is that every effect size value in such an analysis is not equal with regard to the reliability of the information it carries. For a given relationship, for instance, an effect size value based on a sample of five subjects is not as good an estimate as one based on a sample of 500 subjects. If we simply average these two values together, the smaller sample contributes as much to the resulting mean as the larger sample despite its much greater sampling error. This actually makes the combined estimate worse than if we simply took the one based on the larger sample by itself.

The way this problem is handled in meta-analysis is to weight each effect size value by a term that represents its precision. A straightforward approach would be to weight each effect size by its sample size. Hedges (1982b; Hedges & Olkin, 1985) has demonstrated, however, that the optimal weights are based on the *standard error* of the effect size. The standard error is the standard deviation of the sampling distribution (the distribution of values we would get if we drew repeated samples of the same size and estimated the statistic for each). In practice, the standard error for a given statistic is estimated from sample values using a formula derived from statistical theory. Because a larger standard error corresponds to a less precise effect size value, the actual weights are computed as the inverse of the squared standard error value—called the *inverse variance weight* in meta-analysis. Thus, when an effect size statistic is selected for meta-analysis, the formula for computing the associated standard error must also be identified. The coding of each research finding must be designed to yield both the value of the effect size and the inverse variance weight.

One implication of this situation is that meta-analysts are constrained in their choice of effect size statistics for representing research findings of various sorts. While it is generally rather easy to configure a statistical expression that represents the direction and magnitude of a particular kind of research finding, it can be technically challenging to determine the standard error associated with that statistic so that proper inverse variance weights can be calculated. As a practical matter, therefore, meta-analysis is typically conducted using one of a small number of effect size statistics (i.e., the standardized mean difference, the correlation coefficient, and the odds-ratio) for which the standard error formulation and other useful statistical procedures have already been worked out. In addition, some common statistics with known standard error terms that can be readily calculated from the information available in research reports may be used in meta-analysis if the nature of the research findings makes them appropriate. The simple proportion of persons in a sample with a given characteristic, for instance, can be used as an effect size statistic. For research findings that can only be represented with complex or unusual effect size statistics, however, the analyst must either forgo formal meta-analysis or establish the necessary statistical theory prior to the meta-analysis.

With this background, we can now identify and discuss the effect size statistics and their associated inverse variances that are commonly used in meta-analysis, plus several simple, but less commonly used ones, that are applicable to forms of research findings that may be interesting for some purposes. Keep in mind that for a specific meta-analysis the effect size statistic type must remain the same across studies. Multiple meta-analyses can, of course, be performed on the same body of literature, each using a different effect size statistic suited to the nature of the research finding being synthesized and the specific research question being tested.

A NOTE ON NOTATION

Throughout this chapter we use the symbols, ES, SE, and w, to refer to the effect size, the standard error of the effect size, and the inverse variance weight of the effect size, respectively. Subscripts are used to indicate the type of effect size, standard error or weight, such as sm for the standardized mean difference effect size, or p for the proportion effect size.

TYPES OF RESEARCH FINDINGS AND APPLICABLE EFFECT SIZE STATISTICS

A research finding, recall, was defined as a statistical representation of one empirical relationship among variables measured on a single subject sample. To organize the discussion of types of research findings and effect size statistics, we distinguish between one-variable relationships, two-variable relationships, and multivariate relationships (more than two variables). We then consider the different types of relationships within each of these categories and define effect size statistics that can be used to represent each type.

One-Variable Relationships (Central Tendency Description)

The concept of a "relationship" involving only one variable may seem odd, but what we mean by this is a pattern of observations across the categories or values of a single variable. The most widely reported findings of this sort are central tendency descriptions, for instance, the values on a statistic such as a mean, median, or mode. Statistics representing the distribution of values, such as frequencies, proportions, sums, and the like also fall in this category as do those representing variation among the values, e.g., variance, standard deviation, and range.

Research findings in the form of one-variable relationships have not often been meta-analyzed, but the effect size issues are straightforward if two conditions are met. First, all the findings must involve *the same variable operationalized the same way* (or in sufficiently similar ways that the numerical values have comparable meaning across studies). For instance, various forms of self-report operationalizations of subjects' gender resulting in values of "male" or "female" would meet this condition as would the mean values on the same attitude scale used in a number of public opinion polls. Differently operationalized variables representing the same construct, e.g., scores on different mathematics achievement tests, could only be meta-analyzed if they were standardized in some way that made their values comparable, e.g., represented as percentile scores relative to comparable normative distributions.

Second, it must be possible to define an effect size statistic that represents the information of interest *and* to determine the standard error associated with that statistic. Identifying the standard error formula is easy only for established descriptive statistics (for which it can be looked up in reference books) and then it may not be computable from reported information. There are thus constraints on how readily an investigator can meta-analyze research findings for one-variable relationships. Some of the potentially more useful, and usable, one-variable effect size statistics are the proportion and the arithmetic mean; others can be developed by the meta-analyst from established formulations of descriptive statistics and their standard errors.

Proportions

Research findings in the form of the proportion of a sample with a particular characteristic can be represented with the *proportion* as the effect size statistic with values ranging from 0.0 to 1.00. For instance, the proportions of individuals in samples of homeless persons found to be alcohol abusers in studies of various urban areas might be meta-analyzed (Lehman & Cordray, 1993). In such a case, the proportions identified across studies must all represent the same subgroup, e.g., substance abusers, females, persons hospitalized in the last year, and so forth. There are two approaches to generating effect size statistics for proportions, one based directly on the proportion and one based on the conversion of proportions to logits. The applicable statistics for using the proportion directly as an effect size, expressed in terms that presume calculation from sample values, are

$$ES_p = p = \frac{k}{n}, \tag{3.1}$$

$$SE_p = \sqrt{\frac{p(1-p)}{n}}, \tag{3.2}$$

$$w_p = \frac{1}{SE_p^2} = \frac{n}{p(1-p)}, \tag{3.3}$$

where k is the number of subjects in the category of interest and n is the total number of subjects in the sample.

Computer simulations by the authors reveal that, for use in meta-analysis, the foregoing method provides suitable estimates of the mean proportion across studies but underestimates the size of the confidence interval around the mean effect size (proportion) and overestimates the degree of heterogeneity across effect sizes, especially when the observed proportions are less than .2 or greater than .8. This is due to the compression of the standard error as p approaches 0 or 1. If the mean proportion across a collection of similar studies is expected to be between .2 and .8, and only that mean is of interest, then the direct proportion effect size statistic should be adequate.

However, if variation around the mean proportion, i.e., between study differences, is important, the logit method is recommended for analysis. In the logit method, the observed proportions are converted to logits and all analyses are performed on the logit as the effect size. The final results can then be converted back into proportions for ease of interpretation. Unlike the proportion, which is constrained to values between 0 and 1, the logit can take any numerical value. The logit distribution is approximately normal, has a mean of zero, and a standard deviation of 1.83. The proportions .1, .3, .5, .7, and .9 convert into the logits -2.20, $-.85$, .00, .85, and 2.20, respectively; a proportion of .5 equals a logit of zero. The logit effect size for proportions, its standard error, and the inverse variance weight are

$$ES_l = \log_e \left[\frac{p}{1 - p} \right], \tag{3.4}$$

$$SE_l = \sqrt{\frac{1}{np} + \frac{1}{n(1 - p)}}, \tag{3.5}$$

$$w_l = \frac{1}{SE_l^2} = np(1 - p), \tag{3.6}$$

where p is the proportion of subjects in the category of interest and n is the total number of subjects in the sample. The final results, such as the mean logit and confidence intervals, can be converted back into proportions using

$$p = \frac{e^{\text{logit}}}{e^{\text{logit}} + 1}, \tag{3.7}$$

where e is the base of the natural logarithm, or approximately 2.7183, raised to the power of a logit, such as the value of the mean ES_l.

To illustrate, if we had 30 survey studies of urban areas, each reporting the proportion of a homeless sample with alcohol abuse problems, a meta-analysis could be conducted using either those proportions directly or the logit transform of the proportions as the effect size statistic. For statistical analysis, these effect sizes would be weighted by their respective inverse variances. That analysis might examine the effect size distribution for heterogeneity (differences across urban areas), central tendency (the overall mean across all samples and its statistical significance), and the relationship between the effect sizes and various study characteristics, e.g., the type of urban area or the nonresponse rates of the surveys.

Arithmetic Means

A common descriptive statistic for research findings on a single variable is the arithmetic mean expressed in the units of the scale used to measure each individual. A meta-analysis, for example, might investigate the mean number of days of hospitalization for different groups of patients at various hospitals. Since the variable of interest is measured the same way for each individual in each group, that is, as a count of the number of days in the hospital, the means can be compared across groups directly using the mean itself as the effect size statistic, as

$$ES_m = \overline{X} = \frac{\Sigma x_i}{n}, \qquad (3.8)$$

$$SE_m = \frac{s}{\sqrt{n}}, \qquad (3.9)$$

$$w_m = \frac{1}{SE_m^2} = \frac{n}{s^2}, \qquad (3.10)$$

where x_i is an individual score for subject i ($i = 1$ to n), n is the total sample size, and s is the standard deviation of x.

Suppose, for example, that mean days of hospitalization for stroke patients was available for 25 hospitals in a managed care system. Since the operationalization of the variable is the same for all hospitals (days of hospitalization), the mean can be used directly as an effect size statistic. Meta-analysis would proceed using the inverse variance to weight these effect sizes so that the mean across all hospitals, differences among hospitals, and relationships between mean days of hospitalization and characteristics of the hospital could be examined and tested for statistical significance.

Two-Variable Relationships

Two-variable relationships are ubiquitous in social and behavioral research and, correspondingly, constitute the type of research finding that is most commonly meta-analyzed. There are several distinct variations in the nature and form of such relationships with important implications for the effect size statistics that can be used to represent them. In particular, the discussion here distinguishes (a) *pre–post contrasts* in which two variables are compared that differ only with regard to time of measurement, (b) *group contrasts* in which two groups defined by a dichotomous independent variable are compared on a dependent variable, and (c) *association between variables* representing the covariation between two variables measured on a single sample.

Pre–Post Contrasts

A pre–post contrast compares the central tendency (e.g., mean or proportion) on a variable measured at one time with the central tendency of that same variable measured the same way on the same sample at a later time. This is usually done to examine change, e.g., how much better reading scores are for a sample of children at the end of the school year than at the beginning. Two effect size indices are presented here: (a) the unstandardized mean gain and (b) the standardized mean gain. If the pre–post research findings to be meta-analyzed involve the same operationalization, e.g., the exact same attitude scale, then the simple (unstandardized) difference between the Time 1 and Time 2 mean can be used directly as an effect size statistic. If the pre–post research findings include different measurement operationalizations of a construct, such as different measures of drug use, then the mean difference between Time 1 and Time 2 must be standardized.

The Unstandardized Mean Gain. The unstandardized mean gain effect size statistic is applicable to situations in which *all* of the pre–post research findings to be meta-analyzed used the same operationalization of the variable involved (i.e., the same measure) so that the mean scores for findings from different samples are numerically comparable. This might be applied, for instance, to data providing the mean scores at the beginning and end of the school year on the same standardized reading test for a particular grade in a number of schools, say all those in a county or state. A meta-analyst might wish to investigate the distribution of average gain scores in relation to school characteristics. When the same measurement instrument is used for both pre-measures and post-measures for all the samples, there is no need to standardize the values to make them comparable. The effect size statistics can thus be defined as

$$ES_{ug} = \overline{X}_{T2} - \overline{X}_{T1} = \overline{G}, \tag{3.11}$$

$$SE_{ug} = \sqrt{\frac{2s_p^2(1-r)}{n}} = \sqrt{\frac{s_g^2}{n}}, \tag{3.12}$$

$$w_{ug} = \frac{1}{SE_{ug}^2} = \frac{n}{2s_p^2(1-r)}, \tag{3.13}$$

where $\overline{X}_{T1}$ is the mean at Time 1, $\overline{X}_{T2}$ is the mean at Time 2, $\overline{G}$ is the mean Time 2 minus Time 1 gain score, s_p^2 is the pooled variance of the Time 1 and Time 2 scores specifically $(s_{T1}^2 + s_{T2}^2)/2$, s_g^2 is the variance of the gain scores, n is the common sample size at Time 1 and Time 2, and r is the correlation between the Time 1 and Time 2 scores. This situation should not be confused with the more common analysis of the difference between the means of two independent groups (discussed later under group contrasts). In the situation assumed here there is only one group of respondents, each with two scores, one observed at Time 1 and the other at Time 2. Correspondingly, the inferential statistics reported for a pre–post difference will be generated from the correlated (or dependent samples) t-test, the repeated measures analysis of variance, or analogous procedures rather than the more common varieties designed for independent samples.

Estimation Procedures. Computation of the unstandardized mean gain effect size and the associated inverse variance weight involves only one term likely to be difficult to obtain or estimate: the correlation between the Time 1 and the Time 2 values. Otherwise, all that is required are the respective means, or their difference, and the standard deviations. Appendix B provides helpful information for estimating standard deviations when they are not reported directly. Care should be taken, however, to use the correct procedures. Application of procedures appropriate to the more common comparison of means between two independent groups will result in an incorrect value for the standard deviation.

Obtaining or estimating the correlation between the Time 1 and Time 2 values in each study presents special difficulties since sufficient information on this issue is not generally reported. Most often the meta-analyst will need to estimate it from outside sources. For instance, since the variables at issue differ only with regard to time of measurement, the correlation between them should approximate the test–retest reliability, a figure that may be available from other sources, such as from studies examining the psychometric properties of the measure or from other studies included in the meta-analysis. Note that this correlation affects only the inverse variance weight, not the value of the effect size statistic. Since the mean effect size estimate is robust to modest variations in the weights given to individual effect sizes, any reasonable value for the correlation will be suitable for calculation of the mean effect size. On the other hand, the inferential statistics, specifically the confidence interval around the mean effect size and the assessment of the degree of effect size heterogeneity, are affected by variations in the weights and caution should be used in interpreting them if very uncertain estimates of the correlation between the Time 1 and Time 2 values are used.

Example. Suppose we have a set of studies of reaction time to a visual stimulus before and after consumption of alcohol. The reaction times are all measured as the time in milliseconds between presentation of the stimulus and the subject's response, e.g., a button press. The meta-analyst is interested in synthesizing the results of these studies with regard to the magnitude of the impairment produced by alcohol consumption, how it is associated with the age of the subjects and the amount of alcohol used in the studies, and whether different reaction time procedures influenced the results. Because reaction time is measured in comparable ways and in the same numerical units in all the studies, standardization is not needed in the effect size statistic. With a focus on pre–post change across the selected studies, the meta-analyst can use the unstandardized gain effect size statistic to represent the relevant study results and analyze them as a function of study characteristics.

The Standardized Mean Gain. A pre–post contrast, by definition, involves the same operationalization of the variable at both times of measurement for each sample. However, if that operationalization is different for different samples, the resulting numerical values will not be comparable if they are combined in a meta-analysis. In such circumstances it is necessary to standardize the pre–post contrasts in such a way that the values can be meaningfully compared across samples and studies. An effect size statistic for pre–post contrasts in the form of the standardized difference between the Time 1 and Time 2 means was developed for meta-analysis applications by Becker (1988) and is defined as

$$ES_{sg} = \frac{\overline{X}_{T2} - \overline{X}_{T1}}{s_p} = \frac{\overline{G}}{s_g/\sqrt{2(1-r)}}, \tag{3.14}$$

$$SE_{sg} = \sqrt{\frac{2(1-r)}{n} + \frac{ES_{sg}^2}{2n}}, \tag{3.15}$$

$$w_{sg} = \frac{1}{SE_{sg}^2} = \frac{2n}{4(1-r) + ES_{sg}^2}, \tag{3.16}$$

where $\overline{X}_{T1}$ is the mean at Time 1, $\overline{X}_{T2}$ is the mean at Time 2, $\overline{G}$ is the mean Time 2 minus Time 1 gain score, s_p is the pooled standard deviation of the Time 1 and Time 2 scores, specifically $\sqrt{(s_{T1}^2 + s_{T2}^2)/2}$, s_g is the standard deviation of the gain scores, n is the common sample size at Time 1 and Time 2, and r is the correlation between the Time 1 and Time 2 scores. As with the unstandardized mean gain effect size statistic described earlier, care should be taken with the computation and interpretation of the statistical information reported for pre–post comparisons that will be transformed into effect size statistics. The statistics that the meta-analyst finds reported for such situations, and the computations the meta-analyst might do for purposes of estimation, should all be those appropriate to one-sample, repeated measures data, i.e., correlated or dependent samples statistics.

Similarly, it must be noted that the form and meaning of the standardized mean gain effect size statistic is different from that of the standardized mean *difference* effect size statistic that is very commonly used in meta-analysis to represent differences between the means for two independent samples (and is described later). In some instances, it may be tempting to view research findings in pre–post form as presenting much the same information as group contrasts, e.g., when the group contrast is a treatment versus control comparison and the pre–post findings can be interpreted as treatment versus "each subject as his/her own control" comparisons. Comparison of the previous effect size statistics with those presented later for the standardized mean difference should make it evident, however, that these are not comparable formulations and they cannot be expected to yield comparable values. It follows that these two effect size statistics should not be mixed in the same meta-analysis. If the research studies of interest involve findings in both pre–post forms and group contrast forms, those different findings should be separated, each form coded with the appropriate effect size statistic, and each of the resulting sets of effect size values meta-analyzed separately.

Estimation Procedures. The terms required to compute the standardized mean gain effect size statistic and its associated inverse variance are the same as those required for the unstandardized case, previously described. As in that instance, deriving a satisfactory value for the correlation between the Time 1 and Time 2 measures can present problems. Also, the inverse variance term for the standardized mean gain effect size statistic involves the value of that statistic itself. This, of course, is estimated simply by taking the value that is generated by the computation of the effect size statistic for a given sample and using it in the computation of the inverse variance. Other estimation procedures are reviewed in Appendix B.

Example. A meta-analyst is interested in the erosion of mathematics knowledge over the summer vacation for high school students. A set of studies is compiled in which math achievement tests are given to the same sample of students at the end of the school year and again at the beginning of the next school year. Because the study findings of interest represent before and after measures on the same subject samples, a pre–post effect size statistic is suitable for the meta-analysis. The different studies, however, have used different math achievement tests so that their results are not numerically comparable. This situation requires that the study findings on those tests be standardized so that they are comparable across studies. The standardized pre–post mean gain effect size statistic is thus the appropriate way for the meta-analyst to represent these study findings.

Group Contrasts

Research findings in the form of group contrasts involve a variable that is measured on two or more groups of respondents and then compared across groups. The descriptive statistics that typically characterize this situation are the means, standard deviations, and sample sizes for each group on each variable. Alternatively, the groups may be compared on the proportion of each group exhibiting, or not exhibiting, a characteristic of interest. Differences among groups of these kinds are often examined with such familiar statistical tests as the t-test, analysis of variance (ANOVA), chi-square, Mann-Whitney U-test, and the like.

Research involving group contrasts is widespread and frequently meta-analyzed. Most experimental and quasi-experimental studies, for instance, provide findings in this form, e.g., comparison of the experimental group with the control group on one or more dependent variables. Comparison of groups that have not been experimentally assigned is also common, as in survey results that contrast demographic groups on variables relating to attitude, opinion, reported behavior, and the like. Correspondingly, there are a variety of effect size statistics available for representing group contrast findings, each tailored to a somewhat different research situation or form of statistical result. We will discuss four effect size statistics, specifically: (a) the *unstandardized mean difference*, (b) the *standardized mean difference*, (c) the *proportion difference*, and (d) the *odds-ratio*.

When the same operationalization of a variable of interest is used in all the research findings to be meta-analyzed and the variable is continuous, an effect size statistic can be constructed directly from the difference between the group means—the *unstandardized mean difference* effect size statistic. If the variable of interest is dichotomous and similarly measured in all studies, then an analogous effect size is the *difference between proportions*. A more common situation, however, involves group contrasts on some construct or set of constructs operationalized differently in different research studies. For instance, our running example focuses on the effects of challenge programs on juvenile delinquency, as indicated by the differences found between intervention and control groups in experimental studies. The research findings reported on this topic, however, use many different measures of delinquency as dependent variables, yielding results that are not numerically comparable across studies even though they deal with the same construct. To combine such findings in a meta-analysis, it is necessary to use an effect size statistic that standardizes the values from the original measures in some manner that makes them comparable. Two different effect size statistics are available for this situation, both widely used and well developed in terms of statistical theory and practical guidance. One is the *standardized mean difference*, which applies to contrasts between groups that are presented in the form of differences between the mean values on some variable for the respective groups. The other is the *odds-ratio*, which is defined for group contrasts presented as differences in relative frequencies or proportions between two groups. Research findings that include contrasts on *both* arithmetic means and differences in relative frequencies or proportions pose special problems for the meta-analyst who wishes to meta-analyze them together. This situation will be discussed after we look at the four group-contrast effect size statistics.

The Unstandardized Mean Difference. When the same operationalization of a variable of interest is used in all the group-contrast research findings to be meta-analyzed, i.e., using the same measurement procedures and numerical scale, and the variable is continuous, an effect size statistic can be constructed directly from the difference between the group means. Such a situation might occur when the meta-analyst is interested only in differences involving a particular measurement instrument that produces a graduated continuum of scores, e.g., scores on the WISC-R intelligence test. For such circumstances, an unstandardized effect size statistic can be constructed simply by differencing the two group means, as

$$ES_{um} = \overline{X}_{G1} - \overline{X}_{G2}, \tag{3.17}$$

$$SE_{um} = s_p\sqrt{\frac{1}{n_{G1}} + \frac{1}{n_{G2}}}, \tag{3.18}$$

$$w_{um} = \frac{1}{SE_{um}^2} = \frac{n_{G1}n_{G2}}{s_p^2(n_{G1} + n_{G2})}, \tag{3.19}$$

where $\overline{X}_{G1}$ is the mean for Group 1, $\overline{X}_{G2}$ is the mean for Group 2, n_{G1} is the number of subjects in Group 1, n_{G2} is the number of subjects in Group 2, and s_p is the pooled standard deviation, defined as

$$s_p = \sqrt{\frac{(n_{G1} - 1)s_{G1}^2 + (n_{G2} - 1)s_{G2}^2}{(n_{G1} - 1) + (n_{G2} - 1)}}, \tag{3.20}$$

where s_{G1} is the standard deviation for Group 1 and s_{G2} is the standard deviation for Group 2.

Estimation Procedures. Computation of this effect size statistic is straightforward, requiring only the two means at issue (or their difference directly), the standard deviations, and the sample sizes upon which they are based. Where one of these values is not reported (most likely the standard deviation), derivation or estimation may be possible from other statistics that are available, e.g., t-values from a t-test, one-way ANOVA tables, and the like. Appendix B provides guidance for such procedures.

Example. The Addiction Severity Index (ASI) is widely used as an intake measure for patients entering substance abuse treatment. A meta-analysis might examine gender differences on the ASI using descriptive statistics from a number of patient samples collected from studies at various treatment facilities. Because all the scores come from the same measurement instrument (ASI), the difference between the means for males and females in each study can be used without standardizing to create effect sizes that are comparable across studies.

The Standardized Mean Difference. This effect size statistic applies to research findings that contrast two groups on their respective mean scores on some dependent variable that is *not* operationalized the same across study samples. The most common situation of this sort is comparisons between the means of outcome measures for experimental and control groups in treatment effectiveness research. Another appropriate application, however, is comparison of mean scores between nonexperimentally defined groups, e.g., males and females in gender-differences research. There is significant literature on the statistical properties of this effect size statistic and far larger literature reporting its use in diverse meta-analyses (e.g., Cook et al., 1992; Cooper & Hedges, 1994; Hedges & Olkin, 1985). The standardized mean difference effect size statistic is calculated from the statistical information reported in a research study according to

$$ES_{sm} = \frac{\overline{X}_{G1} - \overline{X}_{G2}}{s_p}, \qquad (3.21)$$

where the terms are defined as in the earlier text for Formulas 3.17 through 3.20. However, this effect size index has been shown to be upwardly biased when based on small sample sizes, particularly samples less than 20 (Hedges, 1981). Hedges provided a simple correction for this bias and all subsequent computations will use this corrected or *unbiased* effect size estimate as follows:

$$ES'_{sm} = \left[1 - \frac{3}{4N - 9}\right] ES_{sm}, \tag{3.22}$$

$$SE_{sm} = \sqrt{\frac{n_{G1} + n_{G2}}{n_{G1} n_{G2}} + \frac{(ES'_{sm})^2}{2(n_{G1} + n_{G2})}}, \tag{3.23}$$

$$w_{sm} = \frac{1}{SE^2_{sm}} = \frac{2n_{G1} n_{G2}(n_{G1} + n_{G2})}{2(n_{G1} + n_{G2})^2 + n_{G1} n_{G2}(ES'_{sm})^2}, \tag{3.24}$$

where N is the total sample size $(n_{G1} + n_{G2})$, ES_{sm} is the biased standardized mean difference shown in Formula 3.21, n_{G1} is the number of subjects in Group 1, and n_{G2} is the number of subjects in Group 2.

By convention, when treatment and control groups are contrasted, a positive sign is assigned to the effect size when the treatment group does "better" than the control group; a negative sign is assigned when the treatment group does "worse" than the control group. Note that these signs do not necessarily correspond with the arithmetic sign that will result from simply subtracting the means. When high scores on the dependent variable indicate better performance, the signs work out according to this convention; but when low scores indicate better performance, the signs must be reversed. Similar considerations may apply to contrasts between nonexperimental groups.

In some applications of meta-analysis to experimental studies, the standard deviations for the treatment groups may themselves be affected by the treatment. For instance, treatments that are differentially effective for individual subjects increase the variation on the dependent measure in the treated group. In other situations the effect of treatment may be to decrease variation. An effective instructional program, for example, might bring students who were initially diverse in their ability up to a common performance ceiling. Under such circumstances, it is best to estimate the effect size using only the standard deviation of the control group since it is presumably unaffected by the treatment and, hence, a better estimate of the respective population variance. Smith and Glass (1977; Smith, Glass & Miller, 1980) used this technique as a precaution in their classic meta-analysis of the effects of psychotherapy, though it is not clear that it was necessary in that instance. When there is any doubt on this matter, it is wise to separately code the standard deviations for the two groups at issue (e.g., treatment and control) so that later analysis can examine whether there is any systematic difference. If not, both can be pooled to provide the advantages of larger sample size in the variance estimate (Hedges,

1981). If there is a significant difference, however, the more representative value can be used alone in the denominator of the effect size.

Estimation Procedures. It is not unusual for studies to fail to report the means or standard deviations (or variances) needed to compute the effect size. In such cases, the effect size can sometimes be estimated from other statistics that are reported. For example, the standardized mean difference effect size can be calculated directly from a t-value based on an independent t-test or from an F-ratio from a two-group one-way analysis of variance. There are several degrees of approximation to this effect size, depending upon what information is available. For two-group comparisons, these categories, from least to most approximate, are as follows:

(a) descriptive data are provided from which means and standard deviations can be computed,

(b) complete significance testing statistics are available; for instance, t-values and df from a t-test or F-values and df from a one-way ANOVA, along with sample sizes,

(c) an exact p-value is reported for a t-test or one-way ANOVA and the sample size for each group, or the total for both, is available, and

(d) a categorical p-value is reported (i.e., $p < .01$, $p < .05$, etc.) for a t-test or one-way ANOVA and the sample size for each group, or the total for both, is available.

In addition, there are some cases where information from other statistical tests or more complex ANOVAs is reported for which effect size estimation is sometimes possible. Appendix B provides a set of guidelines for estimating standardized mean difference effect sizes for a range of circumstances. A computer program developed by Shadish, Robinson, and Lu, (1999) is also very useful for estimation of standardized mean effect size statistics from various sorts of information found in study reports.

Example. The meta-analysis of challenge programs described in Chapter 2 focuses on studies involving comparison of a group of subjects in a challenge program with a control group in experimental or quasi-experimental designs. The primary outcome construct of interest is delinquent behavior. Eligible studies present variables related to this outcome with many different operationalizations, e.g., number of arrests over a given time period, various forms of self-report questionnaires, counts of school disciplinary actions, standardized measurement instruments such as the child behavior checklist (CBCL), and so forth. Because these operationalizations of delinquent behavior are different in the measures used and the associated numerical scales, their results are not directly comparable even though they deal with the same general construct. The standardized mean difference effect size statistic is thus an appropriate way to represent the effects of challenge programs on delinquency. By standardizing the difference between intervention and control group means on the corresponding pooled standard deviation, treatment effects are represented in terms of standard deviation units irrespective of the nature of the original operationalization and can be meaningfully combined and compared across studies.

The Proportion Difference. Group contrast findings may appear in the form of differences between proportions. For example, a meta-analysis may collect various studies of prisoners to examine the difference between violent and nonviolent offenders with regard to the proportion abused as children. Given comparable definitions of what constitutes being abused as a child, an effect size statistic can be constructed from the simple difference between the proportions associated with the respective groups using

$$ES_{pd} = p_{G1} - p_{G2}, \tag{3.25}$$

$$SE_{pd} = \sqrt{p(1 - p)\left(\frac{1}{n_{G1}} + \frac{1}{n_{G2}}\right)}, \tag{3.26}$$

$$w_{pg} = \frac{1}{SE_{pd}^2} = \frac{n_{G1}n_{G2}}{p(1 - p)(n_{G1} + n_{G2})}, \tag{3.27}$$

where p_{G1} is the proportion for Group 1, p_{G2} is the proportion for Group 2, n_{G1} is the number of subjects in Group 1, and n_{G2} is the number of subjects in Group 2, and p is the weighted mean of p_{G1} and p_{G2}, specifically $(n_{G1}p_{G1} + n_{G2}p_{G2})/(n_{G1} + n_{G2})$.

Estimation Procedures. Computation of this effect size statistic requires only the values of the two proportions being differenced and the sample size upon which each is based. These values will typically be reported in a study contrasting two groups or easily estimated from tabled values or frequency distributions. If not presented in such relatively direct form, there are not likely to be other statistics available from which estimation will be possible.

The proportion difference is both simple and intuitive. As Fleiss (1994) pointed out, these may be its only virtues. A disadvantage of the proportion difference is that the possible values of ES_{pd} are dependent on where p_{G1} (or p_{G2}) occurs between 0 and 1. That is, if p_{G1} equals .5, then the maximum value for ES_{pd} is also .5; if p_{G1} equals .1, then the minimum value of ES_{pd} is −.1 and the maximum value is .9. According to Fleiss, this may produce an apparent heterogeneity across studies, making it difficult to interpret between-study differences. We confirmed this expectation with a computer simulation that showed a consistent overestimation of the amount of heterogeneity across effect sizes and an underestimation of the confidence interval around the mean proportion difference. Therefore, it is recommended that the odds-ratio effect size be used in situations in which the variable of interest is dichotomous unless the study findings are quite similar with regard to p_{G1} values and the only analysis of interest is the mean ES_{pd}. Complex analyses, such as weighted multiple regression, also should be performed using the odds-ratio method.

The Odds-Ratio. The *odds-ratio* is an effect size statistic that compares two groups in terms of the relative odds of a status or event, e.g., death, illness, successful outcome, receipt of treatment, gender, exposure to a toxin, and so forth (Berlin, Laird, Sacks, & Chalmers, 1989; DerSimonian & Laird, 1986; Fleiss, 1994). The odds-ratio is often mistakenly interpreted as the ratio of two conditional probabilities (the rate ratio, also called the risk ratio). To understand the odds-ratio it is worth clarifying the meaning of *odds*. The odds of an event are defined as

$$\text{Odds of an event} = \frac{p}{1-p},$$

where p is the probability of the event. For example, if the probability of a successful outcome of treatment is .25, then the *odds* of that outcome are .33, that is, $.25/(1 − .25)$. Thus, the odds of a successful outcome, given treatment, are 1 to 3 (one success to three failures), whereas the probability of a successful outcome is 1 in 4 (one success in four cases). Suppose that, for the control group, the probability of a successful outcome is .20. The odds of a successful outcome, given no treatment are then .25, that is $.20/(1 − .20)$. From the odds of success for the treatment and control groups, we can calculate the *odds-ratio*, which is the ratio of those two odds, that is, $.33/.25$ or 1.33. For this fictitious data, the odds of a successful outcome are 1.33 times greater for the treatment group than the control group.

The odds-ratio is applicable to research findings that use dichotomous variables and are presented in the form of relative frequencies and propor-

Table 3.1

	Frequencies		Proportions	
	Status A	Not Status A	Status A	Not Status A
Group 1	a	b	$p_a = a/(a+b)$	$p_b = b/(a+b)$
Group 2	c	d	$p_c = c/(c+d)$	$p_d = d/(c+d)$

tions, e.g., in cross-tabulation tables. It is particularly well suited to the study of events, for instance, the proportion of a sample who died of a heart attack in a given year. It is widely used in meta-analyses of medical research for just this reason.

The odds-ratio is defined in relation to a 2×2 table of results expressed as either frequencies or proportions where a, b, c, and d indicate the cell frequencies and p_a, p_b, p_c, and p_d indicate the proportion of each group in each status (see Table 3.1). Examples of status variables include recidivated versus not recidivated, pregnant versus not pregnant, passed exam versus failed exam, and abused as a child versus not abused as a child. An odds-ratio can be calculated from either the cell frequencies or proportions in a 2×2 table using

$$ES_{OR} = \frac{ad}{bc} = \frac{p_a p_d}{p_b p_c} = \frac{p_a/p_b}{p_c/p_d} = \frac{p_a(1-p_c)}{p_c(1-p_a)} \qquad (3.28)$$

(If a, b, c, or $d = 0$, add .5 to all cells).

The odds-ratio has the inconvenient form of being centered around 1 rather than zero, with 1 indicating no relationship, values between 0 and 1 indicating a negative relationship, and values greater than 1 indicating a positive relationship. An odds-ratio of .5 therefore has the equivalent strength of relationship as an odds-ratio of 2 (the inverse of .5) but in the opposite direction. To compensate for this peculiarity, all analyses are performed on the natural log of the odds-ratio. The distributional form of the logged odds-ratio is approximately normal with a mean of 0 and a standard deviation of 1.83. Thus, a negative value reflects a negative relationship and a positive value reflects a positive relationship. An additional advantage of using the logged odds for calculation purposes is that the standard error becomes easy to calculate. The logged odds-ratio, standard error and inverse variance weight are calculated as

$$ES_{LOR} = \log_e(ES_{OR}), \tag{3.29}$$

$$SE_{LOR} = \sqrt{\frac{1}{a} + \frac{1}{b} + \frac{1}{c} + \frac{1}{d}}, \tag{3.30}$$

$$w_{LOR} = \frac{1}{SE_{LOR}^2} = \frac{abcd}{ab(c+d) + cd(a+b)} \tag{3.31}$$

(If $a, b, c,$ or $d = 0$, add .5 to all cells),

where the terms are defined in Table 3.1. Summary statistics such as means and confidence intervals can be converted back to odds-ratios by taking the antilogarithms,

$$ES_{OR} = e^{ES_{LOR}}, \tag{3.32}$$

where e is the base of the natural logarithm, or approximately 2.718, and ES_{LOR} is any logged odds-ratio.

The logged odds-ratio can be expressed in another form that illustrates its connection to the standardized mean difference effect size statistics more familiar to many social scientists. Specifically, the logged odds-ratio can be computed as the difference between the logit for each group (see Eq. 3.4, presented earlier), stated symbolically as

$$ES_{LOR} = \log_e\left[\frac{p_{G1}}{1 - p_{G1}}\right] - \log_e\left[\frac{p_{G2}}{1 - p_{G2}}\right], \tag{3.33}$$

where p_{G1} is the proportion of persons in Group 1 in the more desirable category, and p_{G2} is the proportion of persons in Group 2 in the more desirable category. Thus, the logged odds-ratio can be interpreted directly as the difference between the log transformed odds of "success" in each group.

Cell Frequencies Equal to Zero. A problem in using the odds-ratio as the effect size statistic in meta-analysis occurs when cell frequencies equal zero. Note that formulas 3.28 and 3.30 can only be successfully calculated if all terms are greater than zero. Adding .5 to the cell frequencies solves this problem by eliminating any zeros but creates a downward bias (Fleiss, 1994). If few of the 2 × 2 contingency tables representing the findings in a set of studies contain zeros, then adding .5 to the cell frequencies for those few is workable and produces reasonably accurate estimates. At worst, these few estimates will tend to be conservative, slightly understating the strength of the relationship. However, if cell frequencies of zero are common in the research domain of interest, then the Mantel–Haenszel method of combining odds-ratios should be used (Hauck, 1989). This method does not rely on individually calculated odds-ratios, thus avoiding the problem of zeros. Unfortunately, the Mantel–Haenszel method does not lend itself to the generic framework for configuring and analyzing meta-analytic data presented throughout this book and, without the individual odds-ratios, the full complement of analysis options presented in Chapter 6 cannot be performed. See Fleiss (1994) for specifics on the Mantel–Haenszel approach if your meta-analysis involves small sample sizes ($n < 100$) and numerous cell frequencies equal to zero. The results from the Mantel–Haenszel method and the logged odds-ratio method based on the effect size statistics presented above converge as the sample sizes become large (Fleiss, 1994) and the latter is commonly used as an approximation to the Mantel–Haenszel method.

Example. A researcher wishes to meta-analyze studies of the effectiveness of programs for preventing adolescents from dropping out of high school. The research designs for eligible studies are restricted to experimental comparisons between an intervention and a control group. All the outcome variables of interest are dichotomous indicators of the number or proportion of students dropping out versus those staying in school through graduation. Because both the independent variables (intervention vs. control groups) and the dependent variables (dropping out vs. not dropping out) are natural dichotomies, the odds-ratio is the most appropriate effect size statistic for the meta-analysis.

Mixing Group Differences Measured on Continuous and Dichotomous Scales. A common problem in meta-analyses of group differences research is the inconsistency with which the construct of interest is scaled and measured. That is, a construct that is continuous in nature may be measured by both continuous and dichotomous scales. Continuous constructs may be measured originally in a dichotomous fashion or continuous measures may be artificially dichotomized by the study authors. For example, delinquent behavior following a challenge program intervention may be measured with a multi-item self-report delinquency inventory producing a continuous numeric value or a dichotomous variable indicating whether the juvenile has been arrested 6 months after intervention, and the continuous self-report values may be analyzed and presented in original form or dichotomized by the study author. Because the standardized mean difference and the odds-ratio effect size statistics are not numerically comparable, the aggregation of study findings addressing the same general construct from continuous and dichotomous measures is problematic.

A solution adopted by many meta-analysts is to use the standardized mean difference effect size statistic and, when dichotomous dependent variables are encountered, to apply a transformation that adjusts for the dichotomization. Common methods for doing this are through the probit, logit, and arcsine transforms. The logic of the probit transform is straightforward. The probit of a proportion, p, is the z-value of the standard normal distribution below which p proportion of the distribution falls. In other words, it is the z-value at the cut-point of the normal distribution that reproduces a dichotomy with the observed proportion of "successes" and "failures." The probit of $p = .5$ is 0, since $z = 0$ is the midpoint of the standard normal distribution. The difference between two probits (i.e., difference between the respective z-values) is an estimate of what the standardized mean difference effect size would have been had the variable been continuous and normally distributed. In theory, the probit should be an excellent estimate of the standardized mean difference effect size. However, as the underlying distribution deviates from normality, the probit tends to overestimate the standardized mean difference, except when the cut-point is in the tail portion of a skewed distribution. This overestimate can be extreme, exceeding 75% of the magnitude of the corresponding standardized mean difference.

The logit method is based on the logged odds ratio (Formulas 3.28, 3.29, 3.33). The logistic distribution is approximately normal with a standard deviation of 1.83. A logged odds ratio can be rescaled by dividing it by 1.83 (or multiplying it by .55) to make it directly comparable to a standardized mean difference effect size and a close approximation to the probit transformation. If a majority, but not all, of the studies in a meta-analysis use a dichotomous measure to examine group differences, then using the logit transformation for the dichotomous measures and the standardized mean difference for the continuous measures may be the best approach (see Hassleblad & Hedges, 1995, for more detail on combining logged odds ratios and standardized mean difference effect sizes).

The arcsine method is borrowed from statistical power analysis (Cohen, 1988) and the corresponding effect size is defined as the difference between the arcsine of the proportion in one group and that in the other group. This method creates an effect size for the difference between proportions whose statistical power is independent of the location of p and $1 - p$ between 0 and 1 and which is approximately equivalent to the standardized mean difference effect size. However, the arcsine method will always yield a smaller estimate of the standardized mean difference effect size than the probit method and, except under conditions of extreme skew, will underestimate the standardized mean difference.

What is a meta-analyst to do? There are several reasonable approaches. First, the meta-analyst may simply choose to synthesize the continuous and dichotomous dependent variables for a construct separately. If the respective sets of variables are inherently continuous and dichotomous, i.e., the underlying distributions they represent are in fact actually continuous in the one case and dichotomous in the other, this is the most statistically defensible procedure. While maintaining statistical purity, however, separate analyses with different effect size statistics have the disadvantage of reducing the number of effect sizes in each analysis for the often interesting between-studies comparisons. In addition, there are not many cases where the same dependent variable construct has both an inherently continuous and inherently dichotomous expression in research findings. More typically in cases of mixed measures, the actual construct at issue has a continuous underlying distribution that is simply reduced to a dichotomy by some measurement operationalizations.

When the construct can be assumed inherently continuous, the meta-analyst may use the arcsine, logit, or probit method of estimating the standardized mean difference effect size for dichotomous dependent variables and the standardized mean difference for continuous ones, then analyze all effect sizes together. This must be done carefully, however, and the results examined to assess the extent to which it may affect any important conclusions from the meta-analysis, e.g., to ensure that those conclusions are stable irrespective of what effect size method is used for the dichotomous variables.

We believe that for most purposes the more conservative arcsine method should be preferred. When we have used the arcsine estimates along with standardized mean difference effect sizes in our meta-analyses, sensitivity analyses have shown that the arcsine effect sizes for the dichotomous variables have been somewhat smaller but not greatly different. As a safeguard, we include a dummy variable for whether the effect size used the arcsine or not in all regression analyses of between study differences. That dummy variable has sometimes been statistically significant and of a meaningful magnitude in these analyses, reinforcing the need to take care that differences associated with the effect size approximation are not confused with substantive differences between studies. Of course, if the construct of interest is expected to be normally distributed in all the study samples, then the probit method, or its approximation, the logit, should provide a better estimate. Further theoretical and empirical work is needed to assess the appropriateness of each of these methods under varying conditions.

As an aid to selecting the appropriate effect size statistic for research findings that represent group contrasts on dependent variables, Figure 3.1 presents a decision tree that summarizes the discussion and advice provided in the foregoing text.

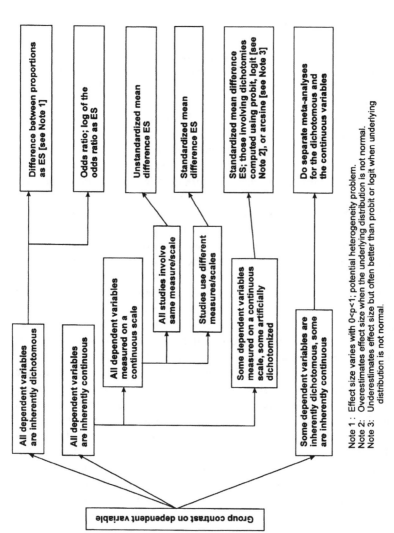

Figure 3.1.   Effect size decision tree for studies involving group contrasts on dependent variables.

Association Between Variables

Another common situation in which a meta-analyst may require an effect size statistic involves study findings that deal with the covariation between two variables. There are many such situations, especially when data from surveys, interviews, or records are analyzed. One might, for instance, examine the association between family socioeconomic status and students' English grades in high school or be interested in the relationship between reports of prior substance abuse and severity of symptoms among mental health patients. Or, the association at issue may be predictive, as in the relationship between a risk variable measured at one time and the subsequent appearance of behavioral problems. Many measurement issues involve association as well. Reliability, for example, is often assessed by the correlation between scores on the same measure taken on two occasions and validity can be investigated by the correlation between a measure and a criterion variable. In such cases the effect size index used in meta-analysis is usually the familiar *Pearson product-moment correlation coefficient* and its variants. Other relevant effect size statistics for some situations include the *odds-ratio* and the *standardized mean difference* discussed in the preceding text.

Before discussing the particulars of the effect size statistics for the association between two variables, a short digression is needed to put in perspective the various forms of research findings that can be viewed as essentially bivariate correlations. In particular, we must recognize that any two-variable relationship can be viewed as a bivariate correlation. Research findings on group contrasts, for instance, can be presented as the correlation between a dichotomous independent variable (group) and a dependent variable. When the dependent variable is a continuous measure, we have the situation to which the standardized mean difference effect size statistic is typically applied. When the dependent variable is dichotomous, we have the situation to which the odds-ratio effect size statistic is typically applied. While those effect size statistics provide a more natural representation of findings that focus on differences between groups, such findings could alternatively be represented as correlational relationships between a dichotomously coded independent variable (e.g., group = 0 or 1) and a dependent variable, which also may be dichotomous.

The standard product-moment correlation is computed on two continuous variables, i.e., variables whose values are graduated from some low to some high score. When that same computation is done on variables that depart from this form it produces distinct variations of the correlation coefficient. The *point-biserial* correlation coefficient, for instance, is the product-moment correlation computed for the relationship between a dichotomous and a continuous variable and, similarly, the *phi* coefficient (also known as the fourfold point correlation) is the product-moment correlation computed for the relationship between two dichotomous variables.

Correlation coefficients computed with dichotomous variables, however, have some quirks. If the dichotomous variable is assumed to have an underlying continuum that is normally distributed, then the observed correlation will be less than it would be if a continuous measure had been used (Hunter & Schmidt, 1990a; McNemar, 1966). For example, a correlation between social support, measured dichotomously as high and low, and depression, measured continuously, would be smaller than if social support had been measured continuously. For a 50-50 split on the dichotomous measure, the correlation is attenuated to .80 of the value it would have with a continuous measure, assuming an underlying normal distribution. The amount of attenuation increases as the skew on the dichotomy increases. The correlation for a 90-10 split on one measure would be .59 of the corresponding correlation without the dichotomization. The effect of dichotomization is compounded when both variables of the correlation are dichotomized.

One consequence of this circumstance is that correlation coefficients with one or both of the variables dichotomized will not be numerically comparable to those using continuous variables. When considering effect size statistics for research findings in the form of bivariate correlations, therefore, some attention must be given to the way in which the variables are scaled. With this in mind, we consider the various possibilities for bivariate correlations and their implications for effect size statistics.

Two Dichotomous Variables (The Odds-Ratio and the Phi Coefficient). Research findings in the form of relationships between two inherently dichotomous variables (e.g., male vs. female, dead vs. alive, arrested vs. not arrested) can be represented by the odds-ratio effect size statistic (described earlier) and by the product moment correlation coefficient (described later), which, in this application, will yield phi coefficients. The basis for choosing between these is not cut and dry, but there are some salient considerations. Most important, perhaps, is the extent of the disproportionality between the number of cases taking each value of the dichotomous variables. When the split is fairly extreme on one of the variables, e.g., 70-30 or more, and not comparably extreme on the other, the phi coefficient is sharply restricted in its maximum value so that it can be considerably less than 1.00 even with the strongest relationship that is mathematically possible between the variables (Guilford, 1965). For example, the maximum possible phi value for a 2 × 2 table with a 90-10 split on one variable and 50-50 split on the other is .33; considerably less than 1. For an 80-20 split the maximum only climbs to .5. The odds-ratio, on the other hand, is insensitive to changes in the marginal proportions, that is, the proportion split for each dichotomy, and is therefore well suited to represent low frequency events.

However, the odds-ratio is generally interpreted as the comparison between two subsamples on a dichotomous dependent variable whereas the phi coefficient is more naturally interpreted simply as the relationship or predictive strength between two variables measured on a given sample. Thus, when the research findings of interest focus on the differences between two readily distinguishable groups on a dichotomous dependent variable (e.g., gender differences in mortality rates), the odds-ratio may be more easily interpreted even though the phi coefficient would carry similar information. Conversely, when the findings of interest focus on the relationship between two variables (e.g., pass–fail relations between two items on an achievement test), the correlation coefficient may be more readily interpretable. These differences in perspective (group difference vs. relationship between variables) are likely to be reflected in the statistics that are typically reported for the research findings of interest, which can have practical implications. If most of the studies report correlation coefficients, the meta-analyst would be wise to select that as the effect size statistic. If cross-tabulation tables or similar presentations showing differences in frequencies or proportions for subsamples are most common, it will generally prove easier to compute odds-ratios as the effect size statistic.

Finally, the odds-ratio has statistical properties that lend itself to meta-analysis, whereas the phi coefficient is problematic (Haddock et al., 1998). In particular, the sensitivity of the phi coefficient to variations in marginal proportions produces "excess" heterogeneity (Fleiss, 1994). That is, given a collection of phi coefficients that are known to be estimating a common correlation, their distribution will incorrectly appear heterogeneous. This also affects the confidence interval for a mean phi coefficient. The odds-ratio, on the other hand, conforms nicely to statistical theory. Computer simulations show that the findings from repeated meta-analysis using odds-ratios converge on the population value and produce an accurate homogeneity statistic and confidence interval.

Example. Suppose a meta-analyst is working with a set of studies of gender differences in mortality among patients with lung cancer for purposes of determining if the probability of death is greater for males. Because both gender and mortality are inherently dichotomous variables, and most studies can be expected to report their relationship in 2×2 tables or equivalent form, the odds-ratio is an appropriate effect size statistic for representing the findings of interest.

A Dichotomous and Continuous Variable (The Point-Biserial Coefficient and the Standardized Mean Difference). Research findings in the form of a relationship between an inherently dichotomous variable (e.g., male–female, treatment–control) and a continuous variable (e.g., test scores, days of hospitalization) can be appropriately represented as a standardized mean difference effect size statistic or as a product moment correlation coefficient, which, applied to variables of this sort, takes the form of a point-biserial correlation coefficient. This situation is much like that discussed above for two dichotomous variables. The point-biserial correlation coefficient is subject to sharp range restrictions if the dichotomous variable has a relatively extreme split, e.g., 80-20 or worse, and thus does not have especially desirable properties under those circumstances (Hunter & Schmidt, 1990a; Guilford, 1965; McNemar, 1966). The standardized mean difference, on the other hand, does not suffer from this problem and has superior statistical properties for meta-analytic purposes. Therefore, it is recommended that if the association of interest is between a dichotomous and a continuous variable, then the standardized mean difference effect size be used. For purposes of interpretation, the standardized mean difference effect size and related statistics (e.g., mean, confidence intervals) can be converted into the metric of a point-biserial correlation coefficient with

$$r_{pb} = \frac{ES_{sm}}{\sqrt{(1/p(1-p)) + ES_{sm}^2}}, \qquad (3.34)$$

where ES_{sm} is any standardized mean difference effect size, p is the proportion of subjects in Group 1, and $1 - p$ is the proportion of subjects in Group 2. If the two groups are equal in size, that is, if $p = 1 - p = .5$ or equivalently $n_{G1} = n_{G2}$, then the preceding formula simplifies to

$$r_{pb} = \frac{ES_{sm}}{\sqrt{4 + ES_{sm}^2}}. \qquad (3.35)$$

Likewise, the standardized mean difference can be computed for any study reporting a point-biserial coefficient with

$$ES_{sm} = \frac{r_{pb}}{\sqrt{p(1-p)(1-r^2)}}, \qquad (3.36)$$

where r_{pb} is the correlation coefficient and p is defined above. In a similar fashion, when p equals .5, this formula simplifies to

$$ES_{sm} = \frac{2r_{pb}}{\sqrt{1 + r^2}}. \qquad (3.37)$$

Two Continuous Variables (The Product-Moment Correlation). When the research findings to be meta-analyzed involve bivariate relationships in which both the variables are continuous, the product-moment correlation coefficient is the straightforwardly appropriate effect size statistic. Indeed, virtually all such research findings will be reported in terms of the correlation coefficient in the original studies, so it will rarely be sensible to consider any other effect size statistic to represent them. The correlation coefficient for the relationship between variable x and variable y is defined as

$$r_{xy} = \frac{\sigma_{xy}^2}{\sigma_x \sigma_y}, \qquad (3.38)$$

where σ_{xy}^2 is the covariance between x and y, and σ_x and σ_y are the standard deviations of x and y, respectively. The product-moment correlation, therefore, is the covariation between x and y divided by the product of the standard deviations of each of the variables. The correlation coefficient is already a standardized index and therefore is usable as a meta-analytic effect size statistic in its raw form even if the variables being correlated are differently operationalized. It is this inherent standardization that yields correlations varying from -1 to $+1$ no matter what the range of numerical values on the variables to which it is applied.

In its standard form, however, the product-moment correlation coefficient has some undesirable statistical properties, including a problematic standard error formulation (Alexander et al., 1989; Rosenthal, 1994). Recall that the standard error is used to determine the inverse variance weight needed for analysis. When used as effect sizes, therefore, correlations are usually transformed using Fisher's Z_r-transform (Hedges & Olkin, 1985), defined as

$$ES_{Z_r} = .5 \log_e \left[\frac{1 + r}{1 - r} \right], \qquad (3.39)$$

where r is the correlation coefficient and $\log_e$ is the natural logarithm. The transformed values can either be calculated using this equation in an appropriate computer program or looked up in a table of Z_r-transformed values, e.g., Cooper and Hedges (1994, p. 552), Hedges & Olkin (1985, p. 333), and Hays, (1988, p. 942). Any Z_r-transformed correlation or mean correlation can be transformed back into standard correlational form for ease of interpretation. This is done using the inverse of the Z_r-transformation[1] (Hedges & Olkin, 1985), shown as

$$r = \frac{e^{2ES_{Z_r}} - 1}{e^{2ES_{Z_r}} + 1} \tag{3.40}$$

where r is the individual or mean correlation, ES_{Z_r} is the corresponding individual or mean Z_r-transformed correlation, and e is the base of the natural logarithm or approximately 2.718. Expressed in the forms we have used for other effect size statistics, we can now present the correlation coefficient as an effect size statistic as

$$ES_r = r, \tag{3.41}$$

$$ES_{z_r} = .5 \log_e \left[\frac{1 + ES_r}{1 - ES_r} \right], \tag{3.42}$$

$$SE_{z_r} = \frac{1}{\sqrt{n - 3}}, \tag{3.43}$$

$$w_{z_r} = \frac{1}{SE_{z_r}^2} = n - 3, \tag{3.44}$$

where r is the correlation coefficient, and n is the total sample size.

Estimation Procedures. Since most studies that investigate the correlations among variables report their results directly in terms of the product-moment correlation coefficient, effect size coding generally will require no more than simply recording that correlation. However, the meta-analyst is likely to encounter some instances where correlational information is presented in some other form, most often as a cross-tabulation table. In such cases it may be possible to compute or estimate the desired correlation coefficient. As with the standardized mean difference effect size statistic discussed earlier, estimation can also sometimes be done from p-values or other such information generated by statistical significance testing. Appendix B presents some useful procedures for these situations.

Example. A meta-analyst wishes to investigate the validity of the ratings made by personnel managers during an employment interview. An appropriate set of studies is assembled which report the strength of association between interviewer ratings and measures of subsequent job performance for a variety of jobs and employment settings. The relationship of primary interest to the meta-analyst is a correlational one, most of the studies report their findings as correlation coefficients, and both interviewers' ratings and job performance are typically measured as continuous variables. The product-moment correlation is an appropriate effect size statistic for this situation. For convenience in conducting some of the analyses, the researcher may use the Fisher's Z_r-transformed version of this effect size statistic, then convert the results back into regular correlation coefficients for interpretation.

Mixed Pairings of Dichotomous and Continuous Variables. In the creatively untidy world of research, what meta-analysts most often find among the studies reporting the bivariate relationships they wish to analyze is a variety of variable types and statistical forms. Even with a relatively narrow definition of the constructs and variables whose relationship is of interest, the pertinent bivariate research findings may well include both continuous and dichotomous versions of each variable in assorted combinations. A further complication is that when variables of interest are configured as dichotomies in the original study, they may be artificial. That is, the variable may not be inherently dichotomous in the way that male–female is but, rather, be a pair of dichotomous categories imposed on an underlying continuum. For example, if relevant research findings are those that report the relationship between academic achievement and drug use for youth, both these variables are most appropriately viewed as naturally continuous—a youth has some degree of academic achievement and some degree of drug use. The operationalization of these constructs in some studies, however, may dichotomize academic achievement into "high" versus "low" or "passing" versus "failing" and may dichotomize drug use into, say, "been arrested for a drug offense" versus "never been arrested" or "user" versus "nonuser."

This situation presents two problems. First, when a variable in a bivariate relationship is naturally continuous but artificially dichotomized in measurement or analysis, the standard product-moment correlation coefficient is technically not the most appropriate statistic to represent it. If one of the two variables is artificially dichotomized, the biserial correlation provides a better representation and, with both variables artificially dichotomized, the tetrachoric correlation is more appropriate (Guilford, 1965; McNemar, 1966). These coefficients, however, are not produced simply by applying the computational formula for the standard product-moment coefficient to dichotomous values. Moreover, they both have distinct standard error terms and hence require distinct inverse variance weights and make rather strong assumptions regarding the normality of the underlying continuous variables. Because they are a different sort of beast from standard product-moment correlation coefficients, combining them in the same analysis with standard coefficients is questionable.

In practice, the technical distinction between a natural dichotomy and an artificial one imposed on a natural continuum is widely ignored in meta-analyses working with correlation coefficient effect size statistics, except in the area of measurement generalization and validity. What remains, however, is the problem associated with the constraint on the numerical value of standard correlation coefficients when they are computed on dichotomous variables, especially those with splits that are not close to 50-50. This means that the meta-analyst might have two research findings representing the same strength of relationship but, if one or both variables are dichotomized in one finding and not the other, they will yield numerically different effect size values. Moreover, since the correlation coefficient by design is constrained within a fairly narrow range (absolute values from 0 to 1), the amount of distortion associated with dichotomization can be large relative to the general magnitude of the correlations at issue. This, of course, can introduce considerable bias into the set of effect size values the meta-analyst wishes to analyze with regard to the strength of the bivariate relationship of interest.

Fortunately, correlation coefficients can be adjusted to correct for attenuation due to artificial dichotomization if the assumption of an underlying normal distribution is tenable. This correction only requires information about the proportion of cases in the lower and upper halves of the dichotomy, which is often available from research reports or can be estimated from information that is reported. This correction is discussed in detail in Hunter and Schmidt (1990a) and summary formulas are provided later in Chapter 6. In cases where bivariate relationships between the same two constructs are reported using both dichotomized and continuous measures, therefore, the correlation coefficient effect size statistic can be used to represent all the findings on the assumption that the dichotomies are artificially imposed on the same general continuum that the continuous variables measure. Each correlation that involves a dichotomous variable can then be adjusted using the Hunter and Schmidt (1990a) procedure so that the values they yield will be more appropriately comparable to those resulting from the correlation of two continuous variables.

As an additional precaution in any situation involving a mix of effect size values derived from somewhat different statistical forms or types of variables, it is wise to code information about which forms and types are the basis for each effect size value. For instance, information could be coded to indicate which variables in a given correlation were dichotomous, how extreme the split was on that variable (i.e., 90-10, 80-20, etc.), and whether a correction for dichotomization was applied by the meta-analyst to that particular correlation. When the effect size values are analyzed, the meta-analyst can then examine the extent to which the variation among the effect size values is associated with the presence of dichotomous variables, the skew in their distributions, or inconsistencies in applied corrections. This not only provides diagnostic information about any distortion introduced into the effect size values by mixing correlations based on continuous and dichotomous variables but permits additional adjustments to be made by treating these diagnostic items as covariates during the analysis phase in ways explained in Chapter 6 of this volume.

As a guide to recognizing different mixes of correlational relationships and selecting appropriate effect size statistics, Figure 3.2 presents a decision tree for the situations likely to be encountered in meta-analyses of association between variables.

Multivariate Relationships

There are many interesting research findings involving more than two variables, that is, multivariate relationships. For example, some research questions are explored through multiple regression, structural equation modeling, factor analysis, discriminant analysis, and the like. Multivariate relationships present special challenges to meta-analysis. However, there are approaches to handling research of this type. For example, Greenwald, Hedges, and Laine (1994) were interested in synthesizing the quantitative multivariate models of the relationship between resource inputs and school outcomes. The findings of interest were the regression coefficients for resource inputs (per pupil expenditure, teacher salary, and other resource inputs) predicting school achievement. Although standardized regression coefficients are, as the name implies, standardized, the varying sets of independent variables across regression equations complicates their synthesis. In particular, the standardized regression coefficient from each analysis is assumed to be estimating a different population parameter. Also, the standard error, and hence the inverse variance weight, of each regression coefficient generally cannot be computed from data reported in published studies. Thus, effect size meta-analysis of the type presented throughout this book was not possible. Greenwald et al. approached this situation in two ways. First, they conducted a combined significance test analysis. This allowed a determination of whether the aggregate data showed a significant effect, that is, rejection of the null hypothesis that there is no relationship between resource inputs and school achievement. Second,

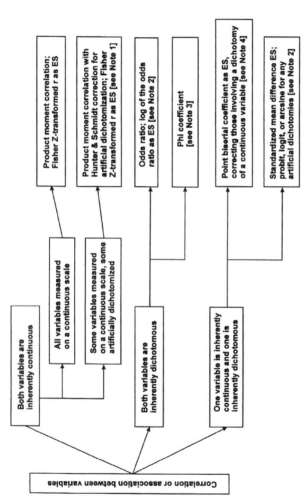

Figure 3.2. Effect size decision tree for studies involving correlation or association between variables.

Greenwald et al. conducted a "limited" analysis of the standardized (and "half-standardized") regression coefficients, calculating the median regression coefficient for each independent variable of interest (i.e., per pupil expenditure, faculty salaries, and other resources). While this analysis did not allow for the assessment of heterogeneity and between studies effects (discussed in Chapter 6), it allowed for a stronger set of conclusions than would have been possible from a qualitative or vote-counting review that relied solely on the statistical significance of regression parameters.

This example illustrates some of the difficulties with meta-analyzing multivariate relationships, these being that the effect size statistics of interest depend on what other variables are in the multivariate analysis and the difficulty in constructing inverse variance weights from information available in published reports. Thus, it is not generally feasible to do a full, proper effect size oriented meta-analysis of multivariate relationships, although for some purposes it might be informative to do some simple aggregation and descriptive comparison as was done by Greenwald et al.

An alternative approach, and the direction that meta-analytic practice is likely to go, is to use meta-analysis to synthesize the statistics upon which the multivariate analysis is based, generally correlations, from the original studies. Multivariate analyses can then be performed on the synthesized correlation matrix. Illustrative examples of this approach to multivariate meta-analyses in the literature are Becker (1992), Premack & Hunter (1988), and G. Becker (1996). Becker (1992) synthesized correlations among predictors of science achievement separately for males and females and performed multivariate analyses to assess whether or not the same set of variables was important for both sexes. Premack and Hunter tested a model of employee decisions about unionization involving five predictors while Becker (1996) synthetized correlation matrices for factor analysis. While this approach is promising, the omission of the full correlation matrix from most reports of multivariate research limits its applicability. Meta-analysis of multivariate findings will be greatly facilitated by a change in the publication norms such that reporting correlation matrices becomes standard.

Reports of Nonsignificance and Missing
Data Problems in Coding Effect Sizes

A frustration in coding studies for meta-analysis is eligible findings for which insufficient information is available to calculate an effect size. For example, a study may simply report that an effect was not statistically significant or that is was statistically significant but not report quantitative information such as means and standard deviations or a t-value. As with all missing data, the concern is that the missingness is not random. That is, the meta-analytic findings will be biased if small or zero effects are less likely than larger ones to be reported with sufficient information for effect size calculations. Meta-analysts have approached this problem in several ways.

The easiest approach, and one adopted by many meta-analysts, is to ignore the problem altogether, considering only those effect sizes for which all of the necessary information is available. While tempting, this may not always be best.

A second approach is to impute a value for the missing effect sizes, such as zero. That is, if a study merely reports that the effect size was nonsignificant, the effect size could be coded as zero. For statistically significant effects without an exact probability level, the effect size can be estimated based on an assumption that $p = .05$. In other words, using methods discussed in Appendix B, the minimum effect size value necessary to attain a $p = .05$ for a given sample size can be determined. This approach is admittedly conservative, resulting in a downward bias in the mean effect size across studies. This is adequate only for purposes of rejecting the null hypothesis that the effect of interest is zero in the population. This downward bias becomes problematic when answering the questions "How big is the effect?" and, "Is the effect different for different types of studies?" It is recommended that analyses aimed at answering these latter questions not use effect sizes imputed as zero from reports of statistical nonsignificance. For a discussion of the problems with this method, see Pigott (1994).

A third approach is to code the direction of effect for relevant findings for which an effect size cannot be calculated, e.g., positive, negative, no difference, and unknown. The distribution of the direction of effects for the "missing" effect sizes can be compared to the distribution of direction for the observed effect sizes. Thus, this method provides a simple, although imperfect, means of assessing the seriousness of the missingness problem. The lack of any serious bias due to missing effect sizes in the observed effect size distribution is plausible if the two distributions of directions are similar. This approach is related to the vote-counting method of synthesis (see Bushman, 1994). Bushman and Wang (1995, 1996) have developed a statistical procedure for combining vote-counts of direction of effect with standardized mean difference or correlation type effect sizes to produce an estimate of the overall mean effect size. This approach can facilitate an assessment of the robustness of meta-analysis results based only on effect sizes.

The problem of noncalculable effect sizes is also related to the "file drawer" problem discussed in Chapter 8. Not only may studies selectively report significant effects but studies producing significant effects may be more likely to be written-up and published. There currently are no easy methods of assuring that the findings from your meta-analysis are not biased due to the absence of unobserved and unobservable effect sizes. The aggressive tracking down of unpublished manuscripts, clear criteria regarding the boundaries for eligible studies and eligible effect sizes, and careful attention to coding and analysis are ultimately the best hedge against serious bias.

Kraemer, Gardner, Brooks, and Yesavage (1998) proposed a radical approach to reduce the potential effects of publication bias and the file drawer problem. They recommended restricting a meta-analysis to studies with adequate statistical power, that is, studies with large sample sizes. This approach makes poor use of the available empirical evidence on a topic and ignores one of the great advantages of meta-analysis: the ability to attain high statistical power from a collection of underpowered studies. The recommendation of Kraemer et al. is based on the assumption that only statistically significant findings will become published. Under this extreme assumption, the bias in mean effect sizes estimates would be substantial under typical conditions. Examination of the data from almost any meta-analysis will show, however, that statistically nonsignificant findings do get published, just at a lower rate than significant ones.

SUMMARY OF EFFECT SIZE STATISTICS

For convenience, Table 3.2 summarizes the different effect size statistics that have been discussed in this chapter, along with the associated standard error and inverse variance weight terms. These effect size statistics should be used, however, only after consulting the sections of this chapter which discuss them and their applications.

NOTE

1. We should note that not all meta-analysts favor using the Z-transformed correlation effect sizes. Hunter and Schmidt (1990b) argued that it is biased upward and prefer combining correlations without the Z-transform. However, this approach introduces some complications in other computations the meta-analyst will want to conduct, e.g., those involving effect size variances and weights. We will present subsequent formulations using the more convenient Z-transformed correlations but the interested analyst may wish to consult Alexander, Scozzaro and Borodkin (1989), Hedges and Olkin (1985), Hunter and Schmidt (1990b), Rosenthal (1994), and Shadish and Haddock (1994) for more discussion of this issue.

Table 3.2

Effect Size, Standard Error and Inverse Variance Weight Formulas for each Effect Size Type

Effect Size Type	Effect Size Statistic	Standard Error	Inverse Variance
One Variable Relationships—Central Tendency Description			
Proportion—direct method	$ES_p = p = \dfrac{k}{n}$	$SE_p = \sqrt{\dfrac{p(1-p)}{n}}$	$w_p = \dfrac{n}{p(1-p)}$
Proportion—logit method	$ES_l = \log_e\left[\dfrac{p}{1-p}\right]$	$SE_l = \sqrt{\dfrac{1}{np} + \dfrac{1}{n(1-p)}}$	$w_l = np(1-p)$
Arithmetic mean	$ES_m = \bar{X} = \dfrac{\sum x_i}{n}$	$SE_m = \dfrac{s}{\sqrt{n}}$	$w_m = \dfrac{n}{s^2}$
Two Variable Relationships—Pre-Post Contrasts			
Mean gain—unstandardized	$ES_{ug} = \bar{X}_{T2} - \bar{X}_{T1} = \bar{G}$	$SE_{ug} = \sqrt{\dfrac{2s_p^2(1-r)}{n}} = \sqrt{\dfrac{s_g^2}{n}}$	$w_{ug} = \dfrac{n}{2s_p^2(1-r)}$
Mean gain—standardized	$ES_{sg} = \dfrac{\bar{X}_{T2} - \bar{X}_{T1}}{s_p} = \dfrac{\bar{G}}{s_g/\sqrt{2(1-r)}}$	$SE_{sg} = \sqrt{\dfrac{2(1-r)}{n} + \dfrac{ES_{sg}^2}{2n}}$	$w_{sg} = \dfrac{2n}{4(1-r) + ES_{sg}^2}$
Two Variable Relationships—Group Contrasts			
Mean difference—unstandardized	$ES_{um} = \bar{X}_{G1} - \bar{X}_{G2}$	$SE_{um} = s_p\sqrt{\dfrac{1}{n_{G1}} + \dfrac{1}{n_{G2}}}$	$w_{um} = \dfrac{n_{G1}n_{G2}}{s_p^2(n_{G1}+n_{G2})}$
Mean difference—standardized	$ES_{sm} = \dfrac{\bar{X}_{G1}-\bar{X}_{G2}}{s_p}$ $ES_{sm}^l = \left[1 - \dfrac{3}{4N-9}\right]ES_{sm}$	$SE_{sm} = \sqrt{\dfrac{n_{G1}+n_{G2}}{n_{G1}n_{G2}} + \dfrac{(ES'_{sm})^2}{2(n_{G1}+n_{G2})}}$	$w_{sm} = \dfrac{2n_{G1}n_{G2}(n_{G1}+n_{G2})}{2(n_{G1}+n_{G2})^2 + n_{G1}n_{G2}ES_{sm}^2}$
Proportion difference	$ES_{pd} = p_{G1} - p_{G2}$	$SE_{pd} = \sqrt{p(1-p)\left(\dfrac{1}{n_{G1}} + \dfrac{1}{n_{G2}}\right)}$	$w_{pd} = \dfrac{n_{G1}n_{G2}}{p(1-p)(n_{G1}+n_{G2})}$
Logged odds-ratio	$ES_{LOR} = \log_e\left(\dfrac{ad}{bc}\right)$	$SE_{LOR} = \sqrt{\dfrac{1}{a} + \dfrac{1}{b} + \dfrac{1}{c} + \dfrac{1}{d}}$	$w_{LOR} = \dfrac{abcd}{ab(c+d) + cd(a+b)}$
Two Variable Relationships—Association between Variables			
Product-moment r	$ES_r = r$ $ES_{Zr} = .5\log_e\left[\dfrac{1+ES_r}{1-ES_r}\right]$	$SE_{Zr} = \dfrac{1}{\sqrt{n-3}}$	$w_{Zr} = n - 3$

Note. See text for definition of terms.

4

Developing a Coding Scheme and Coding Study Reports

The coding procedures for meta-analysis revolve around a coding protocol that specifies the information to be extracted from each eligible study. A coder will read through a study report and fill out the coding protocol with the appropriate responses for that study. Coding studies for meta-analysis is essentially like survey research. A questionnaire is prepared and a research report is "interviewed" by a coder who fills out the questionnaire according to the information provided by the research report. As in survey research, it is important to prepare the questionnaire carefully, train the interviewers (coders), and monitor the completeness, reliability, and validity of the data that are obtained. In this chapter we discuss preparation of a coding protocol, procedures for using it to code studies, and the training of coders.

DEVELOPING A CODING PROTOCOL

There are some general issues that should be considered before turning to the important matter of what content might be included in the coding protocol. First, we must distinguish between two rather different parts of the coding protocol: the part that encodes information about study characteristics (study descriptors) and the part that encodes information about the empirical findings of the study (effect sizes). Conceptually, this distinction is similar to that between independent and dependent variables. Study findings, represented in the form of effect size values, are the dependent variables of a meta-analysis—they are the "output" of empirical research studies. Study characteristics, e.g., methods, measures, samples, constructs, treatment, context, etc., are the independent variables of a meta-analysis—they represent factors that may influence the nature and magnitude of the findings. Among study characteristics, we want to further distinguish those that represent the phenomenon under study, e.g., the kind of treatment whose effects on certain constructs among certain populations are being studied, and those that represent the research methods that are used, e.g., the particular designs, measures, procedures, researchers, research context, etc. Ideally, the latter would be neutral; that is, typical variations would not greatly influence the findings of the research. Unfortunately, this is not generally the case so it is important that the meta-analyst code sufficient information about the research procedures to at least partially disentangle those differences in study results related to variations in the phenomenon of interest from those related to differences in method and procedure.

At the practical level, we distinguish study descriptors from effect sizes because they represent different levels of coding within a study. Study descriptors typically apply to the entire study, e.g., a particular design was used, data were obtained from a sample of certain characteristics, and so forth. Effect size values, however, represent the empirical relationships found among measured variables in the study. Since a study can include numerous measured variables (e.g., multiple outcome measures in a treatment study) representing various constructs, there are potentially numerous distinct effect sizes to be coded for each study. The coding protocol thus must generally be developed in modules: one module to code information that applies to the whole study and another to code effect size information. A complete coding would include the study-level module and as many of the effect size modules as needed to code all relevant quantitative findings the study reported.

Also, since the goal of coding is to build a database for statistical analysis, it is best that the coding protocol use closed-ended items as much as possible. The meta-analyst should attempt to predetermine the likely options for each coding item and set the protocol up in such a way that the coder can simply check off the appropriate response or enter a specific bit of information (e.g., a sample size). Unfortunately, there are times when appropriate categories for a variable cannot be predetermined. In these situations we have used open-ended questions to which the coder records information from the study relevant to the issue at hand. These responses must then be examined later for commonalities and coded into a manageable set of categories or rated along one or more dimensions. This can be time consuming and may require reference back to the original article if insufficient information was recorded. Therefore, open-ended questions should only be used for critical issues and when absolutely necessary.

A related consideration is to design the coding protocol in such a way that it is easy for the coder to use. This generally means clustering items that deal with similar themes together and formatting the items so that they are convenient to complete. Well-trained coders generally will need only abbreviated descriptive information on the protocol to identify each item and each response option. Keeping coding forms as short as possible and organizing them so that the parts the coder must fill in are easy to mark help make the coding more efficient.

On the other hand, it is important to have a full definition of each item and guidelines for coding it to assist the coder in appropriately handling ambiguous, unusual, or borderline cases. It is a good practice, therefore, to first construct a detailed *coding manual* that spells out what information each item is attempting to capture, gives full definitions of the various response options, and provides guidelines for handling ambiguous cases. This coding manual then becomes a reference guide for the coder to consult when difficulties are encountered. With such a manual on hand, the coding forms themselves can be streamlined. In Appendix E we have provided, as an example, the coding manual and the corresponding coding forms for the meta-analysis of studies of challenge programs that constitutes our running example.

We should caution the neophyte meta-analyst against developing an overly ambitious coding scheme. While there are many variables that might be interesting and useful to code about the selected studies, what can actually be coded successfully is very much dependent upon what is routinely reported in study documents. Unfortunately, study reports frequently omit information of potential interest to the meta-analyst. Also, some potentially interesting features may not vary across studies. Because meta-analysis yields an across-study database for analysis, there is little point in coding information that is either infrequently reported or common to all studies. Scattered information available for only a small proportion of the studies cannot usually be aggregated or compared in a meaningful way in the eventual data analysis and, hence, the effort required to code it is not productive. One possible exception is when items are coded only for descriptive purposes to document how infrequent or universal they, in fact, are. To control any tendency to develop a code sheet that includes items that cannot generally be obtained from the studies of interest, it is best to review a sample of representative studies first to determine what information appears often enough to permit relatively complete coding.

Units of Analysis and Hierarchical Levels of Coding

A good way to begin laying out a coding form is to first establish the definition of the major coding unit, then specify the various levels or components of coding required for that unit. In almost all cases the primary coding unit will be a study; that is, the database to be developed for the meta-analysis will be one organized around distinct studies, each described by a profile of study descriptors and effect sizes. While this may seem obvious, it should be noted that a careful definition is required to identify what constitutes a study. A good working definition is that a study consists of a set of data collected under a single research plan from a designated sample of respondents. Note that this definition distinguishes a study from a written report. It is possible for one written report to present the results from several studies. It is also possible for one study to be described in multiple written reports. The first step, then, is to determine what specifications identify the study unit in the research domain of interest and develop guidelines that instruct coders about how to identify the study unit to be coded.

It is wise to assign a distinct study identification number (ID) to each study unit once it is identified. We favor using the same ID numbers assigned in the master bibliography of candidate studies since this makes it easy to cross-link the study coding and the original bibliographic information. Where multiple studies are reported in a single document, additional codes can be added to the basic document ID. For instance, if report number 105 in the master bibliography describes two distinct studies, they could be separately coded under ID numbers 105A and 105B or 105.1 and 105.2. If several reports in the bibliography all describe the same study, the study can be coded under the ID number for the most comprehensive (or earliest published, etc.) report and the coding form could include a place to identify the ID numbers of the other reports that contributed to the coding. However the details are handled, it is important that the meta-analyst find a way to separately identify each study, as distinct from each report, but still carry the bibliographic information that identifies all written sources of information used in the coding. It is this information that enables both the meta-analyst and those who wish to examine the meta-analysis to determine where the data came from.

Once the primary study unit is defined, attention should turn to what distinct components of the typical study structure are of interest for coding. Earlier we identified two broad categories: study-level information and effect size information. We should now consider whether these need further differentiation. Usually this will not be the case for study-level information. The meta-analyst should be able to identify all those items of desired information that describe the overall study and collect them in one place in the coding protocol. The distinguishing feature of study-level information is that it need be coded only once for a given study and does not vary for different variables, effects, follow-ups, sample breakdowns, and the like. Such items as the date of earliest publication, the design used, and the treatment studied (if a treatment study) usually fall in this category. More detailed suggestions about possible items in this category are presented later under the heading "study descriptors."

Effect size information refers to aspects of a study that are distinct to a particular quantitative relationship or study finding that the meta-analyst wishes to code. The specific constructs and measures involved in the relationship, for instance, fall in this category. A given study may yield numerous findings, each different from the others in some of its particulars. This means there may be many possible variations of effect sizes that can be coded and the meta-analyst must identify the range of possibilities, decide which are important to code, and design the coding protocol so that the variations can be distinguished and properly coded.

We have generally found it useful to work through a hierarchy of possible effect size categories defined by different constructs, measures, samples, and times of measurement when considering what to code and how to construct coding protocols. We will describe each in turn.

Constructs

It is not unusual for studies to collect measures on more than one construct. A treatment effectiveness study, for example, may examine treatment effects on, say, interpersonal skills, quality of social relationships, self-esteem, and employment status. A correlational study of drug abuse might examine the interrelations among symptom severity, prior drug history, age, gender, and socioeconomic status. The meta-analyst must decide if all the constructs represented in all the eligible studies, or only a subset, are of interest and hence appropriate to code. In some cases, there may be only one construct of interest. For instance, a meta-analysis of studies of remedial reading programs may only examine reading ability as an outcome, even though eligible studies may measure other constructs as well, e.g., attitudes toward reading. If effects on all constructs are to be included, some consideration should be given to the frequency with which various constructs are represented in the body of eligible studies. Constructs that appear in only a few studies cannot be separately analyzed in any meaningful way in meta-analysis and thus may not be worth coding unless there is a clear rationale for doing so. One rationale may be that the meta-analyst wants to aggregate across all available constructs, rather than keep them separate (more on this later). Another might be that the meta-analyst wishes to document descriptively what constructs are present and in what frequencies, even if there are too few in some categories for further analysis. Decisions must be made, however, before a proper coding procedure can be constructed. In addition, if not all constructs are to be coded, specific guidelines must be drafted as to which are to be included and which are to be excluded to help coders make reliable judgments on this matter.

Measures

It is important to distinguish the operationalizations or measures represented in a study from the constructs those measures are presumed to index. Often different measures representing the same construct appear in a research study, as when therapist ratings, parents' ratings, and self-ratings of a child's behavior problems are obtained. The first decision the meta-analyst must make is whether all the measures of the constructs of interest that appear in the eligible studies are to be coded, or if some criteria are to be applied to differentiate measures the meta-analyst wishes to include from those to be excluded. In some specialized cases, only one measure of a construct may be of interest. For instance, Dobson (1989) conducted a meta-analysis that focused entirely on the effects of cognitive behavioral therapy as measured by the Beck's depression inventory. In other cases, it may be desirable to omit measures of a particular construct that are unconventional, known to be of poor quality, or deficient or inappropriate on some other grounds. It should be noted, however, that the meta-analyst who decides not to code certain measures forgoes the opportunity to examine empirically whether those measures yield results different from those that are chosen for coding.

The second decision the meta-analyst must make is how to code situations where more than one measure is used to index the same construct in the same study. The most inclusive approach is to separately code every measure, keeping track of which construct it is presumed to index, and sort out in later analysis which groupings, selections, or combinations are most interesting or meaningful. This is the approach that permits the fullest empirical examination of the relationship between the particular ways in which a construct is operationalized and the nature of the findings from different studies. Alternatively, the meta-analyst may want to avoid the complications of having multiple measures of some constructs in some studies and only single measures in other situations, or may want to select measures that produce the most uniformity across studies. In such cases, it is appropriate to establish criteria for selecting only one measure to code per construct per study. This selection might, for instance, take the most commonly used measure, if available, to maximize comparability with other studies, or simply exercise random selection. Another approach is to establish quality criteria that allow the best measure by some definition to be selected in cases where more than one measure is available. Sometimes meta-analysts will code results from multiple measures of the same construct, but average them together to get a single effect size for each construct in each study. This approach has some advantages in simplifying the coding of multiple measures but it precludes any later analysis of the influence on study findings of differing operationalizations of a construct.

Samples

Meta-analytic effect sizes are calculated for effects or relationships involving some measurement applied to some sample of respondents, e.g., a correlation between a measure of test-anxiety and high school math grades for a sample of adolescent students or the difference between the means on a measure of bulimic symptoms for a treated group versus a control group of women referred for eating disorders. In addition, study results are often also presented for subgroups of respondents. For instance, the test-anxiety and grades correlation may be presented separately for males and females or the mean differences on bulimic symptoms may be broken out for older versus younger patients. Sometimes multiple, nonindependent breakouts will be presented using different cross-tabulations of the same data, e.g., breaking results out separately by age, by ethnicity, and by gender.

Results presented separately for distinct subsamples are often of particular interest—the corresponding effect sizes can be used to compare strength of relationship or treatment effects for respondents with different characteristics. If every treatment study, for instance, not only reported overall results but broke out the separate results for males and females, the corresponding effect sizes would be of great value for investigating gender differences in response to that treatment. More typically, some studies break out their results for subsamples and others do not. Moreover, those studies that do present breakout results will not necessarily break out the same subsamples. Breakouts on certain demographic characteristics may be relatively common in some study populations, but many studies will present unusual or idiosyncratic breakouts that may not be comparable to those in other studies.

In preparing the coding protocol, therefore, the meta-analyst must decide if effect sizes will be coded only for results on the aggregate sample, i.e., the entire original study sample, or if effect sizes will also be coded for results presented for subsamples. If subsample results are to be coded, then a decision must be made as to which subsamples. The meta-analyst might decide to separately code effect sizes for all breakouts involving gender, age, and ethnicity, for instance, on the basis that these are the only types of subsamples reported often enough to permit any analysis. Alternatively, there may be reasons for coding results for any breakout that is presented in a study. In either case, the meta-analyst must develop a set of codes that will identify the breakout variables involved (e.g., gender, ethnicity) and the status of the separate subsamples on that variable (e.g., male–female; White–Black–Hispanic). Without this information in systematic form, it will be extremely difficult to organize the multiplicity of resulting effect sizes for any meaningful analysis.

Time of Measurement

A given measure of a given construct may be taken on the same group (or subgroup) of respondents at more than one time. In treatment studies, for instance, there may be measurement before treatment begins, after it ends, and for various subsequent follow-up periods. Longitudinal panel studies, by definition, collect data from the same respondents at different times and typically repeat some of the same measures. For study populations where an appreciable number of the studies report results from measures taken at more than one time, the meta-analyst must decide whether to code separate effect sizes for all times of measurement or to select only one or some designated number of measurement times. For treatment studies, for instance, some meta-analysts code only the results for the first outcome measurement after treatment ends. This is the most commonly collected and reported information in such studies and may be deemed sufficient for the purposes of the meta-analysis. Alternatively, the duration of treatment effects may be of interest and the meta-analyst may want to code follow-up results for later times of measurement if enough studies report them. In this latter case, it is unlikely that the follow-up intervals will be the same for all studies. The meta-analyst thus must be sure to also code the timing information, e.g., by counting from the end of treatment so that there might be 1 month results, 6 month results, and so on for a particular study.

The Hierarchy of Effect Sizes

What has been described above is a rough hierarchy, or branching tree, of possible effect sizes that might be codable in a set of studies selected for meta-analysis. Any given study might examine effects or relationships on multiple constructs, each construct may be operationalized with multiple measures, the results on each measure may be reported for subsample breakouts as well as for the aggregate sample, and the aggregate sample and subsample results for each measure may be reported for multiple times of measurement. Additionally, overarching the various effect size possibilities, we have study-level information descriptive of the entire study, including all effect size variations. To organize an effective coding protocol, the meta-analyst must be aware of all these variations and decide which need to be represented in the meta-analytic database. Distinct sections of the coding protocol then need to be tailored to the different types of information in each of these categories and, most especially, include the identifiers needed to interpret what is coded. Those identifiers must give the analyst such information as which construct and measure is represented, the distinguishing characteristics of the sample or subsample measured, and the time of measurement in a uniform format that permits aggregation or comparison across studies. We show later, when we discuss data analysis, how essential such information is to organizing an interpretable analysis.

The coding manual and corresponding coding forms for our example involving challenge studies, provided in Appendix E, shows a coding format for multiple outcome constructs and multiple times of measurement.

Effect Size Coding

Each statistical finding in a study that is ultimately selected for coding in the meta-analysis must be recorded in the form of an effect size value with an accompanying profile of associated information describing the particulars of that effect size. Chapter 3 described effect size statistics that can be used to represent research findings of different types. The coding of effect sizes consists of computing the value for each research finding of interest on the selected effect size statistic using the appropriate statistical formulation for that statistic. Where insufficient information is presented to permit a direct calculation of the effect size value, it may be possible to derive a reasonable estimate of that value. Chapter 3 provided an overview of the estimation procedures associated with each effect size statistic and Appendix B discusses in detail effect size estimation for the more common effect size statistics. We have created a computer spreadsheet calculation program that incorporates all of these formulas (see Appendix C for details). For the widely used standardized mean difference effect size, Shadish, Robinson, and Lu (1999) have also developed a very useful computer program called the *Effect Size Calculator* that is available from Assessment Systems Corporation (http://www.assess.com/).

The supporting information that must be coded along with each effect size value falls into several overlapping categories. First, information that describes the nature of the variable represented by each effect size (or variables in correlational studies) must be coded, such as the general construct measured, the specifics of the measurement operationalization, and the statistical nature of the variable (e.g., dichotomous, discrete ordinal categories, or continuous). The meta-analyst may choose to identify variables only at the broad construct level (e.g., "self-esteem"), or at the more specific operational level (e.g., Coopersmith self-esteem scale), or both.

Second, the point in time when a variable was measured may also be important descriptive information, e.g., pretreatment and posttreatment measurements in an intervention study or waves of data collection in a longitudinal study. In addition, the time period covered by a variable may be pertinent, e.g., the period over which the number of postintervention events is counted when assessing recidivism for treated subjects.

Third, effect sizes based on a subsample of the study-level sample, such as males only, if coded, will need specific sample descriptors. If such subsample effect sizes are to be coded, we recommend careful planning of the coding protocol such that at the analysis stage, effect sizes based on the full study sample can be easily distinguished from subsample effect sizes. Full sample and subsample effect sizes are statistically dependent and therefore should not be included in the same analysis (see Chapter 6). However, two nonoverlapping subsamples, such as boys and girls, are independent and can be included in a single analysis.

Fourth, the coding needs, at a minimum, to include statistical information about the effect size value and the related inverse variance weight, e.g., means, proportions, sample sizes, variances or standard deviations, pre–post correlations, correlations, etc. The meta-analyst may wish simply to record the effect size and inverse variance weight, or to include information about the values of the terms that went into the effect size and inverse variance computation. In addition, the coding protocol might include statistical information needed to make corrections or adjustments to the effect size values for unreliability, dichotomization, range restrictions, and the like, such as reliability coefficients, scale type (e.g., if a dichotomy or whether there are other limitations on the values a variable can take), and standard deviations or variances from norming populations (see the discussion in Chapter 6 on correcting for artifactual bias in effect sizes). Other statistical information that a meta-analyst may wish to code includes (a) elaboration of the statistical significance of the finding, e.g., what type of statistical test was used in the original study and whether statistical significance was found; (b) information bearing on missing data, e.g., the amount of attrition represented in the sample size upon which the effect size value is based relative to the size of the sample at the beginning of the study; and (c) information to facilitate any later checking on the effect size value, e.g., the page number in the research report where the information for the effect size was found, availability of any worksheets showing computations, etc. Exhibit 4.1 provides a list of items that may be appropriate to code as supporting information for effect sizes.

Variable(s)/construct(s) represented in the effect size
Point in time when variable(s) measured; time lag; time covered
Subsample information, if relevant
Sample size(s) (effect size specific)
Means or proportions
Standard deviations or variances
Calculation procedure (effect size specific) including estimation methods
Confidence rating in computed effect size value
Amount of attrition (effect size specific)
Reliability of variable(s) represented in effect size
Dichotomization of variable(s) in effect size
Range restriction on variable(s) in effect size
Type of statistical test of effect used in study; whether significant
Page number in study report where effect size information found

Exhibit 4.1. Information that may be desirable to code for each effect size.

Study Descriptors

As noted previously, one level of coding involves characteristics of the entire study, what we have called study descriptors. This section provides some general guidelines and suggestions for the items a meta-analyst may wish to consider for the portion of the coding protocol dealing with these descriptors. Here we must also caution that describing everything one might want to know about the studies in a meta-analysis almost always requires more information than studies typically report. This is a limitation of meta-analysis, to be sure, but, more fundamentally, it is a limitation of the reporting practices for the studies meta-analysts code. It is best, when developing the coding protocol, to review a broad sample of the studies to be coded and determine what information is reported frequently enough to justify the coding effort. Ideally, for instance, one might like to find and code considerable detail about the experimental designs used in treatment studies—experimenter and subject blinding, how random assignment was made, pretest differences on critical variables, and the like. In practice, one may be fortunate to be able to code studies into rough categories of design type. Many of the details of interest to a discerning researcher will not be regularly reported. With this caveat, we turn to specific suggestions of study descriptors that might be considered.

Our suggestions are organized with a set of categories that identify study descriptors of different types. First, we want to consider descriptors that have to do with *substantive* aspects of the study, e.g., the nature of the persons in the samples, treatments applied, cultural or organizational context, and so forth. These are the variables that have to do with the phenomenon under study and which will generally be most interesting when the meta-analyst attempts to account for different results across studies. Variables in this category permit examination of whether some treatment variants produce larger effects than others, whether some types of persons respond more to treatment, and the like. The meta-analyst usually wants to code all the information that is generally available in studies that might represent significant variations in the substantive aspects of the study.

The second category of study descriptors to consider has to do with study *methods and procedures*. These variables may be of interest in their own right since they are the basis for an investigation of the relationship between methodological variation and study findings that may reveal bias and artifacts stemming from certain methodological practices. Even when methodological issues are not of direct interest, it is essential that the meta-analyst code the major methodological and procedural characteristics of the studies under consideration. Experience in meta-analysis has revealed that differences in study findings are often strongly related to methodological differences among the studies (Wilson, 1995). If methodological differences are not coded and examined, the meta-analyst might easily misinterpret their effects as substantive differences, since methodological variables may be confounded with substantive ones. We will have more to say on this issue when we discuss data analysis and interpretation of results (Chapters 6–8). For now, we only emphasize that it is a wise practice to include in the coding protocol all those methodological and procedural variables that can be coded from the studies and that could conceivably affect study results.

The final category of study descriptors is somewhat miscellaneous and, for lack of a better name, we will call it *source descriptors*. This category includes factors that have to do with the general study context, the particulars of the publication, researchers, and so forth that are neither directly substantive nor methodological. These variables are often valuable simply for descriptive purposes, e.g., to indicate the balance of published versus unpublished studies in a meta-analysis database, to show the distribution of dates of publication, and the like. Sometimes, however, variables in this category are proxies for a substantive or methodological variable that might not otherwise get reported and coded in the studies. In this regard, they are often as useful in the analysis as the straightforwardly substantive or methodological variables, though generally more difficult to interpret. For example, one might find that studies conducted by researchers from different disciplines (say psychology vs. psychiatry) yield systematically different results. In such a case, it might be plausible that discipline is a proxy for different research practices adopted by researchers with different training, even though the nature of those differences may not be evident in the methods sections of the research reports.

Substantive Issues
  Sample source
  Sample descriptors
    demographics (e.g., SES, age, sex, education, ethnicity)
    personal characteristics (e.g., cognitive abilities, personality traits)
    diagnostic characteristics or special features (e.g., clinical
      patients, juvenile delinquents)
  Independent variable(s) (e.g., intervention or treatment)
    general description and type
    theoretical orientation
    levels represented (e.g., dose, intensity, duration, etc.)
    organizational characteristics (e.g., age, size, administrative structure)
    mode of treatment delivery
    characteristics of intervention staff or personnel
Methods and Procedures
  Sampling procedures or method (e.g., random probability sample)
  Survey design (e.g., mail, phone, interview, longitudinal, cross-sectional,
    prospective, retrospective, archival)
  Attrition
  Threats to external validity
  Statistical power
  Quality of measures
  Forms of data analysis
  Independent variable(s) (e.g., intervention or treatment)
    method of assignment to conditions
    nature of control group (e.g., received no treatment, placebo,
      alternate treatment)
    blinding of experimenter and/or subjects to assigned condition
    role of experimenter in treatment (independent, provider)
    threats to internal validity
Source Descriptors
  Publication form (journal, book, dissertation, technical report, dissertation, etc.)
  Year of publication
  Country of publication; language
  Study sponsorship and/or funding
  Characteristics of the researcher (gender, disciplinary affiliation, etc.)

Exhibit 4.2. Study descriptors that may be appropriate for coding.

It is generally appropriate to code study descriptor variables from each of these three categories. Which particular variables should be coded will differ according to the purposes of the meta-analysis and the nature of the studies to be included. As a stimulus, however, Exhibit 4.2 lists some of the items that are commonly coded or (in some cases) that we think should be commonly coded. In addition, recall that Appendix E presents a sample coding scheme for our running example of treatment of adolescent behavior problems with challenge programs. Other useful sources of advice about selecting items to include in a coding protocol appear in Orwin (1994), Stock (1994), and Stock, Benito, & Lasa (1996). Review articles in the area of interest are also invaluable in identifying important variables for consideration.

CODING INFORMATION ABOUT
THE CODING PROCESS ITSELF

Before we leave the topic of coding studies for meta-analysis, we must give some attention to a special category of procedures. This category has to do with documenting important aspects of the judgment process that the coder necessarily applies when interacting with a study report. Since that judgment process may vary from coder to coder and, for one coder, from study to study, it influences the resulting meta-analysis data in ways that the meta-analyst is well advised to monitor.

One issue of this sort is the reliability of the coding that is done on the studies contributing to a meta-analysis. Coder reliability typically has two dimensions: the consistency of a single coder from occasion to occasion, and the consistency between different coders. In a small meta-analysis, there may be only one coder for all the studies, making consistency between coders seem less important. Even in such cases, however, it is not desirable for one coder to code so idiosyncratically, even if consistently, that another coder could not easily reproduce the results. Both these reliability issues, therefore, apply to all meta-analyses.

Coder reliability is checked by drawing a subsample of the coded studies, having the coder(s) code them again, and comparing the results. For reliability of a single coder across occasions, this requires that studies that a person has coded be coded again, after sufficient time has passed so they are not fresh in mind, without reference to the original coding. For reliability between coders, the procedure is to have different coders code the same sample of studies, again without reference to what the other has done. To generate a relatively stable reliability estimate, it is desirable for the reliability samples to consist of 20 or more studies, with 50+ being more desirable. Since many meta-analyses do not have this many studies total, such samples are not always possible. For small meta-analyses, it may be necessary to use all the studies in the reliability check.

Once the appropriate double-coding has been done on a sample of studies, the two sets of results are compared item by item. Yeaton and Wortman (1993) recommend that the items be first clustered according to how independent the coder's judgment is. Many items in meta-analysis are contingent; that is, once a judgment is made on one item, the range of responses to a subsequent item may be constrained. If, for instance, one item asks if the research design involves random assignment or not, other items that ask about the details of the assignment process will be nested under that more general one. Reliability of those independent items at the top of such hierarchies should be determined separately from that of those items that are constrained by them. Once the desired comparisons are organized, any of a range of familiar reliability indices may be applied, depending on the format of the item. Percentage of agreement is the most often reported index, though arguably others are often better (e.g., kappa, weighted kappa, r, and the intraclass correlation; Orwin, 1994).

Even coders who exercise sound judgment and code with a relatively high degree of reliability are often going to be confounded by the poor reporting common in research studies. To glean what information one can, and avoid excess missing data, it is often necessary for coders to make reasonable inferences and informed guesses about the proper response to some items on the coding protocol for some studies. The downside of this practice, of course, is that any systematic bias in those guesses, or in the nature of the studies that require guesswork, introduces some distortion into the resulting meta-analytic data. It is useful for the meta-analyst, therefore, to attempt to document whether key information is coded on the basis of explicit information in the report or some degree of inference.

Orwin and Cordray (1985) suggested that coders give a confidence rating for the most important items in a coding protocol. That is, after they complete a key item, they use a separate rating scale on which they indicate how confident they are in their judgment on that item. Such a scale can range from high confidence, indicating that the coder coded what was explicitly indicated in the report, to low confidence, indicating that relatively crude estimation or guesswork was required. The sample coding forms in Appendix E give some examples of coder confidence rating items. It is especially appropriate that such an item be used for the coding of effect size magnitudes, since those are the central variables in meta-analysis and reporting of the necessary statistical information for their computation varies widely among studies.

Once collected, confidence ratings become part of the meta-analytic database and can be used in data analysis along with all the other items in the coding protocol. When certain relationships among study features or findings are found to be correlated with the confidence rating for an item involved in that relationship, it signals the meta-analyst that further investigation is needed. Such relationships may be substantive and meaningful, but the possibility that they result, in some part, from bias in coder inference must also be considered.

A final matter related to study coding has to do with missing data. Inevitably it will not be possible to code certain items for some of the studies in a meta-analysis. If an item cannot be coded for a large proportion of the studies, it may be best to drop that item from the coding protocol or, later, from the resulting database. Meta-analysis can only work with what is reported regularly in research studies and one of the frequent frustrations of the meta-analyst is that information judged important and relevant simply cannot always be coded from what is reported in studies.

For many items, however, there will be sufficient information to justify coding, but some studies will nonetheless not report what is needed. In such a situation, the meta-analyst must consider the possibility that the studies that do report a specific item of information may be systematically different from those that do not report that item. Drawing conclusions only from those that do report, therefore, may be misleading. In addition, the higher the proportion of missing data, the greater the potential for distorted results. It is thus wise for the meta-analyst to code missing data very carefully and incorporate that information in the data analysis. For each item to be coded, the coding protocol should have an explicit option the coder can use to indicate that he/she cannot tell what the status of the study is on that item. In some research domains, it may also be desirable to distinguish situations where the information is missing because it is not applicable to that particular study from those where it appears to be applicable, but is not reported. We routinely provide both a "missing" and "not applicable" option to items in our coding protocol. Later analysis can reveal the differences between studies with and without missing data for various reasons on key items by comparing their profiles on other major items in the protocol.

TRAINING OF CODERS

Coding research reports is one of the most technically demanding aspects of meta-analysis. An effective coder must not only understand the coding protocol in detail and depth, but must have the knowledge and skills to properly read and interpret research reports that may use a wide range of specialized methods and procedures and report their findings in terms of the jargon of their fields and often in complex statistical form.

Coders must, therefore, have considerable background in social science methodology and some familiarity with the specific research domain at issue to perform the coding task well. Even then, it is our experience that some studies will challenge the most expert researcher or methodologist. Potential coders in meta-analysis, therefore, must generally be at least at the level of doctoral graduate students in a social science discipline to have much likelihood of performing this difficult task adequately. Indeed, in some specialized research domains it may be possible to attain the necessary coding standard only with more experienced researchers, e.g., Ph.D. level specialists in the research field at issue.

Given appropriate background, specific instruction in the tasks and issues of the particular meta-analysis is essential. We recommend that consideration be given to two different phases of such instruction. One phase, of course, should be training in the use of the coding protocol and the accompanying coding manual. Such training should consist of careful, line-by-line reading and discussion of the protocol and the manual to ensure that coders have a clear understanding of the items to be coded and the proper use of the response options. In addition to preparing the coders, this exercise may also reveal some ambiguities or difficulties with the coding materials that can be corrected at this stage.

Once coders are familiar with the coding material, they should begin practice coding. We suggest first selecting several diverse reports and having each coder code each report. This makes it possible for them to compare their coding with each other afterward and to participate in a discussion about difficulties encountered, disagreements among the coders about how certain items were coded, and the like. This process should be repeated as many times as necessary for coders to feel comfortable with the task, to refine the coding materials, and to attain a high level of agreement among coders coding the same studies. At that point, they should be ready to code "for real." It is advisable, however, to have provisions for continuing training, e.g., in the form of regular meetings in which the coders discuss any unusual situations they have encountered, seek clarification of the proper coding, and reach some common understanding of how such situations are to be handled.

Reliability checks on the coding, discussed earlier, can also be used as part of the continuous training procedure. Rather than wait until all studies are coded and then come back to recode for the reliability sample, such checks can be made periodically throughout the coding process. For example, every nth report a coder is to code might be duplicated and given to another coder; the previous nth report might also be recycled to that same coder. Prompt examination of these recodes by the research supervisor yields a running check on the quality of the coding and identifies items with which coders are having difficulty. The latter problems can then be discussed in the periodic coder meetings and further instruction or other corrective action (e.g., modifying the coding protocol) can be taken.

The other phase of coder training to which we alluded may not seem necessary for coders with the requisite research backgrounds we described. It has been our experience, however, that where the details of research studies are concerned, even knowledgeable students and researchers can have gaps or inconsistencies in their understanding of certain research terms, methods, and procedures. We have seen fierce arguments among informed coders, for instance, about just what constitutes a "true experiment" in contrast to a "quasi-experiment" and have uncovered many gaps in statistical understanding as coders struggled to interpret study results and compute effect sizes.

It is our recommendation, therefore, that training of coders for meta-analysis include some number of seminars that provide instruction and discussion on the methodological and statistical procedures and practices characteristic of the body of research involved in the meta-analysis. This might consist of refresher readings, lectures, and discussions on variations of the designs used, the meaning of key terms (e.g., blinding, attrition, stratified sampling, matched designs, etc.), and the range of statistical formats and presentations likely to be encountered in the studies at issue. With regard to statistical presentations, it is critical that coders understand the concept of the effect size index to be used in the meta-analysis and how it relates to the various sorts of statistical results that studies may present. A series of seminars of this sort prior to coding for the meta-analysis will not only refresh and clarify the methodological issues, but should result in some common understanding of those issues among the coders that will translate into greater validity and reliability in the eventual coding.

The discussion above assumes a large meta-analysis. In small meta-analyses, the coding will be done entirely by the researcher(s). A good strategy is to have two researchers code all studies and then discuss and resolve any differences between the two coding protocols.

5

Data Management

Although data management and analysis for a small meta-analysis could be done manually, most meta-analyses require the use of a computer. The choice of software will depend in part on the skill level of the personnel working on the meta-analysis, the software resources available, and the nature of the meta-analysis. Several meta-analysis software programs are available (e.g., *Advanced Basic Meta-Analysis* by Mullen, 1989, and Mullen & Rosenthal, 1985; *DSTAT* by Johnson, 1989; *Meta-Analysis* by Schwarzer, 1996; *MetaDOS* by Stauffer, 1996; *Metawin* by Rosenberg et al., 1997; and *RevMan* by the Cochrane Collaboration, 2000). However, these programs generally have somewhat limited data management and analytic capability and lack the flexibility needed for some applications.

Meta-analysis also can be accomplished using standard statistical software, such as SPSS, SYSTAT and SAS, and specialized multilevel statistical modeling programs such as HLM and MLn/MLwiN. These programs provide greater control over the organization of the data and allow for a greater variety of analysis options. These advantages come, of course, at the cost of somewhat greater complexity in implementing the computations used in meta-analysis. A comprehensive meta-analysis program developed with support from the National Institute of Mental Health is in beta-testing as this book goes to press and may integrate both data management and analysis capabilities well enough to be useful for general application (Borenstein, 2000).

For generality and flexibility, we will discuss data processing on the assumption that a commonly available statistical package will be used (SPSS) rather than specialized meta-analysis software. Strategies and techniques for conducting analysis using standard statistical software are discussed in Chapter 6. This chapter will discuss the creation and manipulation of meta-analytic data files.

CREATING META-ANALYTIC DATA FILES

The original creation of one or more data files of coded data can be done in several ways. The simplest approach is to create an ASCII data

```
100 2 92 15.5 6 4 4 1 3
131 3 88 15.3 1 2 5 2 8
132 3 88 15.5 6 4 4 1 3
158 3 89 15.0 1 3 4 1 3
127 2 80 11.4 1 3 7 1 3
172 2 92 14.8 1 3 4 1 2
255 2 87 16.7 9 9 5 1 2
308 2 68 16.5 1 4 4 1 3
251 3 83 14.1 9 2 9 1 2
250 2 87 10.6 5 4 2 2 4
502 2 72 15.5 9 4 4 1 4
161 3 88 15.3 5 3 4 1 2
537 4 67 18.9 9 4 4 1 2
```

Exhibit 5.1. Example of fixed field ASCII data file.

file in a word processor or text editor. In such a data file, the data would be entered in a fixed length format, with or without spaces between different variables. The results would look something like the data shown in Exhibit 5.1, drawn from the challenge meta-analysis. In this exhibit, the first column records the study ID, the second column is publication type, the third column is publication year, then mean age of the study sample, and so forth. Although ASCII data files are easy to create, they are difficult to edit and time consuming to check for accuracy.

A second approach to creating data files is to use a spreadsheet program, such as Lotus 123, Microsoft Excel, or Quattro Pro. In spreadsheet programs the columns represent variables and the rows represent records or cases with the first row generally used for variable names. An example of a simple spreadsheet data file is presented in Exhibit 5.2. It is useful to use variable names that meet the requirement of the statistical software package you will be using to analyze the data, for example, eight digit

	A	B	C	D	E	F	G	H	I
1	StudyID	PubType	PubYear	MeanAge	Race	Sex	Risk	Unit	Assign
2	100	2	92	15.5	6	4	4	1	3
3	131	3	88	15.3	1	2	5	2	8
4	132	3	88	15.5	6	4	4	1	3
5	158	3	89	15	1	3	4	1	3
6	127	2	80	11.4	1	3	7	1	3
7	172	2	92	14.8	1	3	4	1	2
8	255	2	87	16.7	9	9	5	1	2
9	308	2	68	16.5	1	4	4	1	3
10	251	3	83	14.1	9	2	9	1	2
11	250	2	87	10.6	5	4	2	2	4

Exhibit 5.2. Example of a sample Excel spreadsheet data file.

STUDYID _____ 1. Study Identification Number

PUBTYPE _____ 2. Type of Publication
1 Book
2 Journal Article/Book Chapter
3 Thesis/Dissertation
4 Technical Report
5 Conference Paper
6 Other

PUBYEAR _____ 3. Publication Year (enter 9999 if missing or unknown)

MEANAGE __ __.__ __ 4. Mean Age of Sample (enter 99.99 if missing or unknown)

RACE _____ 5. Predominate Race of Sample
1 > 60% White
2 > 60% Black
3 > 60% Hispanic
4 > 60% Other Minority
5 Mixed (none more than 60%)
6 Mixed, but can't estimate proportion
9 Can't tell

Exhibit 5.3. Sample page of the study-level coding form from the meta-analysis of challenge programs (see Appendix E for the full coding form).

alphanumeric labels. Many statistical software packages can read spreadsheet data files directly and are able to name the variables based on the labels in the first row. A disadvantage to using spreadsheets is that column labels or variable names are often short and cryptic, which can produce ambiguity during data entry. This problem can be reduced by including the variable name directly on the coding form and maintaining consistency in the order of the variables between the coding form and the spreadsheet columns. To facilitate data entry, it is a good idea to configure the coding form so that all the data elements are coded in a column down either the left or right margin of the form. A portion of a coding form illustrating this format is shown in Exhibit 5.3 (and also in Appendix E).

A third approach is to use a database program, but it is important to choose one that can export data in a format acceptable to your statistical software. The use of a database program has several advantages. First, it can create "views" or screen layouts that look like a coding form so it is clear what database fields correspond to the data elements on the form. Another advantage is the ability to associate "edits" with a data field that specify the type of data valid for entry into that field. A warning beep is emitted when an out-of-range value or incorrect data type is entered to help avoid data entry errors. Database programs also have the ability to search for records that meet specified criteria as an aid to identifying coding errors. They also permit the meta-analyst to code directly into the computer rather than transferring the data from a coding form to the database. The disadvantages to using a database for data entry are that it can be labor intensive to set up and requires greater computer skills than a spreadsheet or text editor.

Several popular database programs, such as FileMaker Pro, Paradox, and Microsoft Access, are capable of creating relational databases that handle hierarchical data of the sort often produced by meta-analysis (more on this later). They have the ability to display and to edit data at multiple levels of the hierarchy in a single "view" or computer screen. The files cannot, however, be exported in their relational form to statistical software packages but, rather, must be exported separately and merged using the statistical software as discussed later in this chapter.

Several popular statistical software packages have their own data entry modules. Using these is a fourth approach. Essentially these are spread-sheets built into the statistical package. This approach has the same pros and cons of using a spreadsheet except that the data do not need to be translated or converted between the spreadsheet and the statistical analysis programs.

CODING DIRECTLY INTO
THE COMPUTER

Coding studies for meta-analysis is a time-consuming task. Careful planning and pilot testing of the coding procedures are therefore critical. An important consideration in this process is whether to code directly into a computer database or onto paper forms and then transfer the data into a computer file. The latter approach has the advantages of ease of imple-mentation and creation of a permanent record that cannot be deleted with a few keystrokes. Coding directly into the computer has the advantage of efficiency. Also, computer coding makes it easy to change the coding form and to revise the coding for all studies. This is useful since coding is often iterative, with new categories and variables emerging as the data in the studies becomes better known.

Exhibit 5.4 shows a sample coding screen from the meta-analysis of challenge programs. This screen was developed in FileMaker® Pro and is one of several used for entering effect size data (this screen shows items 8–14 of the effect size coding; see Appendix E). An advantage of database

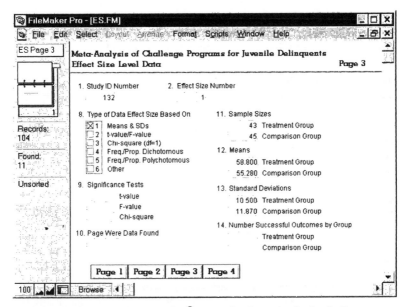

Exhibit 5.4. Example FileMaker Pro® screen for data entry in the challenge meta-analysis.

programs is that the data for computation of an effect size can be entered and the computer can often perform the actual calculation, thus decreasing computational errors. The data entered into this database can be exported to a dBASE file and imported into most popular statistical programs. An advantage of the dBASE file format is that it keeps the variable names used by the database program. Although this example uses FileMaker Pro, other suitable database programs include dBASE, Microsoft Access, FoxPro, and Paradox, among others.

USING THE COMPUTER TO
MAINTAIN THE BIBLIOGRAPHY

A task easily overlooked is the maintenance of the bibliography of study reports related to a meta-analysis. The use of a computer can facilitate several phases of bibliography management. During the search phase, the results of computerized literature searches can be downloaded and manipulated in a word processor or text editor for inclusion in a bibliographic database. Potentially relevant studies can be assigned an identification number and carried forward for further consideration. We have found that sorting references by journal name greatly facilitates library retrieval. A second task is tracking the status of each reference. In our meta-analyses, we include a field in the bibliographic database to indicate whether a study report has been retrieved, reviewed for eligibility, and coded. Other information captured is the source of each reference (e.g., PsychLit, review article, etc.), the study identification number assigned, and the coder's initials. When the meta-analysis is done, the list of studies ultimately included in it can be readily printed from this database.

STRUCTURE OF META-ANALYTIC DATA FILES

Statistical analysis software packages for the computer generally use flat data files. A flat file has one record per unit-of-analysis (a research study in meta-analysis), each with a uniform number of data fields for values on the variables characterizing that unit of analysis. Most meta-analytic data, however, are hierarchical and have a one-to-many structure; that is, one record at one level of the hierarchy is associated with many records at another level. For example, each study record may include one or more subject subsamples and each subsample may involve one or more effect sizes. This hierarchical structure is illustrated, for instance, in a meta-analysis of parent effectiveness training by Cedar and Levant (1990) that focused on changes in knowledge, behavior, and self-esteem for both parents and children. Their data structure consisted of three levels: the overall study data, the subsample data (i.e., the parent data and the child data), and the effect size data (i.e., effect sizes for each outcome construct for either parents or children). To further complicate matters, the data were inconsistent across studies—one study might report multiple outcomes for the parents and none for the child while another would report a single outcome for both parents and child. The meta-analysis of challenge programs used as our running example has a two level hierarchy: study-level data and effect size level data with varying numbers of effect sizes for each study.

An important concern in managing meta-analytic data, therefore, is deciding how to handle its hierarchical structure in a way that allows for appropriate analysis. There are two basic file structures to consider. The first is a single data file with one record per study that includes separate fields or variables for each effect size and its associated data. This method is useful when the meta-analysis involves a limited and predetermined set of effect sizes. The second approach is to create multiple data files, one for each data level. The data in the multiple files can then be linked for specific analyses using study identifiers, called *keys*. This latter structure is well suited to meta-analyses where the number of effect sizes per study and the constructs represented by these effect sizes are not well known prior to study coding or are potentially large and diverse. While it has greater flexibility, this second approach requires greater effort and skill.

Creating a Single Flat File to Use for Analysis

An example of a single flat file structure is a meta-analysis of laboratory studies investigating the effect of alcohol on aggression (Lipsey, Wilson, Cohen, & Derzon, 1996). In this meta-analysis, we were interested in the effect sizes on aggression measures for a set of experimentally manipulated contrasts: (a) alcohol versus no alcohol, (b) alcohol versus a placebo drink, (c) placebo versus no alcohol, and (d) antiplacebo versus no alcohol. Because we had specified in advance the four effect size variables of interest, we created a single data file with a fixed set of fields for each type of effect size and its associated descriptive data. Exhibit 5.5 shows selected data from this file. As seen in this exhibit, there is one row of data per study and each of the four effect size variables has a separate column (ES1, ES2, etc.) with an associated column identifying the type of aggression variable represented in the effect size (DV1, DV2, etc.). Note that only a few studies had all four effect size variables.

Merging Multiple Files to Use for Analysis

The single data file structure is unwieldy when the potential number of effect sizes from any study is large. In the challenge program meta-analysis, for instance, the number of effect sizes available and the outcome constructs they represented varied considerably from study to study. Therefore, two data files were created: (a) a *study descriptors file* for variables characterizing the study design, sample, treatment approach, etc., and (b) an *effect size file* for variables characterizing each effect size, e.g., the outcome measure, sample size, and effect size value. Other meta-analyses may require more data files. A meta-analysis we conducted on longitudinal studies of antisocial behavior (Lipsey & Derzon, 1998) needed four files: (a) a study file with one record per study that included study-level variables (e.g., design, setting); (b) a wave and cohort file with

ID	DESIGN	ES1	ES2	ES3	ES4	DV1	DV2	DV3	DV4
023	2	0.77	.	.	.	3	.	.	.
031	1	-0.10	-0.05	.	-0.20	5	5	.	11
040	1	0.96	.	.	.	11	.	.	.
082	1	0.29	.	.	.	11	.	.	.
185	1	0.65	0.58	0.48	0.07	5	5	5	5
204	2	.	0.88	.	.	.	3	.	.
229	2	0.97	.	.	.	3	.	.	.
246	2	.	0.91	.	.	.	3	.	.
295	2	0.03	0.46	.	0.57	3	3	.	3
326	1	0.87	-0.04	0.10	0.90	3	3	3	3
366	2	.	0.50	.	.	.	3	.	.

ES = Effect Size
DV = Dependent Variable Type

Exhibit 5.5. Flat data file with multiple effect size variables from a meta-analysis of laboratory studies of the effect of alcohol on aggresive behavior (Lipsey, Wilson, Cohen, & Derzon, 1996).

one record describing each measurement wave on each study cohort; (c) a measures and constructs file of records characterizing each construct measured and the methods of measurement; and (d) an effect size file with a record for each effect size. The effect size records are linked through identification keys to the study, wave–cohort, and measures–constructs data files. That is, for each effect size, identification keys entered in designated fields in each record could be used to indicate which two measures were being correlated and which cohort and waves were represented.

To conduct statistical analysis on meta-analysis data in multiple files, a merged file must be created that includes the data relevant to the analysis planned. As we discuss in the next chapter, the recommended approach to the basic analysis of effect sizes is to examine only one effect size construct per analysis. Furthermore, to avoid statistical dependencies, each study should contribute only one effect size representing that construct to each analysis. Thus, for each analysis, a merged data file is created with one record per study that contains one effect size per construct (with its associated variables) plus the study descriptor data.

When using the multiple data files approach, therefore, the initial files are used primarily to archive the data, not as direct input for analysis. They are the source files from which other working files are derived. Most statistical software packages, such as SPSS, SAS, and SYSTAT, analyze only single flat data files. However, each of these packages can create a flat data file from multiple linked files. In particular, they can interleave the data from one file (e.g., study-level data) with each linked data record in another file (e.g., effect size data). However, the process of creating this merged data file varies according to whether the effect size file contains no more than one effect size per construct per study or, for at least some studies, has multiple effect sizes representing the same construct. The procedures for handling each of these two situations will be illustrated using SPSS with our challenge program data. Although the command language will differ for other software packages, the logic will be the same.

No More Than One Effect Size Per Construct Per Study

The nature of the studies, or the meta-analyst's coding of those studies, might be such that no study has more than one effect size for any effect size construct in the effect size data file. This would occur if the original studies simply did not report more than one effect per construct, e.g., presented results for only one dependent variable on each outcome construct examined. Or, it might result from a selection among multiple effects on the same construct that the meta-analyst made at the time of coding each study. Still another possibility is that the meta-analyst would average the effect sizes for each construct within a study at the time of coding and record only the resulting mean. However it occurs, merging a study descriptor and effect size file for analysis is quite straightforward when there is no more than one effect size per construct per study.

Study Descriptor File

STUDYID	PUBYEAR	MEANAGE	TX_TYPE
0100	92	15.5	2
0161	88	15.4	1
7049	82	14.5	1

Effect Size File

STUDYID	ESNUM	OUTCOME	TXN	CGN	ES
0100	1	1	24	24	-.39
0161	1	4	18	22	-.11
0161	2	3	18	22	-.19
0161	3	1	18	22	-.46
7049	1	2	30	30	.34
7049	2	4	30	30	.78
7049	3	1	30	30	.00

Exhibit 5.6. Selected study-level and effect size level data with one effect size per construct per study from the challenge meta-analysis.

```
** SPSS/WIN Command Language
** Merges study level data file and effect size
** data file, linking the records on the study ID.

   MATCH FILES
     /FILE = 'C:\DATA\ES.SAV'
     /TABLE = 'C:\DATA\STUDY.SAV'
     /BY STUDYID .

** Specifies the two files that are to be merged by the
** linking variable STUDYID.  The /TABLE = subcommand
** instructs SPSS to repeat the study level data for
** each link with the effect size level data.

   EXECUTE .
** Runs the Command.
```

Exhibit 5.7. SPSS commands for joining two linked data files.

This situation is illustrated in Exhibit 5.6 with an excerpt of data from the study descriptor and effect size files of the challenge program meta-analysis (see Appendix E for the variable labels and definitions). Note that the study ID number links a single record in the study descriptor file to the potentially multiple records in the effect size file (e.g., study 0100 has one effect size record whereas studies 0161 and 7049 each have three). Also note that for this illustration, none of these studies has more than one effect size for any one construct (the outcome construct is coded in the variable OUTCOME).

Because there is no more than one effect size per construct per study in this case, the simplest approach to creating a merged file suitable for analysis is to attach the study-level data to all the effect size records for that study. That is, the study-level data record is repeated for each associated effect size record so that the resulting data file has one record for each effect size that also includes the study descriptors associated with

STUDYID	PUBYEAR	MEANAGE	TX_TYPE	ESNUM	OUTCOME	TXN	CGN	ES
0100	92	15.5	2	1	1	24	24	-.39
0161	88	15.4	1	1	4	18	22	-.11
0161	88	15.4	1	2	3	18	22	-.19
0161	88	15.4	1	3	1	18	22	-.46
7049	82	14.5	1	1	2	30	30	.34
7049	82	14.5	1	2	4	30	30	.78
7049	82	14.5	1	3	1	30	30	.00

Exhibit 5.8. Merged study and effect size level data from the challenge meta-analysis with one effect size per construct per study (see Exhibits 5.6 and 5.7).

that effect size. For example, the meta-analysis of challenge programs has the study descriptor data in an SPSS data file called STUDY.SAV and the effect size data in a file called ES.SAV. The command language for merging these two data files into a single master data file is shown in Exhibit 5.7. These commands instruct SPSS to join the data in the two specified files on the key variable STUDYID; the study-level file is specified as a table to indicate that the data in it are to be repeated for each match in the effect size file. Results from these commands for the data in Exhibit 5.6 are shown in Exhibit 5.8.

To analyze the data in a merged file of the sort shown in Exhibit 5.8, the meta-analyst need only select the subset of records containing the effect size construct on which the analysis will focus and perform the appropriate statistical manipulations. For instance, the meta-analyst might use the SPSS command SELECT IF OUTCOME = 1 on the data in Exhibit 5.8 to produce the subset of records containing effect sizes with outcome constructs coded with the value of 1 (which refers to delinquency outcomes; see coding scheme in Appendix E). This would select the appropriate records from study 0100, 0161, and 7049 but, since each study has no more than one record for each effect size construct, no study will be represented more than once in the resulting data set. That data set can then be analyzed to examine the delinquency outcomes of challenge programs without concern about statistical dependencies among the effect sizes (see Chapter 6 for further discussion of the problem of statistical dependencies among effect sizes).

More Than One Effect Size Per Construct Per Study

The preceding example assumed that the original coding yielded no more than one effect size per construct per study. If there are multiple effect sizes for some constructs in the effect size file, which is not unusual, intermediate effect size files can be produced for analysis that do have only one effect size per construct per study. These can then be merged with study descriptor files and subsets of effect sizes can be selected for analysis using the procedures described in the foregoing text.

The usual ways of handling multiple effect sizes representing the same construct within a study are to either select a single effect size from among them or average them into a single mean value.[1] For example, in the challenge meta-analysis there are, in fact, multiple effect sizes per study for each of the four major outcome constructs (delinquency, interpersonal skills, locus-of-control, and self-esteem–self-concept). Suppose we decide to produce one effect size per study for each construct by averaging the

```
** SPSS Aggregate Command.
** /OUTFILE specifies the name of a new data file; /BREAK
** instructs SPSS to create one record per OUTCOME per
** STUDYID;/MEANES = MEAN(ES) instructs SPSS to create
** a new variable called MEANES that is the MEAN of all
** ESs with the same STUDYID and OUTCOME values.

        AGGREGATE /OUTFILE 'C:\DATA\WORKINGFILE.SAV'
          /BREAK STUDYID OUTCOME
          /MEANES = MEAN(ES)
          /M_TXN = MEAN(TXN)
          /M_CGN = MEAN(CGN).
        EXECUTE .
```

Exhibit 5.9. SPSS command language to create a mean effect size per construct per study from an effect size data file (see Exhibit 5.6).

effect sizes within a single study when more than one represent that construct. In SPSS this is accomplished with the AGGREGATE command, whereas in SAS the PROC MEANS procedure is used in conjunction with an OUTPUT statement. The SPSS command language for creating an average of multiple effect sizes within a study from data such as that in Exhibit 5.6, *but* with multiple effect sizes per construct per study, is shown in Exhibit 5.9.

The AGGREGATE statement in Exhibit 5.9 instructs SPSS to create a new data file (WORKINGFILE.SAV). The /BREAK parameter tells SPSS what variable to use to group the data. Using the study identification code (STUDYID) and the outcome construct variable (OUTCOME) as break variables results in one record per outcome construct per study being written to the new data file. The remaining commands define the contents of each record in the new data file. For example, the /MEANES = MEAN(ES) syntax specifies that the new variable MEANES be written to the new data file; this is the mean effect size for a single outcome construct and study ID. Note that the only data written to the new data file are the break variables and any aggregate variables specified as part of the command, thus to carry forward the mean sample sizes on which the new mean effect sizes are based or other such effect level information, commands such as /M_TXN = MEAN(TXN) must be included.

Rather than average multiple effect sizes for the same construct within a study, you may choose to select a single effect size per study per construct for a given analysis, either according to some criteria or randomly (see Chapter 6). This is useful for analyses involving variables that are unique to the effect size, such as the nature of the measure, that are lost when effect sizes involving different characteristics are aggregated. Selecting effect sizes from multiples within studies according to some criteria (e.g., those involving the most common or most reliable operationalizations of the construct) generally must be done manually because of the varying combinations within different studies. This process can be aided greatly, however, by sorting the effect size data file on those variables that represent the selection criteria. In the challenge meta-analysis, for instance, suppose that when more than one effect size was available for a construct we decided to select the one with the highest confidence rating for the effect size computation (CR_ES; see Appendix E for coding forms and variable labels) and, if that was equal, then the one with the lowest social desirability bias rating (SOCDESIRE). We could use the procedures for sorting records in SPSS or any other suitable program to sequence the effect size file by STUDYID, OUTCOME, CR_ES, and SOCDESIRE in that order. This would group multiple effect sizes on the same outcome construct within studies together and, within those multiples, sort by confidence rating and, within those groups, by social desirability rating. This would make it relatively easy for the meta-analyst to inspect the effect size records for each study and to select the desired effect size record when

```
**  Assign a random number between 0 and 1 to the
**  variable R .
        COMPUTE R = RV.UNIFORM(0,1) .

**  Sort the cases in ascending order by StudyID and
**  the random number R.
        SORT CASES BY STUDYID R .

**  Compute a new variable called SEL and assign it the
**  value 1 for all cases.
        COMPUTE SEL = 1 .

**  If the current StudyID equals the previous StudyID,
**  then change the value of SEL to 0.
        IF ANY(STUDYID,LAG(STUDYID)) SEL = 0 .

**  Select only those records for which SEL equals 1 .
        SELECT IF SEL = 1 .
        EXECUTE .
```

Exhibit 5.10. SPSS command language to randomly select one ES per study from a file of effect sizes all representing the same construct.

multiples appeared, e.g., by entering a code in a field for a new variable with values of 1 to select and 0 otherwise.

If the meta-analyst wishes to simply make a random selection of one effect size from any multiples on the same construct within a study, this usually can be done directly by the statistical program. The SPSS command language for this procedure is shown in Exhibit 5.10 for effect size files that contain effect sizes on only one construct but have multiples within studies. The logic of this procedure should be applicable to files with more than one construct and to use with other statistical programs. The command language in Exhibit 5.10 (a) assigns a random number between 0 and 1 to the new variable R for each effect size, (b) sorts the cases so that multiple effect sizes within a study (all assumed to represent the same construct) are arranged from the lowest to highest random number; (c) assigns the value of 1 to the variable SEL for the first effect size per study and 0 to all others, and (d) selects those effect sizes with SEL equal to 1. This procedure is well suited to large data sets where it would be cumbersome to implement a manual random selection of effect sizes.

The ultimate purpose of the data management procedures and manipulations the meta-analyst employs is creation of computer files that facilitate statistical analysis. A clear understanding of the nature of the statistical analyses appropriate for meta-analysis data thus contributes essentially to all aspects of data management. The suggestions in this chapter, therefore, should be interpreted in conjunction with the discussion in the next chapter, which deals with the distinctive characteristics of statistical analysis with meta-analytic data.

NOTE

1. An alternative is to maintain the multiple effect sizes and use multivariate analysis techniques that take into account the statistical dependencies among effect sizes based on the same subject samples. This approach is discussed in Chapter 6.

6

Analysis Issues and Strategies

The forms of analysis for meta-analytic data are familiar to researchers, especially those who work with survey data. However, there are certain quirks of meta-analysis data that require special techniques. These are described in more detail later but, for orientation, we first provide an overview of the most important of these distinctive features.

Meta-analysis involves two categories of variables: (a) effect sizes, which are usually the variables of principal interest and constitute the dependent variables of meta-analysis, and (b) descriptive variables that characterize the effect sizes and the studies that generate them, which constitute the independent variables of meta-analysis. Data analysis usually proceeds by first describing the distributions of selected sets of effect sizes (e.g., means and variances) and then examining the relationships between effect sizes and interesting descriptive variables, e.g., using breakout tables, ANOVA comparisons, multiple regression equations, and the like.

Behavioral science researchers are accustomed to data for which the unit of analysis is the individual person. In meta-analysis, the unit of analysis is the individual research study. The distinctive aspects of data analysis follow from this difference. The first complication is that studies in a meta-analysis often generate more than one effect size. While the meta-analyst may be interested in the full range of these multiple effect sizes, any two or more that come from the same study (i.e., the same subject sample) are statistically dependent. Including them in the same analysis would, therefore, violate the assumption of independent data points that is fundamental to most of the common forms of statistical analysis. Therefore, while it may be tempting to use the effect size as the unit of analysis despite multiple effect sizes from some studies, this procedure potentially introduces substantial error into any statistical inference that is derived. The inflated sample size (N of effect sizes rather than N of studies), the distortion of standard error estimates arising from inclusion of nonindependent data points, and the overrepresentation of those studies that contribute more effect sizes can render the statistical results highly suspect.

A second complication that results from having the study be the unit of analysis is that most collections of studies are "lumpy." That is, different studies generally use different sized subject samples. Since effect sizes are derived from sample statistics (means, standard deviations, correlations), their statistical properties depend in part on the underlying sample size. An effect size based on a large sample contains less sampling error and, hence, is a more precise and reliable estimate than an effect size based on a small sample. If we were to conduct statistical analysis on effect sizes without taking sample size into account, we would be treating them as if they should all make the same contribution to the results. However, effect sizes based on large samples should properly play a larger role in any statistical analysis than those based on small samples because they embody less sampling error. The implication of this state of affairs is that effect sizes should not be treated as if they were equal in statistical analysis. Rather, those based on larger samples should be weighted more in statistical computations than those based on smaller samples. Therefore, in meta-analysis, *all* data analysis involving effect sizes is *weighted* analysis. Each effect size is weighted by an appropriate value, generally the inverse of the sampling error variance, so that its contribution to any statistical analysis is proportionate to its reliability.

Once a set of statistically independent effect sizes is assembled, appropriate weights for each effect size are computed, and any other necessary adjustments are made (more on this later), the analysis of effect size data generally proceeds in several stages. The first task is to describe the distribution of effect sizes and to estimate the population mean with an associated confidence interval or statistical significance test. The next phase of the analysis is to assess the adequacy of the mean effect size for representing the entire distribution of effects. A mean effect size will not be very representative of a distribution with a large variance but may characterize one with a small variance quite well. This assessment, called homogeneity testing, is based on a comparison of the observed variability in effect size values with an estimate of the variance that would be expected from subject-level sampling error alone. If the effect sizes are not found to be homogeneous, the meta-analyst may then examine various descriptive variables to determine if they moderate the effect size.

In the remaining sections of this chapter we discuss each step in a typical analysis. In the next chapter we provide suggestions for the practical aspects of implementing an analysis using readily available computer software and work through computational examples.

THE STAGES OF ANALYSIS

Effect Size Adjustments

In many meta-analyses it may be appropriate to adjust individual effect sizes for bias, artifact, and error prior to any statistical analysis. Issues relating to what effect size adjustments are defensible and how best to carry them out are complex and cannot be fully resolved here. However, some adjustments have become customary, such as the small sample bias correction for the standardized mean difference effect size, whereas others are used infrequently, such as the Hunter and Schmidt corrections for such measurement artifacts as low reliability or range restriction in the variables contributing to an effect size. Each of the most commonly used effect size adjustments is discussed in the following text. For more advanced discussions, see Rosenthal (1994) and Hunter and Schmidt (1990a, 1990b, 1994).

Transformations and Bias Corrections

The three most commonly used effect size statistics, the standardized mean difference, the correlation coefficient, and the odds-ratio, all have transformations or bias corrections that should be customarily applied, as noted in Chapter 3. Specifically, the standardized mean difference effect size suffers from a slight upward bias when based on small samples, which is easily corrected (Formula 3.22 in Chapter 3). Both the correlation coefficient and the odds-ratio are usually transformed into more convenient forms for analysis and then transformed back into their original metrics to present the results. For the correlation coefficient, Fisher's Z_r-transformation is applied (Formula 3.39 in Chapter 3), whereas the odds-ratio is transformed by taking the natural logarithm (Formula 3.29 in Chapter 3).

Outliers

The purpose of meta-analysis is to arrive at a reasonable summary of the quantitative findings of a body of research studies. This purpose is not usually served well by the inclusion of extreme effect size values that are notably discrepant from the preponderance of those found in the research of interest and, hence, unrepresentative of the results of that research and possibly even spurious. In addition, extreme effect size values have disproportionate influence on the values of the means, variances, and other statistics used in meta-analysis and may distort them in misleading ways.

It is generally wise, therefore, to examine the distribution of effect sizes to determine if outliers are present (Hedges & Olkin, 1985). If so, it may be advisable to remove them or adjust them to less extreme values before proceeding with the analysis. Of course, a close examination should be made of the discrepant findings and the studies from which they came to assess whether any valid reason is apparent for their unusual values, which may then argue for their inclusion or other special handling.

One common procedure for handling a few outliers that are not believed to be representative of study findings is to simply eliminate them from the effect size distribution. The trimmed distribution can then be analyzed according to plan and the results compared with those from comparable analysis on the untrimmed distribution. Depending on the results of that comparison and the assumptions made about the source of the discrepant values, an interpretation is then reached about which results are more likely to be valid.

In cases where the extreme values are believed to be unrepresentative or spurious, but the analyst does not wish to lose the data they represent, one approach is to recode the extreme values to more moderate ones. This procedure is sometimes called Windsorizing. For instance, the analyst may identify each effect size that is more than 2 (or, perhaps, 3) standard deviations from the mean of all the effect sizes and recode them to the value at 2 (or 3) standard deviations. Huffcutt and Arthur (1995) provide a more analytically precise technique for identifying outliers that takes study sample size into account. Alternatively, the analyst may look for a break in the effect size distribution and code outliers back to the next largest cluster of effect sizes. The discrepant values thus are included in the analysis, and are included as relatively large values, but they are kept from being so extreme relative to the other effect sizes in the distribution that they greatly distort the analysis.

Hunter and Schmidt Artifact Adjustments

Hunter and Schmidt (1990b, 1994) described a variety of other adjustments to individual effect sizes that meta-analysts may wish to make. These include adjustment for the unreliability of the variable(s) involved in the effect size, for restrictions in the range of those variables, for dichotomization of continuous variables, and for imperfect construct validity. Their objective is to permit the meta-analyst to come as close as possible to estimating the magnitude of the relationship represented in an effect size as it would appear under ideal research circumstances. Unfortunately, the information required to apply most of these adjustments often is not available in the research studies coded for a meta-analysis. Moreover, even when relevant information (e.g., reliability of variables) is available for some effect sizes, it may not be available for all of them or even for a majority. The meta-analyst must then decide if it is better to adjust some effect sizes while not adjusting others or to leave them all unadjusted under the rationale that they are more comparable that way, even if less accurate.

Another complication is that each adjustment rides upon assumptions about the data and the purpose of the meta-analysis. Not all analysts are comfortable with those assumptions and with the notion of working with adjusted effect sizes that represent hypothetical ideal values rather than those actually observed in research studies, warts and all. We will not attempt to resolve these issues here, but recommend that the interested analyst consult Hunter and Schmidt (1990b, 1994) and Rosenthal (1994) for a fuller discussion.

Of the Hunter and Schmidt adjustments, the one most likely to be useful and usable is the correction for attenuation due to unreliability of the variables used in the effect size (Hunter & Schmidt, 1990b). This adjustment is applicable to the standardized mean difference and correlation coefficient effect sizes. For the former, the variable at issue is the dependent variable upon which the two groups (e.g., experimental and control) are contrasted. For a correlational effect size, unreliability in either variable contributing to the correlation, or both, can be adjusted. If the reliability of the dependent variable is known, the unattenuated effect size, ES' (standardized mean difference or correlation) is computed as

$$ES' = \frac{ES}{\sqrt{r_{yy}}},$$

where ES is the observed effect size (either ES_{sm} or ES_r) prior to the small sample size bias correction or the Z_r-transformation and r_{yy} is the reliability coefficient. If the effect size at issue is the correlation coefficient and you wish to correct for the unreliability of both variables, then the unattenuated effect size is computed as

$$ES'_r = \frac{ES_r}{\sqrt{r_{xx}}\sqrt{r_{yy}}},$$

where ES_r is the correlation effect size prior to the Z_r-transformation, r_{xx} is the reliability coefficient for one of the variables in the correlation, and r_{yy} is the reliability coefficient for the other variable.

In both of the foregoing cases, the inverse variance weight must also be adjusted. The correction for measurement unreliability increases the sampling error variance and hence decreases the inverse variance weight. The adjustment in the standard error follows the same forms as the adjustment to the effect size, as shown by

$$SE' = \frac{SE}{\sqrt{r_{yy}}},$$

where SE' is the standard error of the adjusted effect size and SE is the standard error for the unadjusted effect size. If you are correcting for measurement unreliability in both measures of a correlation, the standard error is:

$$SE' = \frac{SE}{\sqrt{r_{xx}}\sqrt{r_{yy}}}.$$

Alternatively, these adjustments can be applied directly to the inverse variance weights using

$$w' = w(r_{yy}),$$

$$w' = w(r_{xx})(r_{yy}).$$

Certain types of research involving correlational relationships are especially likely to provide reliability coefficients for one or both of the variables involved in the correlation, for instance, studies investigating the validity, reliability, or covariates of specific measurement instruments. When reliability coefficients are not available for each effect size, or even for a large proportion of them, it may still be worthwhile to collect whatever reliability information is reported in the studies of interest. If the average reliability for the measures involved in the effect sizes can be estimated, it can be used to adjust any mean values calculated over those effect sizes even if each individual effect size cannot be adjusted.

Hunter and Schmidt also recommend adjusting for restriction of range. An effect size will be attenuated if a variable upon which it is based has a smaller range in the study sample than in the population the sample is supposed to represent. For example, if we are investigating the relationship between intelligence and job performance but our sample includes only persons of above average intelligence, then the observed correlation will be smaller than the corresponding correlation in a population with a full range of intellectual ability. The correction for range restriction is most useful when the effect sizes to be analyzed differ greatly in the range represented in one of their constituent variables. In the example of intelligence and job performance, for instance, all the observed correlations could be adjusted to a common population standard deviation for

IQ. Hunter and Schmidt (1990b) provided the formula for the correction of attenuation due to range restriction as

$$ES' = \frac{(U)(ES)}{\sqrt{(U^2 - 1)ES^2 + 1}},$$

where ES is the observed effect size (either ES_{sm} or ES_r) prior to the small sample size bias correction or the Z_r-transformation and U is the ratio of the study standard deviation to the unrestricted (target) standard deviation (i.e., $sd_{study}/sd_{unrestricted}$).

Note that this formula could also be used to adjust downward a correlation based on a sample with a larger range than that of the respective population. In such a situation, the ratio between the study standard deviation and the target standard deviation would be greater than 1, rather than less than 1. Note also that the standard error and inverse variance weight also must be adjusted when range restriction is adjusted in the effect size, as follows (with ES' and ES the adjusted and unadjusted effect sizes, respectively),

$$SE' = \frac{ES'}{ES} SE,$$

$$w' = \frac{ES^2}{(ES')^2} w.$$

It is important to note that these corrections to the standard error and inverse variance weight are approximations and become less precise as the difference between the restricted and unrestricted standard deviations increase (Hunter & Schmidt, 1990b).

An additional source of attenuation in observed effect sizes that can be corrected is dichotomization of a continuous variable (Hunter & Schmidt, 1990a, 1990b, 1994). For example, an intervention study may dichotomize the outcome into "improved" and "not improved." If the dependent variable is actually a continuous construct, dichotomizing it produces a downward bias in the effect size. The formula to adjust for artificial dichotomization if the underlying distribution can be assumed normal is

$$ES' = \frac{ES}{\Phi_{(z)}} \sqrt{p(1 - p)},$$

where ES is the observed effect size (either ES_{sm} or ES_r) prior to the small sample size bias correction or the Z_r-transformation; p is the proportion of cases in the lower portion of the dichotomy and $\Phi_{(z)}$ is the ordinate of the normal distribution corresponding to the cumulative probability equal to p (note this is the ordinate, not the abscissa of the normal distribution, i.e., the height of the curve, not the z-value). The magnitude of this adjustment increases as the proportions of cases in the two portions of the dichotomy become more imbalanced. The correction for dichotomization is most useful when combining effect sizes based on dichotomized variables with those based on continuous variables measuring the same construct. As with the other adjustments, when this one is used the standard error and inverse variance weight must also be adjusted as

$$SE' = \frac{SE}{\Phi_{(z)}}\sqrt{p(1-p)},$$

$$w' = w\frac{\Phi_{(z)}^2}{p(1-p)}.$$

Analyzing the Effect Size Mean and Distribution

The centerpiece of a meta-analysis is one or more effect size distributions. Depending on the specific meta-analysis, these may represent effect sizes for broadly or narrowly defined construct categories. The steps involved in analyzing a distribution of effect sizes are to (a) create an independent set of relevant effect sizes, (b) compute the weighted mean, weighting by the inverse variance weights, (c) determine the confidence interval for the mean, and (d) test for homogeneity of the distribution. If homogeneity of the distribution is rejected, then it may be necessary to repeat steps (b) through (d) using a different statistical model and additional analyses may be warranted. These latter procedures are discussed in the next section. All the steps and procedures will be described in terms of generic effect size statistics and their corresponding inverse variance weights and, therefore, can be used for any effect size statistic and associated weight discussed in Chapter 3.

Creating an Independent Set of Effect Sizes

Effect sizes can usually be assumed to be statistically independent if, for a given distribution, no more than one effect size comes from any subject sample. This is an admittedly limited view of statistical independence. Some have argued rightly that effect sizes for subsamples from the same study share dependencies, as may effect sizes from different studies conducted by the same research team (see Landman & Dawes, 1982; Wolf, 1990). However, these dependencies are likely to be small in most applications, or at least are assumed small, and the standard practice in meta-analysis has been to define independence at the sample or study level.

In most cases, it is advisable to first separate the effect sizes in each study according to the constructs they represent since analyses over disparate constructs are not generally meaningful. For instance, studies of the effectiveness of psychotherapy for children may present outcome constructs for depression, anxiety, relationship with parent, school performance, and so forth. An effect size distribution can be constructed and analyzed for each such construct using one effect size from each study for each construct.

If a study presents more than one effect size for a construct, e.g., using different measurement operationalizations, they should not be included in the same analysis as if they were independent data points. Multiple effect sizes in this situation can be reduced to a single effect size in one of two ways. First, they can be averaged so that the sample on which they are based contributes only one mean effect size to the distribution. Second, one of the effect sizes may be selected for inclusion in the analysis and the other(s) omitted. The meta-analyst may choose to do this a priori by coding only a single effect size per construct per study or the selection may occur post hoc by selecting from among the coded effect sizes. In either case, there should be some justifiable basis for the selection. For instance, selection may be based on criteria for identifying the best of the available effect sizes, e.g., the one dealing with a particular operationalization of interest, the one representing the most common form of a variable and hence most comparable with those in other studies, the one representing greater measurement quality, and the like. If no criteria are especially suitable for choosing a preferred effect size, a random selection may be the best approach. The data management techniques in Chapter 5 included some procedures useful for averaging or randomly selecting effect sizes when more than one per construct per study was coded.

An alternative to creating a set of independent effect sizes for analysis is to statistically model the dependencies among effect sizes, thus allowing for multiple effect sizes per sample in an analysis. A statistical method for achieving this was developed by Gleser and Olkin (1994) and is discussed later in this chapter (see also Kalaian & Raudenbush, 1996). Unfortunately, however, few meta-analysis situations provide sufficient information to permit this method to be implemented and it requires greater statistical sophistication on the part of the meta-analyst.

The Mean Effect Size

The mean effect size is computed by weighting each effect size (ES_i) by the inverse of its variance or w_i (see Chapter 3). The general formula for the weighted mean effect size is

$$\overline{ES} = \frac{\sum(w_i ES_i)}{\sum w_i},$$

where ES_i are the values on the effect size statistic used, w_i is the inverse variance weight for effect size i, and i is equal to 1 to k, with k being the number of effect sizes. In plain English, this formula shows each effect size value multiplied by its respective weight, then summed and divided by the sum of the weights. Computational examples are provided in Chapter 7.

Confidence Intervals around the Mean Effect Size

Confidence intervals indicate the range within which the population mean is likely to be, given the observed data. For example, a 95% confidence interval of 0.05 to 0.49 around a mean effect size indicates a 95% probability that the population mean effect size is between these two values. This is useful in indicating the degree of precision of the estimate of the mean effect size. Additionally, if the confidence interval does not include zero, then the mean effect size is statistically significant at the level specified by the confidence interval (i.e., $\alpha = .05$ for a 95% confidence interval).

The confidence interval for a mean effect size is based on the standard error of the mean and a critical value from the z-distribution (e.g., 1.96 for $\alpha = .05$; not to be confused with Z_r, the Z_r-transform of the correlation coefficient). The standard error of the mean is computed as the square root of the sum of the inverse variance weights (Hedges & Olkin, 1985), as shown in

$$SE_{\overline{ES}} = \sqrt{\frac{1}{\sum w_i}},$$

where $SE_{\overline{ES}}$ is the standard error of the effect size mean, w_i is the inverse variance weight associated with effect size i with $i = 1$ to k effect sizes included in the mean. To construct the confidence interval, you multiply the standard error by a critical z-value representing the desired confidence level and add the product to the mean effect size for the upper limit, $\overline{ES}_U$, and subtract the product from the mean effect size for the lower limit, $\overline{ES}_L$, as shown in

$$\overline{ES}_L = \overline{ES} - z_{(1-\alpha)}(SE_{\overline{ES}}),$$
$$\overline{ES}_U = \overline{ES} + z_{(1-\alpha)}(SE_{\overline{ES}}),$$

where $\overline{ES}$ is the mean effect size, $z_{(1-\alpha)}$ is the critical value for the z-distribution (1.96 for $\alpha = .05$; 2.58 for $\alpha = .01$), and $SE_{\overline{ES}}$ is the standard error of the mean effect size. If the confidence interval does not include zero, the mean effect size is statistically significant at $p \le \alpha$. A direct test of the significance of the mean effect size can be obtained by computing a z-test (not to be confused with $z_{(1-\alpha)}$ or Z_r) as

$$z = \frac{|\overline{ES}|}{SE_{\overline{ES}}},$$

where $|\overline{ES}|$ is the absolute value of the mean effect size and $SE_{\overline{ES}}$ is the standard error of the mean effect size. The result of this formula is distributed as a standard normal variate. Therefore, if it exceeds 1.96 it is statistically significant with $p \le .05$, two-tailed and if it exceeds 2.58 it is significant with $p \le .01$, two-tailed. A more precise probability level can be obtained by consulting a z-distribution in any statistics textbook. Computational examples for confidence intervals and significance testing are provided in Chapter 7.

Homogeneity Analysis

An important question to ask is whether the various effect sizes that are averaged into a mean value all estimate the same population effect size (Hedges, 1982b; Rosenthal & Rubin, 1982). This is a question of the homogeneity of the effect size distribution. In a homogeneous distribution, the dispersion of the effect sizes around their mean is no greater than that expected from sampling error alone (the sampling error associated with the subject samples upon which the individual effect sizes are based). In other words, in a homogeneous distribution an individual effect size differs from the population mean only by sampling error. A statistical test that rejects the null hypothesis of homogeneity indicates that the variability of the effect sizes is larger than would be expected from sampling error and, therefore, each effect size does not estimate a common population mean. In other words, there are differences among the effect sizes that have some source other than subject-level sampling error, perhaps differences associated with different study characteristics. When effect size distributions are found to be heterogeneous, the analyst has several options, discussed later.

The homogeneity test is based on the Q statistic, which is distributed as a chi-square with $k - 1$ degrees of freedom where k is the number of effect sizes (Hedges & Olkin, 1985). The formula for Q is

$$Q = \sum w_i(ES_i - \overline{ES})^2,$$

where ES_i is the individual effect size for $i = 1$ to k (the number of effect sizes), $\overline{ES}$ is the weighted mean effect size over the k effect sizes, and w_i is the individual weight for ES_i. If Q exceeds the critical value for a chi-square with $k - 1$ degrees of freedom, then the null hypothesis of homogeneity is rejected (a chi-square table can be found in Appendix B or in any standard statistics textbook). A statistically significant Q, therefore, indicates a heterogeneous distribution. A distribution found heterogeneous at this point generally warrants additional analysis as described in the next section.

An algebraically equivalent formula for Q that is computationally simpler to implement is

$$Q = (\sum w_i ES_i^2) - \frac{(\sum w_i ES_i)^2}{\sum w_i},$$

where each of the terms is defined as above. Computational examples and command language for using statistical programs for generating Q-values are provided in Chapter 7.

Hunter and Schmidt (1990b; see also Hunter, Schmidt, & Jackson, 1982) proposed an alternative approach to homogeneity testing that does not rely on formal significance testing. Their approach partitions the observed effect size variability into two components: the portion attributable to subject-level sampling error and the portion attributable to other between-study differences. They then assume the distribution is homogeneous if sampling error accounts for 75% or more of the observed variability. Exploration of study moderator variables, as discussed in the following text, is indicated if the sampling error accounts for less than 75% of observed variability. This "75% rule" is intended as a "rule of thumb," not a strict cut-off point and researchers with explicit a priori hypotheses about specific between study effects are encouraged to test for those relationships even if the 75% rule is exceeded (Hunter & Schmidt, 1990b). The intent of this "rule," however, is to force recognition of the role of sampling error in effect size variability across studies and to discourage post hoc exploration of the relationship between study characteristics and effect size when most of the observed variability is adequately explained by sampling error. The interested reader is referred to the writings of Hunter and Schmidt for further information on this approach.

Analysis of Heterogeneous Distributions of Effect Size

The preceding discussion assumes what is called a *fixed effects model* (Hedges, 1994; Hedges & Vevea, 1998; Overton, 1998). Under a fixed effects model, an effect size observed in a study is assumed to estimate the corresponding population effect with random error that stems only from the chance factors associated with subject-level sampling error in that study, i.e., the "luck of the draw" associated with sampling the subjects in each study from the population of potential subjects. For theoretical reasons, the meta-analyst may not believe this assumption is appropriate for the distribution of effect sizes at issue. For instance, the analyst may believe that there are essentially random differences between studies that are associated with variations in procedures, settings, and the like that go beyond subject-level sampling error. Or it may be assumed that the set of studies in the meta-analysis is itself a sample from a larger population of studies that do not have a common population effect size and, therefore, the observed effect sizes will have study-level sampling error as well as subject-level sampling error associated with them.

Correspondingly, the Q-test for a distribution of observed effect sizes from different studies examines the assumption of a fixed effects model from a statistical perspective. A significant Q rejects the null hypothesis of homogeneity and indicates that the variability among the effect sizes is greater than what is likely to have resulted from subject-level sampling error alone. It thus challenges the assumption of the simple fixed effects model that weighting effect sizes by a term representing only subject-level sampling error will be sufficient to account for their differential precision as statistical estimates of population values. Note, however, that a nonsignificant Q does not always provide great confidence that a fixed effects model is justified. With small numbers of effect sizes, especially if they, in turn, are based on small subject samples, the Q-test will not have much statistical power and may fail to reject homogeneity even when there is considerable variability among the effect sizes stemming from sources other than subject-level sampling error. In any event, if the fixed effects assumptions are rejected, whether for conceptual or statistical reasons, the analyst has three options for handling the situation:

(1) *Assume that the variability beyond subject-level sampling error is random, that is, derives from essentially random differences among studies whose sources cannot be identified.* In this case, the analyst would adopt a *random effects model*. The random effects model assumes that to represent the variation among effect sizes another random component must be included in the statistical model in addition to subject-level sampling error. Since this additional random component is assumed to either be, or act like, study-level sampling error, sampling error in the random effects model represents random variability at both the study-level (studies sampled from a population of studies) and the subject-level (subjects in each study sampled from a population of subjects). The random effects model, therefore,

involves a different inverse variance weight than the fixed effects model (recall that this weight is used to represent the statistical error with which an effect size is estimated). This means that when using the random effects model the weight applied to each effect size in any analysis must represent both subject-level sampling error and the additional random variance component assumed by the random effects model. In particular, it requires that the weighted mean and confidence interval computations described above must be recalculated using a different inverse variance weight. This procedure is described below under the heading "Random Effects Model."

(2) *Continue to assume a fixed effects model, but add the assumption that the variability beyond subject-level sampling error is systematic, that is, derived from identifiable differences between studies.* This added assumption is the basis for further analyzing effect size variation in terms of the characteristics of the source studies that generate the effect sizes. In this case, the analyst demonstrates (or assumes) that the effect size distribution has more variability than can be accounted for by subject-level sampling error, but postulates that the excess variability is not random. Instead, the analyst intends to demonstrate that the excess variability can be explained by showing that it is associated with moderator variables that systematically differentiate studies with larger or smaller effect sizes. For example, it may be expected that when the differences in effect sizes associated with different treatments and research designs are accounted for, what remains will be only subject-level sampling error. In that case, the inverse variance weight based on subject-level sampling error assumed in the preceding discussion will still be appropriate. The procedures for investigating the study and effect size characteristics that may account for between-study variation are discussed below under the heading "Fixed Effects Model: Partitioning Effect Size Variance."

(3) *Assume that the variance beyond subject-level sampling error is derived partly from systematic factors that can be identified and partly from random sources.* In this case, the analyst assumes a *mixed effects model*, that is, that there is effect size variance in excess of what can be attributed to subject-level sampling error which has *both* systematic and random components. This model, like the version of the fixed effects model described in (2) above, assumes that certain identifiable study characteristics act as moderator variables and are associated with systematic differences among effect sizes. These systematic differences are presumed to account for some of the excess variability among the effect sizes. Unlike the model above, however, the mixed effects model allows for a random component of residual variance to remain after the systematic portion is accounted for. In other words, it assumes that the effect size variation in excess of subject-level sampling error can be divided into two components, one representing systematic relationships between study characteristics and effect size and another leftover component representing essentially random study-level dif-

ferences. That leftover component reflects statistical uncertainty and must be incorporated into the weighting function used in effect size analysis, e.g., the weighted mean and confidence intervals described above must be recomputed using different weights. The procedures for fitting this model to effect size data are discussed below under the heading, "Mixed Effects Models."

Random Effects Model

As noted, a random effects model assumes that each observed effect size differs from the population mean by subject-level sampling error *plus* a value that represents other sources of variability assumed to be randomly distributed. In this situation, the variance associated with each effect size has two components: the one associated with subject-level sampling error, as presented earlier, and a second component associated with the random effects variance. The sum of these two variance components, v_i^*, is the total variance associated with the distribution of effect size values and is described by

$$v_i^* = v_\theta + v_i,$$

where v_θ is the estimate of the random or between-studies variance component and v_i is the estimate of the variance associated with subject-level sampling error, as computed in the formulas presented earlier for the respective effect size statistics. A random effects mean effect size, confidence interval, significance test, and Q are all computed by substituting the new variance that includes the random effect component for the variance that was based solely on the sampling error variance (SE^2) presented earlier. The inverse variance weight thus becomes $1/v_i^*$ rather than $1/v_i$ and the calculations then proceed as before using this new weighting function.

The difficulty with the random effects model is obtaining a good estimate of the random effects variance component. There are two basic procedures for this, a noniterative method based on the method of moments and an iterative method based on maximum likelihood (Overton, 1998; Raudenbush, 1994; Shadish and Haddock, 1994). The latter provides somewhat more accurate estimates, but the former is quite serviceable for most purposes and, because it is easier to implement, will be the only method presented here. The method of moments estimate of v_θ is

$$v_\theta = \frac{Q - (k - 1)}{\sum w_i - \left(\sum w_i^2 / \sum w_i\right)},$$

where Q is the value of the homogeneity test, described earlier, k is the number of effect sizes, and w_i is the inverse variance weight for each effect size as defined earlier under the fixed effects model. If this formula returns a negative value, then v_θ is set to zero. This occurs only when the effect size distribution is homogeneous and thus is fit by a fixed effects model. Because of the generality of the random effects model, and its mixed model cousin, it is recommended by some as the preferred strategy (Mosteller & Colditz, 1996). Strategies for implementing random effects models with common statistical software and examples of command language are presented in Chapter 7.

Fixed Effects Model: Partitioning Effect Size Variance

Rather than assuming that effect size heterogeneity (between study differences) is due to unobserved random sources, you may believe that it has systematic sources and can be explained by variables captured in the coding protocol. That is, you may believe that the excess between-studies variability can be explained by the independent variables in your meta-analysis—the study and effect size descriptors. Two approaches to modeling the between-study variance will be discussed: Hedges' (1982a) analog to the analysis of variance and Hedges and Olkin's (1985) modified weighted multiple regression. The former handles categorical independent variables and, as the name implies, is similar to one-way analysis of variance (ANOVA). The latter handles continuous or dichotomous independent variables and can model multiple independent variables in a single analysis.

Analog to the Analysis of Variance. The meta-analysis analog to the analysis of variance is a technique that groups effect sizes into mutually exclusive categories on the basis of an independent variable and tests the homogeneity among the effect sizes within the categories and the differences between the categories. If the between category variance is significant, the mean effect sizes across groups differ by more than sampling error. If the pooled within groups variance is homogeneous, it indicates that there is no further variation among effect sizes other than subject-level sampling error. This latter information is critical for assessing the adequacy of the categorical variable to fully explain the original heterogeneity among the effect sizes. Examples of categorical variables include type of research design (e.g., random vs. nonrandom assignment), intervention type (e.g., cognitive–behavioral or insight therapy), and characteristics of the subject sample (e.g., proportion of males). Each of these variables may account for variability in the observed effect sizes.

The ANOVA analog is best suited to testing a limited set of a priori hypotheses regarding moderator variables. A common but incorrect application of this approach is to test a large number of categorical variables to identify those that are statistically significant. There are many examples of published meta-analyses that performed the analog to the ANOVA on all study descriptor variables coded. This analytic approach is comparable to performing t-tests on a large number of outcome variables in an intervention study. Inevitably, something will be statistically significant simply by chance and will lead to unfounded speculation regarding its meaning and interpretation.

The analog to the ANOVA partitions the total homogeneity statistic, Q, into the portion explained by the categorical variable (Q_B) and the residual pooled within groups portion (Q_W). The homogeneity statistic Q is the weighted sum-of-squares of the individual effect sizes around the grand mean (see page 115). The Q_B is then the weighted sum-of-squares of the mean effect sizes for each group around the grand mean. Likewise, Q_W is the weighted sum-of-squares of the individual effect sizes within each group around their respective group mean, pooled over the groups. The formula for Q_B is

$$Q_B = \sum w_j \overline{ES}_j^2 - \frac{\left(\sum w_j \overline{ES}_j\right)^2}{\sum w_j},$$

where Q_B is the Q between groups, $\overline{ES}_j$ is the weighted mean effect size for each group, w_j is the sum of the weights within each group, and j equals 1, 2, 3, etc. up to the number of groups. Q_W is computed as the sum of the within group Qs. The formula is

$$Q_w = \sum w_i \left(ES_i - \overline{ES}_j\right)^2,$$

where Q_w is the pooled Q within groups, ES_i is the individual effect size, $\overline{ES}_j$ is the weighted mean effect size for each group, w_i is the weight for each effect size, i equals 1, 2, 3, etc. up to the number of effect sizes, and j equals 1, 2, 3, etc. up to the number of groups. The preceding formula is difficult to implement. A simpler strategy is to compute a separate Q for each group of effect sizes and then sum those Qs. The result is Q_W; Q_B is then found through subtraction as the total Q minus Q_W. Each of these Qs is distributed as a chi-square. As with the one-way ANOVA, the degrees of freedom for Q_B is $j - 1$, where j is the number of groups. Similarly, the degrees of freedom for the Q_W is $k - j$, where k is the number of effect sizes and j is the number of groups. This analysis is illustrated using a spreadsheet in Chapter 7.

Weighted Regression Analysis. The analog to the ANOVA presented above provides a method of testing the ability of a single categorical variable, such as treatment type, to explain excess variability in a distribution of effect sizes. Meta-analysts are often interested in exploring the relationships between effect size and continuous variables. For example, it may be of interest to test whether attrition, measured as a proportion of the initial sample size, is related to the variability in observed effect sizes. Furthermore, it may be desirable to test several continuous variables simultaneously, such as attrition and intensity of treatment. This can be done using a modified weighted least squares regression, weighting each effect size by the inverse of its variance, as with the formulas for the mean and confidence interval presented earlier.

Most statistical software programs, such as SPSS, SYSTAT, STATA, and SAS, perform weighted least squares regression. Although these programs correctly estimate the regression coefficients if given the appropriate weights, they may report inaccurate standard errors and, hence, statistical significance when applied to effect size data. This happens if the program interprets the weights as representing multiple effect sizes rather than weightings of single effect sizes and attributes an exaggerated n to the effect size sample. The problem is easily overcome, however. Some side calculations performed on the output of these programs will generate the appropriate significance levels of each regression weight (B-weight). In addition, a test assessing whether there is significant residual variability left after the model is fit can be readily computed. Alternatively, we have written macros that provide instructions for multiple regression with meta-analytic data that will run in SPSS, STATA, and SAS (Wang & Bushman, 1998, have also written a set of macros for use with SAS). These are discussed further in Chapter 7 on computational techniques.

Two indices assessing the overall fit of the weighted regression model can be calculated, a Q due to the regression and a Q error or residual (denoted as Q_R and Q_E, respectively). These reflect a partitioning of the total variability into the portion associated with the regression model, Q_R, and the variability unaccounted for by the model, Q_E. Most weighted regression programs report an analysis of variance table with a sum-of-squares column, including a sum-of-squares for the regression model and a residual sum-of-squares. These are Q_R and Q_E, respectively, and both are distributed as a chi-square. The total of these two values should equal the Q total previously computed. Q_R has p degrees of freedom, where p is the number of predictor variables in the regression equation. Q_R is analogous to the F-test for the regression model and, if significant, indicates that the regression model explains significant variability in the effect sizes. The null hypothesis is that all regression coefficients (B-weights) are simultaneously zero. Therefore, when Q_R is significant, at least one regression coefficient is significantly different from zero. The weighted sum-of-squares residual, Q_E, has $k - p - 1$ degrees of freedom, where k is the number of effect sizes and p is the number of predictors. If Q_E is significant, then variability beyond subject-level sampling error remains across the effect sizes. In other words, after removing the variability associated with the predictor variables, the effect sizes remain heterogeneous. It is quite possible to have both a significant regression model and a significant residual variability. In statistical terms, the regression model is underspecified (we return to this issue under the discussion of mixed models).

Of particular interest are the individual *unstandardized* regression coefficients (B-weights). Hedges & Olkin (1985) showed that a correct standard error (SE_B) for these can be computed using the incorrect standard error and the mean-square residual reported as part of the regression output for meta-analytic data from a statistical program doing standard weighted regression (which interprets the weights as differential sample size). The formula for the corrected standard error, SE_B' is

$$SE_B' = \frac{SE_B}{\sqrt{MS_E}},$$

where SE_B is the reported (incorrect) standard error for each regression coefficient, B, and MS_E is the mean-square residual for the regression model, i.e., the mean-square value for the residual model as reported in the regression summary table. A significance test (z-test) can be constructed by dividing the regression coefficient (B) by its corrected standard error as

$$z = \frac{B}{SE_B'},$$

where B is the unstandardized regression coefficient and SE_B' is the correct standard error of the regression coefficient. The result of this formula is distributed as a standard normal variate.[1] Therefore, if it exceeds 1.96 it is significant at $p < .05$, two-tailed and, if greater than 2.58, it is significant at $p < .01$, two-tailed. A more precise probability level can be obtained by consulting a z-distribution in any statistics textbook. This process is illustrated with examples in Chapter 7.

An alternative approach to testing the significance of individual regression coefficients that yields equivalent results is to compute a Q for each. These Q_p-values are distributed as a chi-square with 1 degree of freedom.

The Q method has the advantage of allowing the statistical significance of a subset of regression coefficients to be tested. The sum of any set of Q_p-values is also a Q, distributed as a chi-square with p degrees of freedom, where p is the number of predictors in the summed Q_p. The Q_p for an individual regression coefficient, B, is computed as

$$Q_p = \frac{B^2}{(SE'_B)^2},$$

where the terms are defined in the foregoing text. Note that the Q_p is the sum-of-squares explained by the associated regression coefficient adjusted for all other effects in the regression model. Therefore, the sum of the Q_p-values (excluding the Q for the regression constant or intercept) will be less than the total Q for the model (i.e., Q_R). The difference is "shared" sums-of-squares, that is, variability in effects size that is jointly associated with more than one independent variable. The greater the correlations between the independent variables, the greater the difference between these values.

Mixed Effects Models

An effect size distribution may remain heterogeneous even after modeling between-study differences through the use of regression analysis or an ANOVA analog model. That is, the residual Q_E or Q_W could still be statistically significant (not homogeneous). This indicates that the assumption of a fixed effects model with only systematic variance (the modeled component) and subject-level sampling error is untenable and a mixed effects model should be considered. A mixed effects model assumes that the effects of between-study variables, such as treatment type, are systematic but that there is a remaining unmeasured (and possibly unmeasurable) random effect in the effect size distribution in addition to sampling error. That is, variability in the effect size distribution is attributed to systematic (modeled) between-study differences, subject-level sampling error, and an additional random component.

Fitting a mixed effects model to effect size data is similar to the method for fitting a random effects model. The critical and difficult step is estimating the random effects variance component (v_θ). As before, that estimate is added to the standard error variance associated with each effect size (v_i), the inverse variance weights are recalculated, and the analysis is rerun with the new weights. In a mixed effects model, the estimate of the random effects variance component is based on the residual variability (Q_E or Q_W) rather than the total variability (Q_T). Unfortunately, the value of the random component in the mixed model must be estimated through matrix algebra; for specifics see Kalaian & Raudenbush (1996), Overton (1998) and Raudenbush (1994). The confidence intervals under a mixed effects model will be larger than under a fixed effects model unless v_θ equals zero. Also, regression coefficients that were significant under fixed effects assumptions may no longer be so. Chapter 7 of this volume discusses computational techniques for applying the mixed effects model.

It is frequently questionable whether a fixed or mixed effects model is most appropriate for a particular heterogeneous distribution of effect sizes (Hedges & Vevea, 1998). The fixed effects model has more statistical power to detect moderator relationships with effect size; that is, it is more likely to identify systematic between-study differences. This comes with a price, however. The fixed effects model will have high Type I error rates when, contrary to its assumptions, there is unexplained between-groups heterogeneity. The mixed effects model has Type I error rates that are more accurate but at the cost of statistical power in identifying moderator effects. Thus, a sensitivity analysis comparing the results from fixed and mixed effects models is usually advisable. Additional research will be needed to sort out the conditions under which the various models, fixed, random, and mixed, are most appropriate, though current perspectives are largely unfavorable toward fixed models when effect size distributions are demonstrably heterogeneous (Mosteller & Colditz, 1996; Overton, 1998).

Analysis of Statistically Dependent Effect Sizes

Our discussion of effect size analysis has emphasized the need to maintain statistical independence by including only one effect size per subject sample in any given analysis. When the research studies under review produce multiple effect sizes for the same conceptual relationship, we advocate that only one be selected, randomly or on the basis of some criteria, or that they be averaged together so that only one value is contributed to any given analysis. This admittedly conservative approach has the disadvantage of ignoring potentially meaningful information which, in some cases, the analyst may be quite reluctant to omit. For such situations, Gleser and Olkin (1994) have developed a method for handling dependent effect sizes in a single analysis. However, this method requires that the covariance between dependent effect sizes be known or estimated so that it can be incorporated into the analysis.

We described analyses of independent effect sizes that are weighted by their inverse variances. Imagine that these variances make up the diagonal of a square matrix with rows and columns for the effect sizes to be analyzed. The off-diagonal values in this matrix represent the covariances between different effect sizes; for statistically independent effect sizes, these are all zeros. For any statistically dependent effect sizes, the Gleser and Olkin method replaces the zeros with the respective covariances between them. If we now take the inverse of the values in each cell, we have the usual inverse variance weights for each effect size on the diagonal and inverse covariance weights for statistically dependent effect sizes in the off-diagonal.

All of the formulas for computing meta-analytic results presented in this chapter can be rewritten in matrix algebra form. The Gleser and Olkin method then simply substitutes the weighting matrix with the inverse covariance terms in the off-diagonals for the otherwise assumed version with all zeros in the off-diagonals. The specifics are presented in Gleser and Olkin (1994); Wang and Bushman (1998) have created macros for SAS that perform the required computations.

A situation where this method would be useful is the synthesis of studies that have more than one experimental group of interest but only a single control group. A statistical dependence among effect sizes in this instance results if effect sizes are computed for all treatment-control comparisons because the same common control group data is used in each calculation. In this case, an estimate of the covariance between the effect sizes is based on the control group sample size (see Gleser & Olkin, 1994). A more common situation for which this method is applicable is when multiple effect sizes are calculated on the same subject sample for inclusion in the same analysis, e.g., the same measure observed at different times or different measures of the same construct observed at the same time. Unfortunately, determining the covariance among the effect sizes in this situation requires knowledge of the correlation between the measures. In our experience, this is rarely reported in most areas of research, which severely limits the practical utility of this approach despite its theoretical and statistical advantages (Kalaian & Raudenbush, 1996).

Additional Analysis Issues

A common frustration in meta-analysis is the uneven reporting practices among researchers. Information that should be reported is often missing or, if reported, is too vague or terse to permit adequate coding for meta-analysis. Conducting a meta-analysis thus routinely requires coders to make judgments based on imperfect information which, in turn, results in data elements that are missing or in which little confidence can be placed. Indeed, in Chapter 4 we recommended that confidence ratings be used for critical items as a means of formalizing this uncertainty. For example, a confidence rating could be associated with the item that codes the basic design of an intervention study. Likewise, a confidence rating could be associated with the data extracted for computation of an effect size. How can these confidence ratings be used in the analysis?

One approach (which we do not recommend) is to weight each effect size in an analysis by the confidence ratings associated with it or, alternatively, by some other index of quality, e.g., methodological quality. Since effect sizes are already weighted by the inverse variance, this approach creates a composite weight in which the two weights are added, multiplied, or otherwise combined. There are two disadvantages to this approach. First, the statistical theory that allows for the analysis procedures described in this chapter requires inverse variance weights that are related to the standard errors for the specific effect size statistic used. Composite weights, properly applied, would necessitate an adaptation of the statistical theory to take into account the variance associated with the confidence or quality weights as well. Second, weighting by confidence or quality ratings obscures the relationship between the ratings and the observed effect sizes. We believe it is far more informative to know whether and how the ratings relate to effect size and, if justified, to use them as control or moderator variables in the analysis. Moreover, if the ratings are strongly related to effect size, it may be more appropriate to omit studies with low ratings on critical items than to presume that the analyst can determine how best to weight them in an analysis with better studies that yield quite different results.

A related issue is missing data. In meta-analysis, some variables may be coded solely for descriptive purposes, that is, to describe the characteristics of the studies included in the meta-analysis. For this purpose, reporting that a given variable was not codable for a certain proportion of the studies is informative. However, variables that are intended to explain between-study variability in effect size present a problem if they have much missing data. For analyses using the analog to the ANOVA, including the "missing" category as one group in the analysis is probably the best choice for most situations. For multiple regression analysis the missing value may be imputed or that case may be excluded from the analysis. The methods used here are no different than in other social science research (Little & Rubin, 1987; Rubin, 1987). If the number of cases with missing values is small relative to the total number of cases, then any reasonable method should suffice. We recommend that, whatever the method of imputation used, a sensitivity analysis be performed to assess the extent to which the results of the analysis depend upon the way missing data are handled. In this regard, it is often informative to include a "missingness" dummy variable in the analysis to assess whether the studies for which that variable could not be coded systematically produced smaller or larger effect sizes after accounting for the other variables in the model.

The analysis strategies described in this chapter can be implemented in various ways, even manually for small meta-analyses. Beyond a very modest size, however, computer analysis is necessary. The next chapter describes some computational techniques and adaptations of statistical software that are helpful for actually performing the analytic procedures previously described.

NOTE

1. Raudenbush (1994) recommends comparing these values with the student's t-distribution, rather than the normal distribution, with $k - p - 1$ degrees of freedom, where k is the number of studies and p is the number of predictor variables in the regression model. Using the t-distribution will yield more conservative confidence intervals and significance levels. However, for analyses with 120 or more effect sizes the two approaches will be virtually identical.

7

Computational Techniques for Meta-Analysis Data

The full range of statistical procedures outlined in Chapter 6 has yet to be built into popular data analysis software programs (but see Borenstein, 2000). With some relatively manageable adaptations, however, most general purpose statistical programs can be used for meta-analysis. It is beyond the scope of this book to attempt to show how this would be done for all the major statistical programs, but the steps and logic of implementing the various meta-analysis procedures are similar for most of these applications. In this chapter, therefore, we illustrate the relevant techniques for a typical statistics program, SPSS for Windows, and spreadsheet, Excel for Windows. We have tried to present sufficient detail to allow users of other software programs to adapt the procedures.

THE MEAN, CONFIDENCE INTERVAL, AND HOMOGENEITY TEST

The mean and related statistics for effect sizes can be computed by creating three new variables that are summed across records and used to compute the desired statistics. For each data record we need an effect size, ES_i, and the inverse variance weight, w_i (see Chapter 3 for formulas). At this point, we assume that any desired adjustments to the effect size have been performed, such as the small sample bias correction for the standardized mean difference or the transformation of correlations via Fisher's Z_r-transform. We are also assuming the effect sizes in the distribution to be analyzed are statistically independent.

Table 7.1 provides illustrative data from the challenge programs meta-analysis. Reported in this table are effect sizes for delinquency outcomes from 10 studies. Note that the effect size values shown in this table are small sample bias corrected standardized mean differences (see Formulas 3.21 through 3.24 in Chapter 3) but the same computational procedures would be applicable to any of the effect size statistics described in Chapter 3.

To begin calculating the basic statistics needed to analyze an effect size distribution, we use ES_i and w_i to compute the following three variables:

(a) the product of w_i and ES_i, which we call wes_i; (b) the product of w_i and the square of ES_i, which we call $wessq_i$; and (c) the square of w_i, which we call wsq_i. These are shown in Table 7.1.

The SPSS command language for computing these new variables for an effect size variable and its associated inverse variance weight is shown in Exhibit 7.1. In a spreadsheet program, such as Excel, these new variables can be calculated by substituting the column label and row number for the variable names in the SPSS compute statements in Exhibit 7.1 and by following the general procedures for specifying formulas in the particular spreadsheet program. In Excel, the composite variable wes_i can be calculated for an effect size (ES_i) in cell C2 and an inverse variance weight (w_i) in cell E2 by typing "=C2 * E2" in the target cell, such as F2. This formula can then be copied down for all rows of the data set. The result of this procedure is shown in Exhibit 7.2.

Next, determine the sum of the variables w, wes, $wessq$, and wsq across studies. In a statistical program this can easily be obtained from the output of a descriptive statistics command, as shown in Exhibit 7.1. In a spreadsheet, simply sum the respective columns. The mean effect size, confidence interval, z, and Q can be computed using these sums, as shown in the following formulas. For instance, the weighted mean effect size is computed as the sum of wes_i divided by the sum of w_i, stated

Table 7.1

Illustrative Effect Size Data from the Meta-Analysis of Challenge Programs for Delinquency Outcomes[a]

Study ID	ES_i	v_i	w_i	wes_i $(w \times ES)$	$wessq_i$ $(w \times ES^2)$	wsq_i (w^2)	Random[b]	Intensity[c]
100	−.33	0.084	11.905	−3.929	1.296	141.729	0	7
308	.32	0.035	28.571	9.143	2.926	816.302	0	3
1596	.39	0.017	58.824	22.941	8.947	3460.263	0	7
2479	.31	0.034	29.412	9.118	2.826	865.066	0	5
9021	.17	0.072	13.889	2.361	0.401	192.904	0	7
9028	.64	0.117	8.547	5.470	3.501	73.051	0	7
161	−.33	0.102	9.804	−3.235	1.068	96.118	1	4
172	.15	0.093	10.753	1.613	0.242	115.627	1	4
537	−.02	0.012	83.333	−1.667	0.033	6944.389	1	5
7049	.00	0.067	14.925	0.000	0.000	222.756	1	6
Total			269.963	41.815	21.240	12,928.205		

[a]Multiple delinquency effect sizes from a single study were averaged if the sample sizes were equal, otherwise the effect size with the largest sample size was selected.
[b]Random assignment to conditions: 1 = yes; 0 = no.
[c]Coder rated intensity of challenge: 1 = very low through 7 = very high.

```
** Compute three new variables: wes,wessq, and wsq. The sum of these
** variables will be used to compute the mean, homogeneity Q, confidence
** intervals, z-test and the random effects variance component.
** Note: es is the effect size and w is the inverse variance weight.

    compute wes  = w*es .
    compute wessq = w*es**2 .
    compute wsq  = w**2 .
    execute .

** Calculate the sum of each variable for use in hand calculations .

    descriptives
    /variables w wes wessq wsq
    /statistics sum.

** Sample output for the 10 cases in the challenge meta-analysis .

    Descriptive Statistics
               N        Sum
    W      10     269.963
    WES    10      41.815
    WESSQ  10      21.240
    WSQ    10   12928.205
```

Exhibit 7.1. SPSS Command syntax for creating variables and the sums of those variables needed to compute a weighted mean effect size, confidence interval, and homogeneity Q.

	A	B	C	D	E	F	G	H
1	studyid	random	es	v	w	wes	wessq	wsq
2	100	0	-0.33	0.084	11.905	-3.929	1.296	141.729
3	308	0	0.32	0.035	28.571	9.143	2.926	816.302
4	1596	0	0.39	0.017	58.824	22.941	8.947	3460.263
5	2479	0	0.31	0.034	29.412	9.118	2.826	865.066
6	9021	0	0.17	0.072	13.889	2.361	0.401	192.904
7	9028	0	0.64	0.117	8.547	5.470	3.501	73.051
8	161	1	-0.33	0.102	9.804	-3.235	1.068	96.118
9	172	1	0.15	0.093	10.753	1.613	0.242	115.627
10	537	1	-0.02	0.012	83.333	-1.667	0.033	6944.389
11	7049	1	0.00	0.067	14.925	0.000	0.000	222.756
12								
13				totals	269.963	41.815	21.240	12928.205
14								
15				totals nonrandom = 0	151.148	45.104	19.897	5549.315
16				totals random = 1	118.815	-3.289	1.343	7378.890
17								

Exhibit 7.2. Example setup for computing a weighted mean effect size, confidence interval, homogeneity Q, and analog to the ANOVA using a spreadsheet.

symbolically as

$$\overline{ES} = \frac{\sum wes_i}{\sum w_i}.$$

For the data presented in Table 7.1 for delinquency outcomes in the challenge meta-analysis, the sums for w_i, wes_i, and $wessq_i$ are 269.963, 41.815, and 21.240, respectively. The weighted mean for those 10 delinquency effect sizes is, therefore:

$$\overline{ES} = \frac{41.815}{269.963} = 0.155.$$

The standard error of the mean effect size, z-test, and the lower and upper bounds of the .95 confidence intervals can then be calculated as

$$SE_{\overline{ES}} = \sqrt{\frac{1}{\sum w_i}} = \sqrt{\frac{1}{269.963}} = 0.061,$$

$$z = \frac{\overline{ES}}{SE_{\overline{ES}}} = \frac{0.155}{0.061} = 2.54,$$

$$\overline{ES}_L = \overline{ES} - 1.96(SE_{\overline{ES}}) = 0.155 - 1.96(0.061) = 0.035,$$

$$\overline{ES}_U = \overline{ES} + 1.96(SE_{\overline{ES}}) = 0.155 + 1.96(0.061) = 0.275.$$

The z-test value of 2.54 exceeds the critical value of 1.96 at $p = .05$ so we conclude that the mean effect size for this sample of studies is statistically significant. Correspondingly, the 95% confidence interval around the mean effect size ($0.035 < \mu < 0.275$) does not include zero and reveals the relative precision of the estimate of mean effect size of the population of studies from which these 10 are presumably drawn.

With the values of w_i, wes_i, and $wessq_i$ we can also compute Q for the 10 effect sizes in Table 7.1 to assess their homogeneity:

$$Q = \sum wessq_i - \frac{(\sum wes_i)^2}{\sum w_i} = 21.240 - \frac{41.815^2}{269.963} = 14.763.$$

The resulting Q-value of 14.763 with 9 degrees of freedom ($k - 1$ where k is the number of studies) is less than the .05 critical value of 16.92 for a chi-square with 9 degrees of freedom. We thus fail to reject the hypothesis of homogeneity at $\alpha = .05$. The variance in this sample of effect sizes is not demonstrably greater than would be expected from sampling error alone.

```
meanes es = es /w = w .

***** Meta-Analytic Results *****

------- Distribution Description ---------------------------------
         N        Min ES      Max ES      Wghtd SD
    10.000        -.330        .640         .234

------- Fixed & Random Effects Model ----------------------------
          Mean ES    -95%CI    +95%CI      SE        Z        P
Fixed      .1549      .0356     .2742     .0609    2.5450    .0109
Random     .1534     -.0146     .3215     .0858    1.7893    .0736

------- Random Effects Variance Component -----------------------
v    =    .025955

------- Homogeneity Analysis ------------------------------------
         Q          df          p
    14.7640      9.0000      .0976

If Q significant, reject null (v=0).

Random effects v estimated via noniterative method of moments.
```

Exhibit 7.3. Sample output from SPSS macro MEANES that computes meta-analytic summary statistics (see Appendix D).

If you have numerous sets of effect sizes to analyze, such as a set for each treatment type, using the previous approach repeatedly is tedious. To reduce this tedium, we created a macro that runs within SPSS for Windows and performs these calculations (see Appendix D; macros for SAS and STATA are also available). Sample output from this macro is shown in Exhibit 7.3. Note that this macro also reports results for both a fixed and random effects model. The latter will be discussed later.

Analysis of Heterogeneous Distributions of Effect Size

Recall that rejecting homogeneity (a significant Q) means that the variability across effect sizes is greater than expected from sampling error alone. As noted earlier, there are three analytic approaches the meta-analyst can take for this situation. First, the excess variability can be assumed to stem from random differences between the studies that cannot be modeled. This approach (random effects model) necessitates the re-estimation of the mean effect size and confidence intervals using an adjusted inverse variance weight that incorporates the random effects variance component, as discussed in Chapter 6. Second, the excess variability can be assumed to be either zero or completely systematic, that is, associated with independent variables (e.g., study descriptors) in the meta-analysis (fixed effects model). The main methods of modeling the systematic variance in effect sizes are the analog to the ANOVA for categorical variables and weighted least squares regression for continuous variables. Third, it may be assumed that a portion of the excess variability is systematic and can be statistically modeled and that another portion is random and cannot be modeled. As described in Chapter 6, this last approach, the mixed effects model, requires fitting a statistical model, either the ANOVA analog model or the modified weighted least squares regression model, with an inverse variance weight that incorporates the random effects component. Computational procedures for each of these approaches is discussed later.

Random Effects Model

In the challenge meta-analysis, we were unable to reject the hypothesis of homogeneity, suggesting that we do not need to fit a random effects model or test for moderator effects. However, the Q-test has low statistical power for rejecting homogeneity when there are few effect sizes, especially when they are based on small samples, as in this example. To be conservative and for purposes of sensitivity analysis (as well as didactic purposes), we will fit a random effects model to this data anyway. First, we must determine the random effects variance component. Using the Q found earlier under fixed effects assumptions, the number of effect sizes, k, and the sums of w_i and wsq_i, the random effects variance component is computed as follows using the method of moments technique (see Chapter 6):

$$v_\theta = \frac{Q - (k - 1)}{\sum w_i - (\sum wsq_i / \sum w_i)}.$$

For our challenge data the random variance component, v_θ. is thus:

$$v_\theta = \frac{14.763 - (10 - 1)}{269.963 - 12928.205/269.963} = \frac{5.763}{222.074} = 0.026.$$

To proceed with a random effects analysis, the preceding random variance component (a constant) is added to the variance of each effect size. Specifically, 0.026 is added to each of the values in the column labeled v_i in Table 7.1. The inverse variance weights (w_i) are then recomputed and all subsequent statistics use these new weights. Note that confidence intervals are wider under a random effects model, since the between-study variability assumed to be attributable to unmeasured between-study differences is added to sampling error variability and thus increases the uncertainty associated with the estimate of the population mean.

Since the Q-test earlier led us to conclude that this distribution of effect sizes was homogeneous, we might wonder why the random variance component computed above does have a value of zero. The failure to reject homogeneity does not mean that the observed variability exactly equals the variability expected from subject-level sampling error. That is, we are almost certain to observe more or less variability than expected, albeit not always enough to be so improbable as to reject the null hypothesis of homogeneity. It is useful to note that the expected value of a chi-square is equal to its degrees of freedom. In other words, the df for Q can be read as the Q-value that would be expected if effect size variability represented only sampling error. In the foregoing example, the Q-value (14.764) is larger than its associated degrees of freedom (9) and, therefore, the observed variability exceeds expectation, just not by enough to be statistically significant at an alpha level of .05.

We must now add the value of the random effects variance component, 0.026, to each v_i in our data set, recalculate the inverse variance weights, w_i, based on this new v_i^*, and recompute all other values and statistics. The new sums for w_i, wes_i, and $wessq_i$ are 135.888, 20.849, and 12.017, respectively. Using the same formulas as in the foregoing text, the random effects weighted mean effect size is then 20.849/135.888, or .153. This is essentially the same as the fixed effects weighted mean of .155.

The standard error is the inverse of the square root of the sum of w_i, which equals $1/\sqrt{135.888}$ or 0.086. Therefore, the lower and upper bounds of the 95% confidence interval are $0.153 \pm 1.96(0.086)$ or -0.015 and 0.322, respectively. This confidence interval is slightly larger than the confidence interval under the fixed effects model and includes zero, suggesting that the earlier interpretation of a positive effect of challenge programs on delinquency may have been unwarranted. (Note that these hand calculations agree with the results reported for the random effects model from the SPSS macro in Exhibit 7.3).

Analog to the ANOVA

Rather than assume a random effects model from the start, you may believe that some or all of the excess variability in effect sizes is systematic and can be modeled with variables captured in the coding protocol. The first approach we illustrate is the analog to the ANOVA, which tests the ability of a categorical variable, such as treatment type or population served, to explain the excess effect size variability. This procedure partitions the total variability into the portion explained by the categorical variable (Q_B) and the residual or remaining portion (Q_W). The Q_B is an index of the variability between the group means and Q_W is an index of the variability within the groups. If significant variability is explained by the categorical variable (a significant Q_B) then the mean effect sizes across categories differ by more than sampling error, that is, show a statistically significant difference. This test also indicates whether the pooled within groups variance is homogeneous. This is critical information in assessing the adequacy of the categorical variable in explaining the excess variability among effect sizes. If Q_W is not statistically significant, the categorical variable represented in Q_B is sufficient to account for the excess variability in the effect size distribution.

The first step in computing the analog to the ANOVA using either a spreadsheet or a statistics program is to sum the previously created variables w_i, wes_i, and $wessq_i$ separately for *each category* of the variable of interest. Next, using these sums, calculate the homogeneity Q for each category (Q_j) using

$$Q_j = \sum wessq_j - \frac{\left(\sum wes_j\right)^2}{\sum w_j},$$

where $\sum wessq_j$ is the sum of $wessq_i$ for each j, $\sum wes_j$ is the sum of wes_i for each j, $\sum w_j$ is the sum of w_i for each j and j identifies each of the j categories of the between-groups variable. The pooled within groups homogeneity statistic (Q_W) is computed as the sum of the $Q_j s$, the homogeneity statistics for each category. This is stated symbolically as

$$Q_W = \sum Q_j,$$

where Q_j is the Q for each j and j equals 1 for the first category, etc. up to the total number of categories. The between-groups homogeneity statistic (Q_B) is the weighted sum-of-squares of the mean effect size for each category around the grand mean effect size. Since Q_B and Q_W partition the total Q_T, Q_B can be solved through subtraction as

$$Q_B = Q_T - Q_W,$$

where Q_T is the total Q and Q_W is the pooled within groups Q. Each of these Qs is distributed as a chi-square. The degrees of freedom for Q_B is $j - 1$, where j is the number of categories. For example, if the categorical variable of interest was the type of treatment, with four treatment categories, then j equals 4 and df_B equals 3. The degrees of freedom for Q_W is $k - j$, where k is the number of effect sizes, and j is the number of categories. For example, if you have 30 effect sizes and the categorical variable has three categories, then df_W is $30 - 3 = 27$. Note that you can also calculate separate means and confidence intervals for each category of effect sizes using the sums of w_i, wes_i, and $wessq_i$ for each category and the formulas presented earlier.

Returning to the challenge data, rows 15 and 16 in Exhibit 7.2 show the sums for w_i, wes_i, and $wessq_i$ for two groups of studies, those using random assignment to conditions and those not using random assignment (rows 8–11 and 2–7, respectively). Using these sums, the Q for the non-randomized studies (Q_n) is

$$Q_n = 19.897 - \frac{(45.104)^2}{151.148} = 6.438,$$

and the Q for the randomized (Q_r) studies is

$$Q_r = 1.343 - \frac{(-3.289)^2}{118.815} = 1.252.$$

The sum of these two Qs $(6.438 + 1.252)$ is the Q within groups, Q_W, which thus equals 7.690. This is distributed as a chi-square with 8 degrees of freedom (the number of effect sizes, 10, minus the number of categories, 2) and is not statistically significant (the critical value of chi-square at $\alpha = .05$ and $df = 8$ is 15.51). Therefore, the residual variability within each category or group is homogeneous. The Q between groups, Q_B, is simply the Q total, found previously as 14.76, minus the Q within, and thus equals 7.07. The degrees of freedom are 1 (the number of categories minus 1). This Q is statistically significant at $p < .05$, indicating a significant between-groups effect (the critical value of chi-square at $\alpha = .05$ and $df = 1$ is 3.84).

The weighted mean effect size can be computed for each group in the same way shown earlier for the full set of effect sizes and yields the following for the nonrandomized and randomized studies, respectively,

$$\overline{ES}_n = \frac{45.104}{151.148} = 0.298,$$

$$\overline{ES}_r = \frac{-3.289}{118.815} = -0.028.$$

In similar fashion, the standard error and confidence interval for each group can be found using the methods outlined earlier for the full set of effect sizes.

```
metaf es = es /w = w /group = random .

******              Meta-Analytic ANOVA            ******

------- Analog ANOVA table (Homogeneity Q)  -------
                 Q           df          p
Between        7.0738      1.0000      .0078
Within         7.6902      8.0000      .4643
Total         14.7640      9.0000      .0976

------- Q by Group -------
   Group        Q          df          p
   .0000      6.4383      5.0000      .2659
  1.0000      1.2519      3.0000      .7406

------- Effect Size Results Total    -------
            Mean ES       SE      -95%CI     +95%CI       Z        P         N
   Total     .1549     .0609     .0356      .2742     2.5450    .0315   10.0000

------- Effect Size Results by Group -------
   Group   Mean ES      SE      -95%CI     +95%CI        Z        P         N
   .0000    .2984     .0813     .1390      .4578      3.6687    .0063    6.0000
  1.0000   -.0277     .0917    -.2075      .1521      -.3017    .7705    4.0000
```

Exhibit 7.4. Sample output from SPSS macro for performing the analog to the ANOVA analysis.

As a meta-analysis increases in size and complexity, the functionality of a spreadsheet for performing the analysis decreases. Therefore, we have written a macro for SPSS that performs the analog to the ANOVA (see Appendix D). Sample output from this macro is shown in Exhibit 7.4 using the data from Table 7.1. Note that this macro produced the same results as previously calculated.

Weighted Regression Analysis

As described in Chapter 6, a modified weighted least squares regression can be used to assess the relationship between effect size and continuous and discrete variables. The predictor variables can be dichotomous, such as a yes–no variable, ordinal, such as low–medium–high, or continuous. Categorical variables can, of course, be "dummy" coded as a set of dichotomous variables, one less than the number of categories (Cohen & Cohen, 1975). Most statistical software programs perform weighted regression analysis and can be used for a meta-analytic purpose, specifying the inverse variance weight (w) as the weight and the effect size (ES) as the dependent variable. Study descriptors, such as subject sample characteristics and treatment type, and effect size descriptors, such as measurement features, are entered as independent variables. Although most statistical software programs fit the regression model correctly (i.e., the regression coefficients, betas, R^2, etc.), the standard errors must be adjusted to be correct and to yield correct assessments of statistical significance. Exhibit 7.5 shows partial output from the SPSS weighted regression procedure for the challenge data in Table 7.1. The independent variables are whether the study used random assignment (Random: 1 = yes; 0 = no) and the rated intensity of the challenge experience (Intensity: 1 = very low through 7 = very high). The homogeneity test for the regression model, Q_R, is the regression sum-of-squares (7.08, with df = 2, in Exhibit 7.5). Comparison with the critical value of 5.99 (α = .05) for a chi-square with 2 degrees of freedom indicates that the regression model is statistically significant. This regression model thus explains significant variability across the effect sizes. Examination of the sum-of-squares residual (Q_E = 7.68, df = 7, p > .05) shows that the unexplained variability is no greater than would be expected from sampling error (the chi-square critical value at α = .05 and df = 7 is 14.07).

It is important to note that the standard errors of the regression coefficients (SE_B), the t-test values (T), and the probability values for the

```
regression /regwgt=w /dependent=es
/method=enter random intensty .

* * * *   M U L T I P L E   R E G R E S S I O N   * * * *

Weighted Least Squares - Weighted By..        W

Equation Number 1     Dependent Variable..    ES

Multiple R            .69253
R Square              .47959
Adjusted R Square     .33090
Standard Error       1.0477

Analysis of Variance
                     DF     Sum of Squares     Mean Square
Regression            2            7.0807          3.5404
Residual              7            7.6833          1.0976

F =       3.2255        Signif F =  .1017

----------------- Variables in the Equation -----------------

Variable          B         SE B        Beta         T    Sig T

RANDOM         -.32978     .136636    -.700013    -2.414   .0465
INTENSTY       -.00409     .051631    -.022953     -.079   .9391
(Constant)      .32233     .314069                 1.026   .3389
```

Exhibit 7.5. Sample output from SPSS weighted regression procedure. (Note that F, Signif F, SE_E, T, and Sig T values are not correct).

t-test (Sig T) are *incorrect* in the printout in Exhibit 7.5. This is because the weighting procedure automatically applied, though using the correct weights, assumes that they represent different numbers of subjects. All the output related to statistical significance testing, therefore, is based on sample size assumptions that are incorrect in application to meta-analysis data. The correct statistical significance of the regression coefficients can be determined by calculating a corrected standard error and using it in a z-test. This is done by first dividing the reported SE_B by the square root of the mean-square residual. In Exhibit 7.5, the mean-square for the residual is 1.0976 and, thus, its square root is 1.0477. Therefore, the corrected SE_B for the variable RANDOM is .136636/1.0477 or 0.1304. A z-test can be calculated by dividing the unstandardized B by its associated SE_B. Using the corrected SE_B, the z-test for RANDOM is $(-.32978)/(.1304)$ or -2.53, $p < .05$. Performing these same calculations for INTENSTY yields a z-value of .08, $p > .05$. Thus, the intensity of the challenge does not appear to add anything to explaining variability across effect sizes beyond that explained by whether or not the studies employed random assignment. The small number of studies precludes the exploration of more complex models, as does the homogeneity of the residuals which indicates that all remaining variability is explainable as subject-level sampling error.

We have created an SPSS macro that performs modified weighted least squares regression for analyzing any type of effect size (see Appendix D). This macro reports correct standard errors and significance levels for the fit of the model and the significance of the regression weights. Sample output from this macro is shown in Exhibit 7.6 and, you will note, agrees with the computations presented earlier.

Mixed Effects Models

Although mixed effects models may sound complicated, they are not. For both the analog to the ANOVA and the modified weighted regression, the approach is the same. The first step is to estimate the random variance component *after* accounting for the moderator variables. That is, the random effects variance component should be based on the residual Q rather than the total Q (for specific formulas see Overton, 1998; Raudenbush, 1994; and Shadish and Haddock, 1994). The SPSS macros for both the analog to the ANOVA and weighted regression include an option to request a mixed effects model (i.e., "/model(mm)" for a method of moments based estimate of the random effects variance component, and "/model(ml)" for a maximum likelihood estimate; see Appendix D).

```
metareg es = es /w=w /ivs = random intensty .

***** Inverse Variance Weighted Regression *****
***** Fixed Effects Model via OLS *****

------- Descriptives -------
    Mean ES      R-Square              N
     .1549        .4796          10.0000

------- Homogeneity Analysis -------
                Q           df            p
Model        7.0807       2.0000       .0290
Residual     7.6833       7.0000       .3613
Total       14.7640       9.0000       .0976

------- Regression Coefficients -------
              B       SE    -95% CI   +95% CI      Z        P      Beta
Constant   .3223    .2998   -.2652    .9099    1.0752    .2823    .0000
RANDOM    -.3298    .1304   -.5854   -.0742   -2.5286    .0115   -.7000
INTENSTY  -.0041    .0493   -.1007    .0925    -.0829    .9339   -.0230
```

Exhibit 7.6. Sample output from SPSS macro metareg that performs weighted least squares regression.

```
metareg ES=es /W=w /IVS=random intensty /Model=mm.

***** Inverse Variance Weighted Regression *****
***** Random Intercept, Fixed Slopes Model *****

------- Descriptives -------
    Mean ES      R-Square              N
     .1571        .4368          10.0000

------- Homogeneity Analysis -------
                Q           df            p
Model        5.5709       2.0000       .0617
Residual     7.1819       7.0000       .4102
Total       12.7528       9.0000       .1741

------- Regression Coefficients -------
              B       SE    -95% CI   +95% CI      Z        P      Beta
Constant   .3311    .3198   -.2958    .9580    1.0351    .3006    .0000
RANDOM    -.3269    .1439   -.6090   -.0448   -2.2712    .0231   -.6724
INTENSTY  -.0068    .0528   -.1103    .0967    -.1292    .8972   -.0383

------- Method of Moments Random Effects Variance Component -------
v        =   .00488
```

Exhibit 7.7. Sample output from SPSS macro metareg showing mixed model results using the option for mixed effects method of moments weighted least squares regression.

These macros estimate the random effects variance component, recalculate the inverse variance weights with the random effects variance component added, and refit the model. Exhibit 7.7 shows output from the metareg macro for the same data used in Exhibit 7.6 with selection of the option for the method of moments estimated mixed effects model.

Note the slight change in the overall homogeneity statistic, the confidence intervals, and the statistical significance of the independent variables as a result of including the random variance component in the error formulation. These differences would be even greater if the random variance component had been larger than in this example. Under a mixed effects model, the Q residual is generally nonsignificant because, by assumption, it is composed entirely of sampling error and the random variation incorporated in the random variance component.

GRAPHING TECHNIQUES

The visual representation of effect size data can be useful both as an analysis aid and as a means of effectively communicating final results. Wang and Bushman (1998) present a thorough discussion of graphing techniques in meta-analysis (see also, Light, Singer, & Willett, 1994) and demonstrate how to produce various types of graphs using the SAS statistical program. Most of the graphing techniques helpful to meta-analysis are adaptations of visual displays common in the social and health sciences, such as histograms, stem-and-leaf displays, scatterplots, error-bar charts, and box-and-whisker plots.

The histogram and related graphic techniques, such as the stem-and-leaf plot, efficiently communicate the central tendency, variability, and normality of an effect size distribution. These displays are especially useful in diagnosing problems with meta-analytic data such as extreme skewness and outliers. The stem-and-leaf plot is often used by meta-analysts to present the effect size distribution and has the advantage that the original data can be recreated from the graphic display. It is not, however, well suited to displaying distributions with large numbers of effect sizes. All the major statistical software and graphics programs readily create these types of graphs and present no special issues or complications when applied to meta-analytic data. Exhibit 7.8 shows how the effect size data in Table 7.1 look as a stem-and-leaf display.

Scatterplots, a familiar method of visualizing the relationship between two variables, are another graphical form useful in meta-analysis. Especially common in meta-analysis is a scatterplot of the effect size by sample size, called a funnel-plot for the expected shape of the scatter (Elvik, 1998; Light, Singer, & Willett 1994; Wang & Bushman, 1998). The funnel-plot is useful for detecting potential bias due to underrepresentation of studies with small subject samples. If a collection of effect sizes is unbiased and

```
.6 │ 4
.5 │
.4 │
.3 │ 129
.2 │
.1 │ 57
.0 │ 0
-.0 │ 2
-.1 │
-.2 │
-.3 │ 33
```

Exhibit 7.8. Stem-and-leaf display of the effect size data from the challenge meta-analysis presented in Table 7.1.

drawn from a single population, there should be greater variability among the effect′ sizes based on small samples than those based on large samples. A scatterplot between sample size and effect size, therefore, should take the shape of a funnel (see Light, Singer, & Willett, 1994, or Wang and Bushman, 1998, for examples). If small sample studies with small effects are underrepresented, a likely reason is publication bias—smaller proportions of small sample studies than large sample studies tend to be published because the low statistical power of small sample studies more often results in nonsignificant results. Publication bias thus tends to censor small effect sizes, reducing the number of effect sizes in that region of the funnel display. Unfortunately, funnel-plots can be difficult to interpret. A meta-analysis of a small number of studies may have too few data points to create the visual effect of a funnel and large meta-analyses may have too much natural heterogeneity in the effect sizes for a clear funnel shape or a clear censoring effect to be visible.

Another helpful graph for meta-analysis data is an error-bar chart. These graphs display the magnitude of a parameter of interest (e.g., a mean) as a dot and its associated confidence interval as a horizontal or vertical line. This type of graph has been adapted to meta-analysis for display of individual effect sizes and their associated confidence intervals. It effectively communicates the precision associated with each effect size and the general pattern of results (Light, Singer, & Willett, 1994). Typically, the display also includes the overall mean effect size and its confidence interval. Exhibit 7.9 shows an example of an error-bar chart from a preliminary meta-analysis of corrections-based adult basic education programs (Wilson et al., 1999). Wang and Bushman (1998) describe the methods for creating such a display using the SAS statistical program. The graph in Exhibit 7.9 was generated using Sigma Plot for Windows version 3.0.

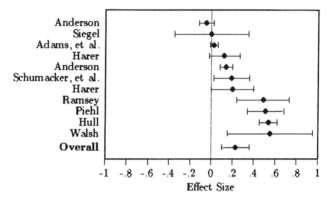

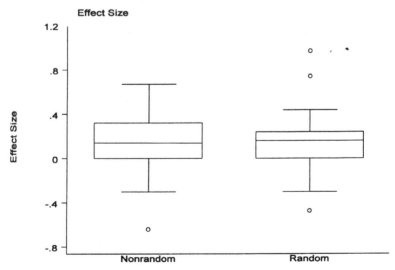

Exhibit 7.9. Error-bar chart with effect sizes and 95% confidence intervals from studies of the effects of education programs on the recidivism of adult offenders (Wilson et al., 1999).

A common graphical display for contrasting both the central tendency and dispersion of a distribution for different levels of a categorical variable is a box-and-whisker plot. A box-and-whisker plot shows the median, 25th percentile, 75th percentile, range and any outliers for two or more groups of effect sizes. Exhibit 7.10 presents a box-and-whisker plot for the effect

Exhibit 7.10. Example of a box-and-whisker plot contrasting effect sizes from randomized versus nonrandomized studies in the challenge meta-analysis (see Exhibit 7.1).

sizes from randomized versus nonrandomized studies in Table 7.1. It was generated using the STATA statistical program. In that plot, the center horizontal line represents the median, the box outlines the 25th and 75th percentiles, and the vertical line shows the range of effect sizes, excluding the outliers represented as small circles. Most major statistical programs create box-and-whisker plots and these displays are particularly effective when combined with analysis of a categorical variable using the analog to the ANOVA procedure.

This discussion of graphing is by no means exhaustive and only focuses on a few visual displays of particular utility in meta-analysis. We have not presented step-by-step instructions for creating these graphs from meta-analysis data, for the details vary greatly across software programs, but most are easily created with those programs once the meta-analyst has decided which type of display to produce.

8

Interpreting and Using Meta-Analysis Results

Meta-analysis yields one or more mean effect sizes representing the average magnitude of the indexed relationship for specific categories of studies, constructs, samples, and the like, depending on the topic and focus selected by the analyst. In addition, it may yield information about the source of variation in effect sizes across studies, e.g., categorical breakdowns of effect sizes by selected study characteristics or multiple regression analysis identifying variables that moderate effect size. In this section, we turn attention to the question of how such results should be interpreted and used. The high level of aggregation characteristic of meta-analysis and the unfamiliar character of effect sizes and study-level units of analysis can make meta-analysis results difficult to comprehend and can obscure their implications for practice, policy, and research.

INTERPRETING EFFECT SIZE VALUES

One difficulty in understanding meta-analysis results is the nonintuitive nature of the effect size statistics that constitute its primary metric. Many researchers, and certainly practitioners and policymakers, for instance, are not familiar with the notion of contrasting groups on standard deviation units or odds ratios and do not have a good sense of what importance to ascribe to a given difference represented in those terms. While product-moment correlations are more familiar, at least to researchers, they too are difficult to appraise in terms of their practical significance.

What is needed to properly interpret effect size results, therefore, is some frame of reference that puts meta-analysis effect sizes in some interpretable context. There are various ways to do this and none is completely satisfactory for every purpose. We summarize some of the more useful approaches here but caution that the meta-analyst must pick and choose among them, or invent others, for the perspective most appropriate to the particular purposes and audiences of interest.

146

Rules of Thumb for Effect Size Magnitude

A widely used convention for appraising the magnitude of effect sizes was established by Cohen (1977, 1988) in his book on statistical power. Cohen reported his general observation that, over a wide range of behavioral science research, standardized mean difference effect sizes fell into the following ranges,

Small	Medium	Large
$ES \leq .20$	$ES = .50$	$ES \geq .80$

The analogous values for the correlation effect size are

Small	Medium	Large
$r \leq .10$	$r = .25$	$r \geq .40$

Cohen did not show any systematic tally of effect sizes from research studies as the basis for his generalizations about what was a typical "small," "medium," and "large" effect in behavioral research. With the widespread application of meta-analysis in recent years, systematic effect size data is available, at least for those research areas selected for meta-analysis. This information permits something of an actuarial approach to appraising the magnitude of effect sizes. That is, an analyst can compare the mean effect size found in his or her meta-analysis with the distribution of mean effect sizes found in other meta-analyses. For the standardized mean difference effect size, Lipsey and Wilson (1993) generated the distribution of mean effect sizes for over 300 meta-analyses of psychological, behavioral, or educational interventions. Exhibit 8.1 shows that distribution for the subset of relatively independent meta-analyses.

If we divide that distribution into quartiles, we get the following benchmarks,

$$\text{Bottom quartile } ES \leq .30$$

$$\text{Median } ES = .50$$

$$\text{Top quartile } ES \geq .67$$

Unfortunately for this purpose, no one has yet compiled such distributions for the correlation effect size applied to either individual differences research or measurement research. For the standardized mean difference effect size, however, the distribution in Exhibit 8.1 allows a meta-analyst to compare the mean effect size found in a meta-analysis of research on

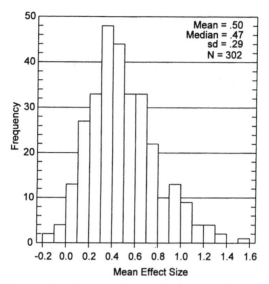

Exhibit 8.1. Distribution of mean effect sizes from 302 psychological, educational, and behavioral treatment studies (Lipsey & Wilson, 1993).

some social or behavioral intervention with the magnitude typically found for such interventions.

Translation of Effect Sizes to Other Metrics

Another approach to interpreting the effect size values that result from meta-analysis is to translate them into some other, more intuitively comprehensible, metric. While many researchers and consumers may not have a good "feel" for the importance of a given number of standard deviation units difference between two groups or the product-moment correlation between two variables, they may better appreciate the equivalent value on some more familiar scale.

Original Metric

In some intervention research areas there is one outcome measure that dominates the research or, at least, is the most frequently used measure, e.g., length of stay in institutional facilities or a particular measure of academic achievement. Alternatively, there may be a mix of measures of the same construct but one common and familiar one can easily be selected, e.g., achievement tests to index educational outcomes. In such cases, it is often informative to translate the effect size results from a meta-analysis into the metric of the particular familiar measurement instrument to reveal what the intervention effect means in terms of those more interpretable units.

To do this, the analyst simply determines the mean and standard deviation on the measure of interest for the control groups providing that information in the studies included in the meta-analysis. Some selection may be necessary to ensure that those control groups use samples that are representative of a population that constitutes a reasonable benchmark. Since the mean and standard deviation of the control group are needed to compute an effect size, these values, or some estimates that can be derived from reported statistics, are generally available. The results from multiple studies can be pooled to generate an overall mean and standard deviation. With this information, it is a simple matter to determine the mean for the intervention group on that same scale. It is the control group mean plus the product of the effect size and the standard deviation value for the metric of interest.

Suppose, for instance, that a meta-analysis found a mean effect size of $+.30$ on client satisfaction measures for medical treatment that was preceded by an orientation session by nurses telling the patient what to expect in contrast to "treatment as usual" without the orientation session. Suppose further that the most commonly used overall client satisfaction measure was a five-point Likert scale with anchor points ranging from "very unsatisfied" to "very satisfied." The meta-analyst might then pull out all the studies using that particular satisfaction measure and determine the control group mean and standard deviation. Let us say that there were k such pairs of values found. The first step in translating the ES value would be to pool those k values into a grand mean and standard deviation for the control group on the particular satisfaction measure. Since the values from each study will generally be based on a different sample size, a weighted average must be computed, with sample size or, more precisely, degrees of freedom, as the weights. The general formulas for this are

$$Pooled \ Mean = \frac{\sum(n_i - 1)\overline{X}_i}{\sum(n_i - 1)},$$

$$Pooled \ sd = \sqrt{\frac{\sum(n_i - 1)s_i^2}{\sum(n_i - 1)}},$$

where $\overline{X}_i$ is the mean of the control group on the measure of interest, n_i is sample size of the control group, s_i is the standard deviation of the control group on the measure of interest for $i = 1$ to j, the number of groups. Let us say that these calculations produce a mean of 3.5 and a standard deviation of 1.5 for the control groups on the five-point client satisfaction scale. Since the effect size for client satisfaction from the meta-analysis was .30, we know that the average experimental group scored .30 standard deviation units higher on client satisfaction than the average control group. Multiplying .30 by 1.5 tells us that this is equivalent to .45 units on the satisfaction scale. With the control group mean at 3.5, the average treatment group scored the equivalent of 3.95, or about 4.0. Thus, the mean effect size of .30 is equivalent to an increase from 3.5 to about 4.0 on this commonly used five-point client satisfaction scale. For most researchers and practitioners, this version of the effect size will be more meaningful than simply knowing that there was a difference of .30 standard deviation units.

An analogous procedure for correlation effect sizes can be carried out very simply by using the properties of bivariate regression. This procedure requires that a mean correlation effect size from a meta-analysis be thought of in terms of two specific familiar variables that are correlated. In a meta-analysis of the relationship between socioeconomic status and children's behavioral problems in school, for instance, we might choose to depict the overall effect size in terms of an income scale ranging from under $5,000 to over $100,000 per year correlated with scores on the Achenbach Child Behavior Checklist (CBCL) completed by parents.

As before, we first determine the mean and standard deviation for each of these measures from appropriate studies in the meta-analysis·(see the previous information for formulas for computing weighted means and pooled standard deviations). We then must identify one of the measures as an independent variable and the other as the dependent variable. In this example, it would be reasonable to treat income as the independent variable and the Achenbach CBCL scores as the dependent variable. With this preparation, we simply turn to the standard formula for a bivariate regression of the standardized dependent variable (Z_y) on the standardized independent variable (Z_x), as

$$Z_y = \beta Z_x,$$

where Z_y is the standardized dependent variable (e.g., Achenbach CBCL), β is the standardized regression coefficient (i.e., slope), and Z_x is the standardized independent variable. As it happens, in the bivariate regression case the standardized regression coefficient is equal to the product-moment correlation between the independent and the dependent variable, that is,

$\beta = r$. Since the standardized regression coefficient gives the slope of the regression line, it tells how many standard deviation units the dependent variable changes for each standard deviation of change in the independent variable. Let us say that in our example the meta-analysis found a mean correlation effect size of .20 for the income-CBCL relationship. Suppose also that income was coded in $1,000 increments (i.e., from 5 to 100) and had a mean of 30 and a standard deviation of 10. The Achenbach CBCL is scored from about 0 to 100 and has, say, a mean of 50 and a standard deviation of 10.0. Since $\beta = r = .20$, we know that for each standard deviation increase in income, there is a .20 standard deviation increase in the CBCL score. In this case, then, for each $10,000 increase in annual income we find a two-point increase (.20 × 10.0) in the CBCL score, i.e., two scale points worse performance on this checklist. We can also depict this relationship in terms of the mean values on each measure. In that case, we note that the typical sample has a mean income of $30,000 per year and children whose score is 50 on the CBCL. For each $10,000 increment above the income mean the CBCL improves by an average of two points; for each $10,000 below the mean the CBCL score worsens by two points.

Generic Success Rate

Another approach to translating effect size results is to use one of several schemes that represent the effect size in terms of overlapping distributions of scores from two groups so that the difference between them can be more clearly visualized. The most widely used of these approaches is the Rosenthal and Rubin (1983) *Binomial Effect Size Display* (BESD). This display translates correlation effect sizes into the equivalent difference in a "success rate" indicator contrasting two populations.

The representation the BESD makes is as follows: Imagine a "success threshold" set at the *median* of the distribution of scores on a dependent variable for the aggregate population. The aggregate population includes all the persons represented in the correlation of interest which, in the case of group comparisons, includes persons from both groups (e.g., treatment and control). We now differentiate the population on the basis of the independent variable, group membership for experimental or two-group comparisons or a median split (high vs. low) on the independent variable for single group situations. We then ask what proportion is above the success threshold in each group and compare the groups to obtain an image of the size of the differential (effect) in simple success rate terms.

Exhibit 8.2 depicts this situation for two distributions of scores on a dependent variable, each group being defined by status on the independent

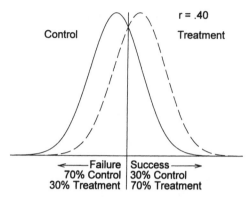

Exhibit 8.2. Distribution showing BESD relation for a correlation of .40.

variable. The presumed success threshold is shown at the median for the combined distributions. That success threshold, by definition, is always at the 50% level for the combined distributions. The useful property of the BESD is that the success rate *differential* between the two distributions at issue is always equal to the correlation effect size the distributions represent. Thus, if the effect size is $r = .40$, there are 40 percentage points between the percent of the lower distribution and that of the upper distribution above the threshold. With the threshold at the overall 50% level, this means 20 percentage points below and 20 percentage points above (equal to 40 points total), that is, a success rate of 30% for the lower group and 70% for the upper group.

Exhibit 8.2 shows the success proportions corresponding to a correlation effect size of .40. As shown, the corresponding success rate for the lower group is .30 (i.e., $.50 - .40/2$) and that for the upper group is .70 (i.e., $.50 + .40/2$). For most readers, it is easier to comprehend the magnitude of a relationship if it is expressed as a difference between a 30% and a 70% success rate than if it is expressed as a correlation effect size of .40. The success threshold is arbitrarily set, of course, and may not correspond to what would actually constitute success on the dependent variable. Similarly, the independent variable may not actually be a group variable so there may be some artificiality in treating it as a group contrast. Nonetheless, this translation into the equivalent values for a success rate differential using a standard format can be informative.

The success rate differential is easy to compute for correlation effect sizes. To use it for standardized mean difference effect sizes, they must first be converted into the correlational equivalent as

$$r = \frac{ES_{sm}}{\sqrt{4 + ES_{sm}^2}}.$$

Perhaps even simpler is to look up the respective success rates for either the correlation or the standardized mean difference in an appropriate table. Table 8.1, provides a range of useful values (along with some others discussed later).

Table 8.1
Standardized mean difference effect size equivalents for r, percent variance
(PV) explained, $U3$, and BESD

ES_{sm}	r	(1) PV (r^2)	(2) U3: % of T above $\overline{X}_c$	(3) BESD: C versus T Success Rates		(4) BESD C versus T Differential
0.1	.05	.003	54	.47	.52	.05
0.2	.10	.01	58	.45	.55	.10
0.3	.15	.02	62	.42	.57	.15
0.4	.20	.04	66	.40	.60	.20
0.5	.24	.06	69	.38	.62	.24
0.6	.29	.08	73	.35	.64	.29
0.7	.33	.11	76	.33	.66	.33
0.8	.37	.14	79	.31	.68	.37
0.9	.41	.17	82	.29	.70	.41
1.0	.45	.20	84	.27	.72	.45
1.1	.48	.23	86	.26	.74	.48
1.2	.51	.26	88	.24	.75	.51
1.3	.54	.30	90	.23	.77	.54
1.4	.57	.33	92	.21	.78	.57
1.5	.60	.36	93	.20	.80	.60
1.6	.62	.39	95	.19	.81	.62
1.7	.65	.42	96	.17	.82	.65
1.8	.67	.45	96	.16	.83	.67
1.9	.69	.47	97	.15	.84	.69
2.0	.71	.50	98	.14	.85	.71
2.1	.72	.52	98	.14	.86	.72
2.2	.74	.55	99	.13	.87	.74
2.3	.75	.57	99	.12	.87	.75
2.4	.77	.59	99	.11	.88	.77
2.5	.78	.61	99	.11	.89	.78
2.6	.79	.63	99	.10	.89	.79
2.7	.80	.65	99	.10	.90	.80
2.8	.81	.66	99	.09	.90	.81
2.9	.82	.68	99	.09	.91	.82
3.0	.83	.69	99	.08	.91	.83

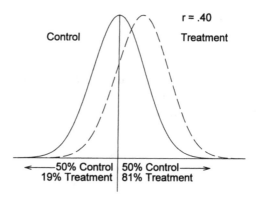

Exhibit 8.3. Distribution showing $U3$ relation for a correlation of .40.

A variation on the BESD format is to set the success threshold at the median of the lower distribution rather than at the grand median for both distributions. Though in both cases the placement of the threshold is essentially arbitrary, there is some appeal to having it at the median, i.e., "middle," of the "control" group in experimental comparisons. Even when the independent variable is not a group variable, there can be a similar appeal to comparing the imagined group that is high on the independent variable to the median of the low group. Exhibit 8.3, depicts this situation. The success rate is now 50% for the lower group (by definition) and we interpret effect size in terms of how much better the success rate is for the higher group.

When the depiction shown in Exhibit 8.3 is used to derive success proportions, the values correspond to a measure Cohen (1977, 1988) called $U3$. Table 8.1 also shows the success rate values corresponding to a range of effect size values for this $U3$ comparison. That table shows, for instance, that if we found a standardized mean difference effect size of .90 in a meta-analysis of treatment effects (equivalent to $r = .41$), it could be depicted as a success rate of 82% in the treatment group compared with 50% in the control group. That is, 82% of the treated subjects are above the control group median whereas, by definition, only 50% of the control subjects are above that level.

Clinical and Practical Significance

Sometimes the meta-analyst may wish to benchmark effect sizes directly against familiar features of a particular clinical or practical setting, especially when intervention effects are at issue (Sechrest, McKnight,

& McKnight, 1996). One way in which this can be done is by use of a *criterion contrast* derived from groups in that clinical or practical setting that represent a familiar difference on some dependent variable of interest. This approach requires that some meaningfully different groups be defined in the setting of interest in such a way that practitioners and other informed observers will readily comprehend the practical significance of the contrast that is generated.

For example, in a mental health treatment setting patients in a given diagnostic category with the most severe symptoms might be contrasted with those with the least severe symptoms. Alternatively, patients judged to have progressed the most under treatment may be contrasted with those judged to have progressed the least, or even to those not yet treated. Patients whose cases are serious enough to require in-patient treatment might be contrasted with those provided only out-patient service. Similarly, referrals with sufficient problems to be eligible for services might be contrasted with those whose problems fall below the eligibility criteria. Such contrasts are generally relatively easy to define in most clinical or practical settings. All that is required is that the difference between the groups selected be clinically or practically meaningful in terms familiar to those most knowledgeable about the treatment setting.

With these *criterion groups* identified, the next step is to obtain information for them on whatever dependent measure(s) are relevant to the meta-analysis. These might be scores on standardized instruments of functional status or psychological functioning, achievement test scores, or whatever corresponds with the constructs and, as much as possible, the particular measures represented in the meta-analysis effect size(s) of interest. Often such information is already available in client records, e.g., as a result of intake or diagnostic procedures. If not, however, arrangements must be made to collect it or find it in published literature.

What is needed from each criterion group are means and standard deviations for whatever measure coincides with that represented in the effect size of interest. With those statistics, a benchmark effect size can be computed for the magnitude of the differential between the criterion groups. This is done as a standardized mean difference, just as in the meta-analysis, but with the criterion group means plugged in instead of the treatment and control group means. This criterion contrast effect size, ES_{sm}, is thus defined as

$$ES_{sm} = \frac{\overline{X}_2 - \overline{X}_1}{s_{\text{pooled}}}$$

where $\overline{X}_2$ is the mean for the criterion group with the higher functioning, $\overline{X}_1$ is the mean for the criterion group with the lower functioning, and s_{pooled} is the pooled within groups standard deviation for the measure of interest, calculated as shown in Formula 3.20 in Chapter 3. What this accomplishes is to convert a clinically familiar contrast between two groups into the effect size metric. The effect size from the meta-analysis can then be compared against the benchmark of this criterion contrast. Since both are in standard deviation units, proportionate comparisons can be made as well. That is, it is legitimate to say that the meta-analysis effect size is half the criterion group effect size, or two-thirds, or three times, etc. Thus we might discover that an effect size of .30, representing the meta-analytic result for the effects of an innovative treatment, was half the size of the contrast between the least severe and most severe patients in the appropriate diagnostic category in a clinical setting in which the innovative treatment might be used. We thus gauge the magnitude of the likely effects of the innovative treatment to be equivalent to having our most severe patients improve to the point where they had moved halfway to the level of our least severe patients. Against this benchmark, it is easier to judge the practical significance for clinical practice of the effect size generated by the meta-analysis.

A variation on this procedure is to compute an effect size value for the contrast between the mean of the treatment group and the mean of a normal group. This "normative effect size," calculated before treatment and after treatment, assesses the magnitude of the initial gap between a treatment population and a normal population and the extent to which treatment closes that gap (Durlak, Fuhrman, & Lampman, 1991; Jacobson & Truax, 1991). This could easily be done in treatment domains that commonly use standardized tests that have been normed on the general population, as is common with many measures of psychological functioning.

CAVEATS IN INTERPRETING META-ANALYSIS RESULTS

While meta-analysis has many advantages as a technique for analyzing and summarizing the quantitative findings of a body of empirical research, it is by no means without problems and limitations, many of which we have mentioned in the course of prior discussion (see also Hall & Rosenthal, 1995). Here we want to focus on some specific issues relevant to properly interpreting the results of meta-analysis for practice, policy, and research.

Methodological Adequacy of the Research Base

Meta-analysis results are only as good as the studies that are included in the meta-analysis. If there are no studies of high methodological quality in the research base, it can hardly be expected that aggregating their findings will yield valid and useful results. Meta-analysts thus must carefully observe and code the key features of the studies judged eligible for the meta-analysis that bear on the validity and credibility of their results. If a large proportion of the studies are seriously flawed, corresponding cautions should be placed on any interpretation of the results and the analysis should be handled especially carefully.

Most typically, meta-analysts find that the studies selected for their meta-analysis represent diversity on methodological quality—some are relatively good, others have larger numbers of weaknesses. In this case, it is especially important for the analysis to explore the extent to which key results differ as a function of study quality. Where the same results appear in the better quality and worse quality studies, greater confidence can be placed on those results. Where there are sizable differences, however, results from weaker studies must be discounted.

Studies often differ in such varied ways on so many methodological dimensions that it is not possible to separate them into simple categories of methodologically "good" and "poor" studies. However, multivariate analysis of the sort described in Chapter 6 may make it possible to estimate the independent contribution of each methodological feature to the study results. Typically the analyst knows which value on a methodological feature is preferred, e.g., randomized designs are better than nonrandomized, reliable measures are better than unreliable, etc. This makes it possible to interpret multivariate results according to their implications for distortion of summary effect sizes. If most methodological features are neutral in their relationships with effect size, then there should not be great distortion in the effect sizes estimated by aggregating studies with different methodological features.

If the methodological features are not neutral, however, those that are most influential must be identified and their net impact on summary effect sizes must be assessed. One approach is to fit weighted multiple regression models in which the various methodological features are used to predict effect size. The resulting unstandardized regression coefficients on the method variables (B-weights) represent the multiplier that weights each value on a method variable. If the best value is plugged in for each important method variable, the equation can be used to estimate the mean effect size that would be expected if all studies had the optimal combination of method features. Similarly, by plugging in the "worst" value for each important method feature, we estimate the mean effect size if all studies were suboptimal on all key method features. The difference between these two estimates should indicate how sensitive the effect size results are to method variation and give the analyst some basis for identifying the summary effect size value associated with best methodological practice. Such sensitivity analyses can go a long way toward preventing erroneous effect size findings from being interpreted as if they were valid indicators of the true strength of the relationship at issue.

Confounding of Substantive and Methodological Features

Just as results based on methodologically weak studies can be misleading, so too can results that are confounded with methodological variables. This occurs when meta-analysts break out their effect size results to compare different categories (see ANOVA analog section in Chapter 6). For instance, meta-analyses of treatment research often break out different treatment variants and compare their mean effect sizes. It is in this way that we might discover that, say, cognitive behavioral therapy has larger effects on anxiety than systematic relaxation techniques. Alternatively, different outcome constructs may be contrasted to find out, say, whether tutoring for elementary students has larger effects on self-esteem or on school performance. Likewise, effects may be contrasted for different population groups (gender, ethnicity, diagnosis), settings, therapist characteristics, and the like. Similar breakouts can be made for correlation effect sizes that index the strength of relationship between variables of interest.

The problem is that if any of the substantive variables used in these contrasts (treatment type, population groups, etc.) are confounded with methodological features in the studies, the differences found may represent the influence of the methods, not the substantive feature to which it is likely to be attributed. Consider, for instance, a situation found in a number of meta-analyses of psychotherapy (Shadish, 1992, p. 131). A simple breakout of mean effect sizes for behavioral versus nonbehavioral therapy generally shows larger effects for behavioral therapy. It happens, however, that studies of the effects of behavioral therapy are more likely to use outcome measures that closely parallel the therapy process itself, e.g., use desensitization therapy for phobias then test the results by measuring tolerance for the feared situation. These are often called "reactive" measures. It is not surprising that such measures are more sensitive to the therapy effects than, say, a paper and pencil standardized anxiety scale would be.

Thus, the behavioral therapies may show larger effect sizes at least in part because they are disproportionately likely to use these reactive measures. When a control variable for reactivity of measures is entered in the analysis, much of the initial difference between the two types of therapy disappears.

It is not our point here to enter the controversy over whether behavioral or nonbehavioral therapies are more effective. Rather, we want to make the point that if valid conclusions are to be drawn from this and analogous matters from meta-analysis, care must be taken to ensure that the comparisons are not contaminated by confounding variables. This may be approached by stratifying studies on key methodological features so that the comparisons of interest are always made between studies "matched" on key methodology. Alternatively, it may be approached in a hierarchical multiple regression format in which important methodological variables are entered first as control variables, then the substantive variables of interest are entered to determine if they add anything significant to the prediction of effect size.

We close discussion of this crucial issue for interpreting meta-analysis results with an example from an actual meta-analysis on the effects of treatment for institutionalized delinquents (Garrett, 1985). Table 8.2, shows the results of different breakdowns of the effect sizes that were found for psychodynamic treatment, behavioral treatment, and life skills training. As the first panel of Table 8.2 shows, a simple breakdown of the treatment types seems to show that behavioral treatments are superior by a wide margin. The analyst might thus recommend that behavioral therapy be universally adopted as the treatment of choice for institutionalized delinquents. In this case, however, such a conclusion would be a grave error.

As panel 2 in Table 8.2 shows, when Garrett separated the results for the "more rigorous" designs from those with the "less rigorous" designs, a quite different pattern emerged. Now we see that the apparent superiority of behavioral therapy was largely a function of overrepresentation of less rigorous designs, in particular, one-group pre–post designs which tend to overestimate effects. Thus, at this point, we might conclude on the basis of the more rigorous studies that behavioral and life skills treatment are effective, and about equally so, while psychodynamic treatment is notably less effective. This conclusion also would be an error.

Panels 1 and 2 in Table 8.2 have collapsed effect sizes across different measurement constructs. Panel 3 of this table shows, however, that we find a still different pattern if we examine effects for various outcome constructs separately using only the more rigorous designs. If we look at

Table 8.2

Mean Effects for Different Treatments of Institutionalized Delinquents
(Adapted from Garrett, 1985)

Treatment Category	Overall Results		
	Mean ES		
Psychodynamic	.17		
Behavioral	.63		
Life skills	.31		

Treatment Category	Mean ES by Design Rigor		
	More Rigorous	Less Rigorous	
Psychodynamic	.17	.16	
Behavioral	.30	.86	
Life skills	.32	.31	

Treatment Category	Mean ES by Outcome Construct for More Rigorous Designs Only		
	Recidivism	Institutional Adjustment	Psychological Adjustment
Psychodynamic	−.01	.30	.48
Behavioral	−.08	.33	.58
Life skills	.30	−.08	1.31

subsequent recidivism, which might be of prime interest to a policymaker, only life skills treatment has a positive effect; both psychodynamic and behavioral treatment have near zero effects. On the other hand, if we look at institutional adjustment, which might be of prime interest to the administrators who manage the facilities in which these delinquents are placed, we see that life skills treatment is the one with near zero effects while psychodynamic and behavioral treatment have relatively good effects. For psychological adjustment, however, which might be of chief interest to the mental health professionals treating these juveniles, we see that all treatments produce positive effects, but that life skills treatment shows the largest effects.

Garrett did not break her results out further than this, but for all we know there are other confounded variables that would need to be examined before we could confidently draw a conclusion about which treatment was most effective for which juveniles under which circumstances for which purposes. The point of this example should be clear, however. Careful examination of possible confounding variables must be made in a meta-analysis before any conclusions are drawn from the results. We want to be as sure as possible, given the data available, that those results reflect the substantive factors of interest and not some undetected confounded variable that may render the findings spurious.

The Importance of Variance

There is an understandable tendency for meta-analysts to crank out the mean effect sizes for the various categories of interest and report those as the major findings. After all, the means represent the simplest and most interpretable summary statistic to characterize the effects of the typical or (by definition) average study at issue. Additionally, this emphasis on mean values is familiar and generally meaningful in "normal" research studies where we average over individual differences among persons rather than over different studies. Nonetheless, it is not a wise practice for meta-analysts to give too much attention to mean values without proper attention to variances. The truism that the average may not adequately represent any single unit combined in that average applies with particular force to meta-analysis.

When doing typical person-level research, we do not expect the individuals involved to be replications of each other on the measured characteristics. We recognize that there is generally a natural distribution (indeed, a "normal distribution") of values across persons on almost any characteristic of interest. If we are to generalize, that is, do nomothetic rather than idiographic research, we must to a large extent suppress some individual differences and instead center the research on what may, admittedly, be mythical average persons, distinguishing them only by categories defined by other relevant measured variables (e.g., gender).

In meta-analysis, however, we define a population of *studies* that we believe investigate the "same" thing, at least by some definition of sameness. It is best under these circumstances to begin with the assumption that the studies are, therefore, replications, at least to an order of approximation. Variation between them in their findings (effect sizes) is not something to be squeezed into some overall average but, rather, is a challenge to the assumption that the studies really do study the same thing that must be met straightforwardly in the analysis.

The tidiest meta-analysis result in this regard is a distribution of effect sizes that are tightly homogeneous under the fixed effects model (see Chapter 6). Given a sufficient number of studies for the homogeneity test to have adequate statistical power, this result tells us that the effect sizes do not differ by more than would be expected from sampling error and, hence, are virtual replications in their findings. Even though the studies may differ on a variety of characteristics, methodological and substantive, none of those differences matter in terms of the magnitude of the effects found by the studies. In this case, the mean effect size is clearly a representative and meaningful summary of the distribution of effect size values.

When the distribution of effect sizes is heterogenous, however, we are alerted to the fact that studies disagree on what the magnitude of the effect is. When studies that presumably examine the same thing disagree, it is neither wise nor especially meaningful to resolve their differences simply by averaging them all together. The average over contrary results is not likely to converge on the truth, just muddle it. What is necessary is to determine *why* study effects differ. This is where a careful and thorough coding of study and effect size descriptors comes in, including methodological, substantive, and source features. It is among these descriptors that we may find the factors that help explain why study findings do not agree. We may discover that different methods produce different effects, or that different effects were produced by different ways of operationalizing variables, different treatments, different types of subjects, or whatever. What we want to do in this circumstance is account for all the meaningful study differences—either by categorizing studies similar on key features that then show homogeneous results within each category, or by fitting a multivariate model (e.g., via multiple regression) that shows effect size as a function of the various study characteristics. Then, using either the categories or the models, we can produce mean effect sizes (or the functional equivalent) that meaningfully summarize the effects of subsets of studies that basically agree in their findings. Of course, the factors that explain the disagreement among studies are often of more interest in this situation than the mean effect sizes, but the latter are nonetheless "clean" and interpretable.

The random effects model provides refuge for the analyst who cannot account for all nonsampling error variance in effect sizes and has plausible reasons for believing that study results will differ by an additional random component. If that random component is very large (relative to sampling error), however, it leaves open the possibility that the differences between studies are, in fact, systematic and the analyst has just not yet discovered the basis for those differences. Mean effect size values purporting to summarize effects of certain treatments, important group differences, strength of relationship between interesting variables, and the like have to be viewed with some skepticism in these circumstances. Departures from that mean may indeed reflect only random factors, but could also represent important differences between studies that produce meaningfully different findings.

Cautious interpretation of meta-analysis results, therefore, just like careful analysis of meta-analytic data, requires close attention to the variation among the effect size values that are found in any distribution of presumably comparable study findings. While the purpose of meta-analysis is to generate robust summary statistics that characterize a set of quantitative research findings, the corresponding mean values can be quite misleading if they aggregate over significant differences among study findings. In short, the more unexplained variance across studies, the more uncertain is the meaning of the summary statistics.

Research Gaps and Generalizability

One valuable by-product of meta-analysis is the summary description it provides of the nature of the body of research under inspection. It is particularly useful in this regard to examine the frequency distribution for the study descriptor variables. Depending on what is coded, this reveals the profile of available research on various methodological and substantive dimensions—what kinds of designs and measures are used, the nature of the samples studied, the range of constructs, and so forth. Often this information reveals gaps and limitations in available research and, sometimes, shows that while there are too few (or none) of some kinds of studies, others are greatly overrepresented. Some treatments, populations, or constructs may be heavily studied, for instance, while others equally promising have been neglected.

It is important that the analyst, and anyone interpreting meta-analysis results, be well aware of the characteristics of the body of research summarized in the meta-analysis. It is, of course, useful for researchers setting a research agenda to know where the interesting gaps are in the research base as well as what sorts of studies are overrepresented. Of more general importance, however, is the issue of the generalizability of the meta-analysis results. It is obvious that meta-analysis cannot summarize research findings for research that is not part of the base of studies included in the meta-analysis. As noted earlier, if there are few studies of high methodological quality in the meta-analysis, the results can represent little more than what methodologically weak studies show. If certain treatments, settings, client populations, constructs, etc. are not well represented in the research base, generalization of the results of the meta-analysis to those circumstances is questionable.

One intrinsic limit to the generalizability of meta-analysis results especially warrants attention, particularly with regard to applied research. By its nature, meta-analysis synthesizes research. This means, of course, that everything that is summarized in a meta-analysis derives from a research situation. The importance of this otherwise trite statement is that the circumstances within which research can be and is conducted, even applied research, are not necessarily representative of those circumstances to which we might wish to generalize, e.g., those in which research is not carried out (or reported in forms accessible to the meta-analyst). One implication of this fact is that the effects we find from meta-analysis regarding, say, the efficacy of a particular treatment with a particular type of client are not necessarily representative of the effects that occur in routine clinical practice in nonresearch settings (Weisz, Weiss, & Donenberg, 1992).

We might think of this particular generalizability issue in terms of a continuum of behavior settings. At one end we have what we might call "laboratory" settings. These are not necessarily actually laboratories, but they are settings in universities, teaching hospitals, demonstration projects, and the like where research is integrated into whatever other services are provided. At the other end of this continuum are routine service settings devoted exclusively to providing service and not involved in systematic research at all. Somewhere between these points are settings in which some research takes place, but not as an intrinsic part of the mission of the facility. For instance, such a setting may be a site for a particular grant research project initiated by an outside researcher, or it may have its own research unit that mostly serves internal information needs but occasionally mounts a more systematic study. We should expect that the nature of the organizations, administration, personnel, training, participants, services, practices, etc. vary across this continuum.

Generally, most of the applied research that finds its way into a meta-analysis comes from the more research-intensive settings at one end of this continuum, the research "laboratories." Of necessity, it cannot ever represent more than the research settings and those service settings that at least occasionally host formal research. Within the full population of service settings, however, the largest number will usually be those where research is conducted very rarely or never. Most practical service settings simply do not have the time, resources, mission, or, often, even the inclination to conduct research. It follows that those meta-analysis results (or any research results for that matter) that seem relevant to routine service settings may not, in fact, generalize to those settings. Great care is therefore required in attempting such generalizations. Potential differences between research and nonresearch settings must be considered and some determination must be made of how they might affect the applicability of findings from the research settings to the nonresearch setting. This particular issue of generalizability from clinical research settings to routine clinical practice settings has received useful discussion in the area of mental health treatment for children (Weisz, Weiss, & Donenberg, 1992). The literature that is generated on that topic is well worth examining as an illustration of the nature of this fundamental generalizability problem. It is important to remember, however, that the problem is inherent in *any* meta-analysis and deserves thoughtful consideration as part of the interpretation of results.

Sampling Bias

A final caveat in the interpretation of meta-analytic findings is the potential upward bias of the mean effect size due to sampling bias or the systematic omission of difficult-to-find studies. It has long been suspected that the published literature is biased toward studies showing statistically significant findings (e.g., McNemar, 1960). Lipsey and Wilson (1993) showed that on average published studies have a larger mean effect size than unpublished ones, providing evidence for a publication bias (see also Smith, 1980). Since published studies are far easier to identify and retrieve than unpublished studies or studies that were never written up due to their negative or null findings, a sample of studies included in a meta-analysis may overrepresent published works. The plausibility of this bias can be reduced by a thorough search for fugitive studies, as discussed in Chapter 2.

Of greatest concern is whether sampling bias is large enough in a given meta-analysis to influence the conclusions drawn. A simple approach to assessing the potential magnitude of this bias is to compare the mean effect size for the published versus unpublished studies included in a meta-analysis. Unless there is reason to believe that the sample of unpublished studies is unrepresentative of the unpublished work in the area, this approach can bracket the potential size of any bias. For example, if the mean effect size for the unpublished studies is .40 and for the published studies it is .50, then it is likely that any sampling bias due to the omission of unpublished studies is less than .10. The actual bias in the estimate of the grand mean effect size across all studies is likely to be less than the difference between the mean for the published and unpublished studies, since unpublished studies represent only a portion of the empirical work in a given area. This approach necessitates that a sufficient number of published and unpublished studies are available to obtain a reliable estimate of the mean for each subset of studies.

If question remains about the plausibility that the observed results are biased due to sampling, then an additional statistic developed by Rosenthal (1979) called the *fail-safe N* can be calculated. The *fail-safe N* estimates the number of unpublished studies reporting null results needed to reduce the cumulated effect across studies to the point of nonsignificance. Rosenthal developed the *fail-safe N* for use with his method of cumulating *z*-values across studies. The formula determines the number of additional studies needed to lower the cumulative *z* below the desired significance level, such as a *z* equal to or less that 1.65 ($p \geq .05$). Orwin (1983) adapted this approach to the standardized mean difference effect size. Orwin's approach, which can also be applied to correlational meta-analyses, determines the number of studies with an effect size of zero needed to reduce the mean effect size to a specified or criterion level. The *fail-safe N* formula for any effect size type is

$$k_0 = k\left[\frac{\overline{ES}_k}{\overline{ES}_c} - 1\right],$$

where k_0 is the number of effect sizes with a value of zero needed to reduce the mean effect size to $\overline{ES}_c$, k is the number of studies in the mean effect size, $\overline{ES}_k$ is the weighted mean effect size, and $\overline{ES}_c$ is the criterion effect size level.

For example, suppose a meta-analysis of 42 studies yielded a weighted effect size of 0.74. Using Orwin's formula shows that 20 studies with an effect size of zero are needed to reduce the mean to 0.50 (see computation later). If a thorough search for unpublished studies had been undertaken, then it is unlikely that with only 42 studies identified a full 20 studies remain "in the file drawer." Furthermore, the criterion effect size of .50, while substantially smaller than .75, is still of a moderate size and likely to be both statistically significant and clinically important. For this example with a criterion effect size of .50, the number of studies in the file drawer with a zero effect would need to be

$$k_0 = 42\left[\frac{.74}{.50} - 1\right] = 20.$$

Although this technique has the advantage of being easy to calculate, it only addresses the issue of whether the observed mean effect size is spurious (i.e., null in the population of studies despite the positive result in the meta-analysis) and not the magnitude of the potential sampling bias. Careful sampling and identification of the fugitive literature are the best protection against a publication bias. For additional discussion of these issues see Begg (1994), Bradley and Gupta (1997), Cleary and Casella (1997), Hedges and Vevea (1998), and Vevea and Hedges (1995).

IMPLICATIONS OF META-ANALYSIS
FOR PRACTICE AND POLICY

The primary purpose of this book is to help researchers without much meta-analytic experience to properly undertake one. Done correctly, meta-analysis can make significant contributions to practice and policy as well as to general knowledge. Meta-analysis has the advantage of moving discussion away from individual studies toward an overview of the whole body of research bearing on a given topic. Given that individual studies will often differ in their results and quality, for reasons already described, they lend themselves to duels and skirmishes in which opposing sides pick and choose the studies that favor their positions and find basis to criticize the studies supporting the opposing view. Though such debates cannot and, generally, should not be silenced, meta-analysis can provide a framework within which better informed debate can take place. When well done, it is even-handed in identifying the methodological flaws of all studies and examining their relationship to what the studies find. Moreover, when studies differ in their findings, good meta-analysis attempts to determine the source of those differences and may well show that one view is correct for one set of circumstances, but another is correct for another set of circumstances.

In addition, meta-analysis results (again, properly derived) have a certain robustness that makes them especially attractive as a basis for policy, practice guidelines, and the like. The high level of aggregation involved in meta-analysis reduces sampling error that accounts for much of the instability of individual study findings (Schmidt, 1992). It also averages over a broad range of settings, researchers, and circumstances, smoothing the resulting picture into a composite, much as a magazine picture looks more crisp and coherent at arms length than when the pixels are examined through a magnifying glass. Additionally, where there are real and meaningful differences among studies, good meta-analysis attempts to make the distinctions that will separate those studies that should be interpreted separately and, hence, differentiates the research domain in ways that may reveal new insights and important differences.

Finally, good meta-analysis is conducted in a fish bowl. All the criteria, data, and procedures are made explicit. Meta-analysis is not like the traditional literature review where the consumer generally does not know on just what basis studies were selected, how many were inappropriately omitted, how information was extracted from them, and, most important, how information was combined into a conclusion. For better or worse, all these steps are documented in meta-analysis. If the results are questionable or controversial, other researchers can replicate the process, systematically try out different decisions and procedures, and compare the results. Meta-analysis even produces a database that permits other researchers to independently confirm, or modify, the coding and to do their own analysis. The pioneering meta-analysis of psychotherapy conducted by Smith and Glass (1977; Smith, Glass, & Miller, 1980) has, for example, been criticized, reanalyzed, and replicated in whole and in parts using Glass's original studies and coding and using alternate study selection and coding (e.g., Matt, 1989; Shapiro & Shapiro, 1982). This process of scrutiny, and the accessibility of meta-analysis to such scrutiny, adds to its credibility and, hence, its persuasiveness in application to policy and practice.

These various advantages of meta-analysis should generally make it the method of choice in circumstances where it is desirable to use quantitative research findings to guide practice and policy. As meta-analysis evolves, we expect to see it used to synthesize empirical evidence that bears on the relationships postulated in practical theory and to undergird policy models that direct the public investment in prevention and intervention. While these latter applications are perhaps some time off, we do not think they are unrealistic. Meta-analysis is certainly no panacea that will solve all problems of integrating and interpreting research for practice and policy, but it is a useful and powerful tool for translating research into insight and action. We think it deserves the close attention of behavioral researchers and hope this volume has helped make it more accessible.

Appendix A

Computer-Based Bibliographic Services and Examples of Relevant Databases

There are a number of useful computer-based resources for locating research studies that can be accessed through university libraries and similar sites or directly via the Internet. DIALOG® Information Services provides one of the most extensive (http://www.dialog.com); other broadband services include ProQuest® (http://www.umi.com) and Lexis-Nexis® (http://www.cispubs.com), and Ovid (http://www.ovid.com).

The following databases have been selected from the DIALOG® catalog. While this is not an exhaustive list of those that might be of interest to a researcher conducting a meta-analysis, it does illustrate the nature and range of searchable bibliographic information available. Increasingly, these resources and similar ones are available on the Internet.

ACADEMIC INDEX: General interest, social sciences, and humanities literature with an emphasis on academic journals.

AGELINE: Indexes journals covering social gerontology—the study of aging in social, psychological, health related, and economic contexts.

AIDSLINE®: Provides access to the medical literature related to AIDS.

BOOKS IN PRINT: Basic bibliographic information on currently published, forthcoming, and recently out-of-print books.

BRITISH BOOKS IN PRINT: Comprehensive indexing of books printed in the English language and published in the United Kingdom; some government publications of general interest.

BRITISH EDUCATION INDEX: Bibliographic references to journal literature relating to education and teaching.

CHILD ABUSE AND NEGLECT: Bibliographic references, research project descriptions, service program descriptions, legal references relating to child abuse and neglect.

CRIMINAL JUSTICE PERIODICAL INDEX: Index of over 100 journals, newsletters, and law reporters relating to a wide range of criminal justice topics.

CURRENT CONTENTS SEARCH®: Online version of *Current Contents*, a weekly service that reproduces the tables of contents from current issues of leading journals; one subset covers the social and behavioral sciences.

DISSERTATION ABSTRACTS ONLINE: Abstracts of all U.S. dissertations since 1861 and citations for some Canadian dissertations; also includes selected Master theses since 1962.

ECONOMIC LITERATURE INDEX: Index of journal articles and book reviews from 260 economics journals and approximately 200 monographs per year.

EMBASE: Source for searching biomedical literature with coverage of over 4000 journals.

ERIC: Research reports, articles, and projects significant to education; full text available on some items.

EXCEPTIONAL CHILD EDUCATION RESOURCES: Literature on all aspects of education of handicapped and gifted people of all ages.

FAMILY RESOURCES: Bibliographic coverage of the psychosocial literature related to the family.

FEDERAL RESEARCH IN PROGRESS: Information about ongoing federally funded research projects in the fields of physical science, engineering, and the life sciences.

GPO PUBLICATIONS REFERENCE FILE: Publications for sale by U.S. Superintendent of Documents.

HEALTH PERIODICALS DATABASE®: Indexing and full text of journals covering a broad range of health subjects and issues.

INTERNATIONAL PHARMACEUTICAL ABSTRACTS: Research and current health-related drug literature including abstracts reporting clinical studies.

LC MARC-BOOKS: Bibliographic records for all books catalogued by the U.S. Library of Congress since 1968.

MEDLINE®: Biomedical literature and research from over 3000 international journals.

MENTAL HEALTH ABSTRACTS: Worldwide information on mental health from 1200 journals plus books, monographs, technical reports, workshop and conference proceedings, and symposia.

NCJRS: National Criminal Justice Reference Service database covering all aspects of law enforcement and criminal justice; full text available on some items.

NTIS: National Technical Information Service database that identifies government sponsored research, development, and engineering projects plus analyses prepared or sponsored by federal agencies.

NURSING & ALLIED HEALTH: Index to more than 300 nursing and allied health journals and selected citations from 3200 other biomedical journals.

PsycINFO®: The online version of *Psychological Abstracts*; indexes published research in psychology and behavioral sciences from approximately 3000 journals and technical reports published throughout the world.

SMOKING AND HEALTH: Bibliographic citations and abstracts for journal articles, reports, and other literature relating to smoking and health.

SOCIAL SCISEARCH®: Index of social science journals throughout the world covering every area of the social and behavioral sciences.

SOCIOLOGICAL ABSTRACTS: Worldwide coverage of sociological research.

Appendix B

Procedures for Computing Effect Sizes Values from Eligible Study Reports

Throughout this volume we have referred to three common effect size indices, the standardized mean difference (ES_{sm}), the correlation coefficient (ES_r), and the odds-ratio (ES_{OR}). A challenge in meta-analysis is obtaining values for the desired effect size statistic from eligible studies. Many studies report only the results of inferential statistics and fail to report the descriptive statistics required for effect size computation, e.g., means, standard deviations, or correlation coefficients. As a result, it is frequently necessary to manipulate the statistical information available in a report to extract or, at least, to estimate the effect size value. This appendix provides formulas and examples for computing or estimating the standardized mean difference, correlation coefficient, and odds-ratio from a variety of statistical data.

STANDARDIZED MEAN DIFFERENCE EFFECT SIZE

The standardized mean difference effect size (ES_{sm}) is used to synthesize results from studies that contrast two groups on measures that have a continuous underlying distribution. The two groups may be different experimental conditions, such as treatment and control, or naturally occurring groups, such as males and females. The definitional formula for this effect size is based on the means and standard deviations for the two groups being contrasted. That formula is presented in Table B10 at the end of this appendix along with a variety of other formulations that are either algebraically equivalent (produce the same result) or yield approximations of varying degrees. These formulas are discussed in the following text and are illustrated with fictitious data.

Direct Calculation of ES_{sm}

The basic formula for ES_{sm} is the difference between the group means divided by the pooled standard deviation (Formula 1, Table B10). For intervention meta-analyses, a positive effect size should reflect a positive effect of treatment. Therefore, if a smaller score on a measure indicates success relative to a larger score, the direction of the subtraction in the numerator of Formula 1 should be reversed (comparison mean minus the treatment mean). For group differences meta-analyses, consistency must be applied in defining groups 1 and 2. If the contrast is between boys and girls, for instance, boys must always be group 1 and girls must always be group 2 (or vice-versa) in Formula 1. Although this may seem obvious, in our experience it is easy to make errors in assigning the algebraic sign to effect sizes during coding.

Example. A study reports the mean self-esteem score on a standardized scale with higher values indicating more self-esteem. For the treatment group of $n = 25$, the mean score is 127.8 and, for the comparison group of $n = 30$, the mean is 132.3. The standard deviations are 10.4 and 9.8, respectively. Using Formula 1 from Table B10, the pooled standard deviation for this data is 10.08 and the effect size is -0.45 (the minus sign indicating that the control group did better on self-esteem than the treatment group).

$$s_{pooled} = \sqrt{\frac{(n_1 - 1)s_1^2 + (n_2 - 1)s_2^2}{n_1 + n_2 - 2}}$$

$$= \sqrt{\frac{(25 - 1)10.4^2 + (30 - 1)9.8^2}{25 + 30 - 2}} = 10.08$$

$$ES_{sm} = \frac{\overline{X}_2 - \overline{X}_1}{s_{pooled}} = \frac{127.8 - 132.3}{10.08} = -0.45$$

Algebraically Equivalent Formulas for ES_{sm}

It is common for a study to report the results of a statistical significance test of the difference between two group means, such as a t-value or an F-ratio, without reporting the means and standard deviations. Formulas 2–5 in Table B10 provide a way to compute effect sizes in this situation. Within rounding error, these formulas produce the same value as Formula 1 and are thus algebraically equivalent. It is important to note that Formulas 2 and 3 only apply to t-values from *independent* t-tests, that is, t-tests performed on the means from two groups of different individuals, and Formulas 4 and 5 only apply to a *one-way* ANOVA testing the difference between two independent group means. A one-way ANOVA with three or more groups or more complex ANOVA designs with multiple factors is discussed later.

Example, t-value. A study reports a t-value of 1.68, favoring the treatment group with treatment $n = 10$ and comparison group $n = 12$. As shown below, using Formula 2 (Table B10), $ES_{sm} = 0.72$.

$$ES_m = t\sqrt{\frac{n_1 + n_2}{n_1 n_2}} = 1.68\sqrt{\frac{10 + 12}{(10)(12)}} = 1.68\sqrt{\frac{22}{120}} = 0.72$$

Example, F-ratio. The difference between a treatment and a control group using a one-way ANOVA is reported as $F = 13.1$, with $df = 1, 98$. Thus, $N = 98 + 2 = 100$. Using Formula 5 (Table B10) for a one-way ANOVA and assuming the groups have equal sample sizes produces an ES_{sm} of 0.72.

$$|ES_{sm}| = 2\sqrt{\frac{F}{N}} = 2\sqrt{\frac{13.1}{100}} = 0.72$$

Be sure to put the correct sign on this effect size value. The preceding formula will *always* return a positive value. Change the sign to negative if group 1 performed less well than group 2. In the absence of reported means for each group, this generally can be inferred from the discussion of results in the report.

Exact Probability Levels for a *t*-value or *F*-ratio

A common situation is the reporting of exact probabilities levels only, such as: "a t-test showed that the effect was statistically significant ($p = .037$), indicating a positive effect of treatment." If the reported probability level is from a t-test or one-way ANOVA based on two groups, the associated t-value or F-ratio can be determined from appropriate tables (e.g., Table B13 at the end of this appendix) or from the inverse distribution function in most newer computer spreadsheet programs, such as Excel or Quatro Pro. With the t-value or F-ratio in hand, ES_{sm} can be determined using the appropriate formula (2–5) as described earlier. Note that $df = N - 2 = (n_1 + n_2 - 2) = 2n - 2$. Since p-values are always positive, the sign of the effect size must be determined from the narrative portion of the report.

Example. You have $n_1 = 10$ and $n_2 = 12$ (i.e., $df = 20$) and are told that the t-test is significant at $p = .037$. Interpolating between the values 2.086 and 2.528 in Table B13, the t-value for $p = .037$ and $df = 20$ is approximately 2.278. Using the procedures described in the preceding text, the effect size is 0.98.

$$|ES_{sm}| = 2.278\sqrt{\frac{10 + 12}{(10)(12)}} = 2.278\sqrt{\frac{22}{120}} = 0.98$$

The above method using the t-distribution (Table B13) also can be used with a probability value associated with a one-way F-ratio based on only two groups, in which case $t^2 = F$.

Calculation of Means and Standard Deviations from a Frequency Distribution

When the dependent measure takes a limited number of values, the frequency distribution for each value or group of values may be reported rather than the means and standard deviations. If the resulting categories are ordered, that is, range from low to high on some dimension, then a mean and standard deviation for each group can be calculated and used in Formula 1 of Table B10. For example, a study of an innovative probation program for juvenile delinquents may report the number of probation violations for the treatment and comparison subjects grouped into the categories 0, 1–2, 3–4, and >4 violations, as shown in Table B1. The only additional statistical information for this outcome measure may be the sample sizes (125 and 104, respectively) and a chi-square test. The chi-square value cannot be used for effect size purposes since it has more than a single degree of freedom ($df = 3$ for a 4 × 2 table) and hence does not represent the central tendency contrast between groups. Means and standard deviations for each group, treatment and comparison, can be calculated using the following procedure.

Step 1. Assign a numerical value to each category of the measure, e.g., the midpoint of the grouping if it involves a numeric range, as in the preceding example, or simply number the categories serially (e.g., 1, 2, 3, 4) starting with the lowest category. For example, you could assign the values 1, 2, and 3, respectively, to the categories low, medium, and high. The actual numeric value is less important than that the values reflect the correct order of the groupings.

Step 2. Convert percentages into actual frequencies if the frequencies are not given. In Table B1, the number of persons in the treatment group with 0 violations was 45% of 125 (*n* of the treatment group) or 56 persons.

Step 3. Multiply the assigned grouping value (denoted as *x*; *Step 1*) times the frequency (denoted as *f*) for that category.

Step 4. Square each grouping value (*x*) and multiply it by the frequency (*f*) for that category. These steps are most easily accomplished by creating a table such as the one illustrated in Table B2. The mean and standard deviations for each group are based on the sums of the values generated in Steps 2, 3, and 4, using Formulas 7 and 8 from Table B10. Using the sums shown in Table B2, the mean for the treatment group is:

$$\overline{X}_T = \frac{\Sigma(xf)}{\Sigma f} = \frac{229}{125} = 1.80$$

Similarly, the mean for the comparison group is:

$$\overline{X}_c = \frac{\Sigma(xf)}{\Sigma f} = \frac{194}{104} = 1.87$$

The standard deviation for the treatment group is:

$$s_T = \sqrt{\frac{(\Sigma f)(\Sigma x^2 f) - (\Sigma xf)^2}{(\Sigma f)^2}}$$

$$= \sqrt{\frac{125(527) - 229^2}{125^2}} = \sqrt{\frac{13434}{15625}} = 0.93$$

Table B1

Violations	Treatment Group (%)	Comparison Group (%)
0	45	40
1–2	35	42
3–4	12	8
>4	8	10

Table B2

Treatment Group

Step 1 Value x	Step 2 Frequency f	Step 3 $x * f$	Step 4 $x^2 * f$
1	56	56	56
2	44	88	176
3	15	45	135
4	10	40	160
Totals	125	229	527

Comparison Group

Step 1 Value x	Step 2 Frequency f	Step 3 $x * f$	Step 4 $x^2 * f$
1	42	42	42
2	44	88	176
3	8	24	72
4	10	40	160
Totals	104	194	450

The standard deviation for the comparison group is:

$$s_c = \sqrt{\frac{(\Sigma f)(\Sigma x^2 f) - (\Sigma x f)^2}{(\Sigma f)^2}}$$

$$= \sqrt{\frac{104(450) - 194^2}{104^2}} = \sqrt{\frac{9164}{10816}} = 0.92$$

Using Formula 1 (Table B10), the effect size, with a positive sign indicating fewer violations in the treatment group, is calculated as

$$ES_{sm} = \frac{-(1.80 - 1.87)}{\sqrt{\frac{(125-1)(.93)^2 + (104-1)(.92)^2}{125+104-2}}} = 0.08$$

Approximations Based on Continuous Data— The Point-Biserial Coefficient

A study may report the relationship between group membership and a multivalued dependent variable as a correlation coefficient (for correlations involving a dichotomous dependent measure, see the following discussion regarding the phi coefficient). This specific type of correlation is the *point-biserial* coefficient, although it can be calculated using the standard formula for the Pearson product-moment correlation. Formula 9 in Table B10 provides an approximation of ES_{sm} from r, the Pearson product or point-biserial correlation coefficient, for equal sample sizes in each group. Formula 10 should be used when the sample sizes are unequal.

Example. A study reports a correlation between the group variable (treatment $= 1$ and control $= 0$) and the dependent variable as $r = 0.27$, with $N = 50$ ($n = 25$ in each group). If higher scores on the dependent variable are more favorable, then this correlation indicates a positive treatment effect, since the treatment group also has the higher value on the independent variable (1 vs. 0). Based on Formula 9, the estimate of ES_{sm} for this data is 0.56, as shown below.

$$ES_{sm} = \frac{2r}{\sqrt{1 - r^2}} = \frac{2(.27)}{\sqrt{1 - .27^2}} = \frac{.54}{.96} = 0.56$$

Estimating $(\overline{X}_1 - \overline{X}_2)$ and s_{pooled}

In thinking about the standardized mean difference type effect size it is useful to consider the numerator and denominator separately. The numerator is an estimate of the mean difference between the groups being contrasted, such as a treatment and a control group, on a specific measure. This estimate may be derived directly by differencing the group means, as is done in Formula 1 in Table B10, but may also be estimated in other ways. The denominator of ES_{sm} serves to standardize the estimated group difference based on the variability of whatever measure it represents. Ideally, this is the pooled standard deviations for the groups being compared. However, when those standard deviations are not available, the pooled standard deviation may be estimable from other data. The following sections discuss methods for estimating the numerator and the denominator of ES_{sm} when the means or standard deviations for each group are not reported.

Estimates of $(\overline{X}_1 - \overline{X}_2)$, the Numerator of ES_{sm}

Situations arise in coding ES_{sm} where means for each group on the measure of interest are not reported but some other statistics relating to the group difference are available, e.g., mean gain scores or covariance adjusted means. The group difference estimates discussed in this section represent "adjusted" effects, typically adjusted for pretest differences. An important issue is the comparability of ES_{sm} based on adjusted, rather than observed, values. It is recommended, therefore, that the meta-analyst keep track of the method used for calculating the effect size and assess at the analysis stage whether or not there is a relationship between effect size calculation method and magnitude of effect size. Although conceptually the use of effects that have been adjusted for sources of pretest nonequivalence in an intervention study can strengthen the overall conclusions, mixing together adjusted and unadjusted effect size estimates may contribute to between-study heterogeneity and thus should be accounted for. Furthermore, this mix may obscure between-study differences if adjustment practices are confounded with other study differences. Note also that the adjusted mean difference is only the "top half" of ES_{sm}, and must be divided by the pooled standard deviation of the outcome measure or an estimate of that value obtained using the methods discussed later. For comparability with other effect sizes, it is important that that pooled standard deviation not be adjusted downward for variance associated with covariates or other adjustments.

Gain Score Estimate of $(\overline{X}_1 - \overline{X}_2)$. The most common adjusted estimate of treatment effects is the gain score. The gain score is simply the posttest or time-two value of a measure minus the pretest or time-one value of the same measure for the same respondents. A little algebra shows that the difference between the mean gain score for the treatment and comparison groups is equivalent to the difference between the posttest means minus the difference on the pretest means. That is, the posttest means are "corrected" by subtracting out any difference at pretest. If there is no difference at pretest, this simply yields the difference between posttest means. If there is a difference at pretest, this yields a "net" group difference at posttest over and above what was already there at pretest. Thus, if a study reports the mean gain score for each group, the difference between those means can serve as an estimate of the numerator of ES_{sm}. To obtain ES_{sm}, however, the pooled standard deviation of the posttest scores must either be provided or be estimated. Note that the standard deviation of the gain scores should not be used as the denominator in Formula 1. That standard deviation reflects the variability in treatment *gains*, not the sample variability on the outcome measure itself. This is discussed in more depth later.

Covariate Adjusted Means Estimate of $(\overline{X}_1 - \overline{X}_2)$. Covariate adjusted means are another form of adjusted means a meta-analyst may encounter.

In its simplest form, a covariate adjusted mean is generated from a one-way analysis of covariance (ANCOVA) with the pretest on the dependent variable as the covariate. A more complex analysis will include multiple covariates. Assuming the adjustments are reasonable for the purpose at hand, these adjusted means can be used in place of observed means. In other words, the difference between the adjusted means can serve as the estimate of the treatment effect. Again note that the pooled standard deviation for the denominator must *not* involve any reductions in variance associated with the covariate.

Regression Coefficient Estimate of $(\overline{X}_1 - \overline{X}_2)$. Algebraically equivalent to the difference between two covariate adjusted means is the unstandardized regression coefficient (denoted as B) for group membership from a multiple regression analysis. Assuming that group membership has been dummy coded (e.g., 0 and 1), the B for group membership is equal to the difference between the two group means, adjusted for the other variables in the regression model. Therefore, B divided by the unadjusted pooled standard deviation of the dependent measure, or an estimate thereof, produces ES_{sm}.

Estimates of the Pooled Standard Deviation, the Denominator of ES_{sm}

A critical element in the comparability of ES_{sm} values based on different measures, as is typical in meta-analysis, is the *standardization* of the difference between the groups via the standard deviation. Thus, an ES_{sm} of .50 indicates that the two groups being contrasted differ by half of the population value of the standard deviation on the dependent variable as estimated from sample values. The use of an incorrect estimate of s_{pooled} in the denominator of ES_{sm}, such as the standard deviation of gain scores instead of the original dependent variable values, therefore, can produce inaccurate estimates. There are several methods of estimating s_{pooled} correctly when the standard deviation for each group is not reported directly.

Full Sample Standard Deviation. The full sample standard deviation can be used as an estimate of s_{pooled}. However, the full sample standard deviation overestimates the pooled standard deviation to the degree that there is a treatment or group differences effect, since the variability across individuals includes variability due to treatment or the group characteristic under investigation. If the expected difference is small to modest, then the full sample standard deviation may be a serviceable approximation to the pooled standard deviation. It is possible, however, to estimate the within groups standard deviation from the full sample standard deviation and the group means using Formula 14 in Table B10. For example, suppose a study comparing satisfaction with treatment for integrated versus nonintegrated mental health services for children reported the means for each group as 6.2 and 5.1, respectively. The study also reported the full sample standard deviation as $s = 2.3$. Using Formula 14, s_{pooled} can be found as below.

$$s_{pooled} = \sqrt{\frac{s^2(N-1) - \frac{\left(\overline{X}_{G1}^2 + \overline{X}_{G2}^2 - 2\overline{X}_{G1}\overline{X}_{G2}\right)(n_{G1}n_{G2})}{(n_{G1}+n_{G2})}}{N-1}}$$

$$= \sqrt{\frac{2.3^2(270-1) - \frac{(6.2^2+5.1^2-2(6.2)(5.1))(130(140))}{(130+140)}}{270-1}} = 2.23$$

Independent t-test. Although ES_{sm} can be computed directly from a *t*-value, there are situations in which a meta-analyst may be interested in also coding the means and standard deviations into the database. Since *t* is a function of the difference between the means, the standard deviation and sample size, s_{pooled} can be calculated from *t* using Formula 15 in Table B10. For example, suppose a study of a drug prevention program reported posttest self-esteem scores for the intervention group ($n = 54$) and the comparison group ($n = 48$) of 93.4 and 89.6, respectively, and a *t*-value equal to 2.359. Using Formula 15, s_{pooled} is determined as follows.

$$S_{pooled} = \frac{\overline{X}_1 - \overline{X}_2}{t\sqrt{\frac{n_1+n_2}{n_1 n_2}}} = \frac{93.4 - 89.6}{2.359\sqrt{\frac{54+48}{(54)(48)}}} = 8.12$$

Standard Error of the Mean. A study may report the standard errors of the individual means, rather than the standard deviations. These are often denoted as s_X, *s.e.*, or *se*. The standard error is used to construct a confidence interval for the mean. If the sample size for each group is known, then the standard deviation for each group can be determined using Formula 16 in Table B10. For example, consider a study comparing boys ($n = 150$) and girls ($n = 139$) on a math achievement test that reports the means (102.3 and 105.4) and standard errors (1.29 and 1.35) for each group. The standard deviation for each group can be found using

Formula 16, as shown below.

$$s_{boys} = se_{boys}\sqrt{n_{boys} - 1} = 1.29\sqrt{150 - 1} = 15.75$$

$$s_{girls} = se_{girls}\sqrt{n_{girls} - 1} = 1.35\sqrt{139 - 1} = 15.86$$

These standard deviations and the means can now be used in the definitional Formula 1 for ES_{sm}.

It may occur that, rather than standard errors, a study reports confidence intervals. The standard error of the mean can be determined from the confidence interval by dividing the confidence interval in half and then dividing again by the critical value associated with the confidence interval (e.g., 1.96 for a 95% confidence interval). For example, suppose a study reports a confidence interval of the mean gross-motor mobility score for the intervention condition (physical therapy) of 19.1 to 23.5. The standard error is thus:

$$se = \frac{.5(CI)}{z_\alpha} = \frac{.5(23.5 - 19.1)}{1.96} = \frac{.5(4.4)}{1.96} = 1.12$$

The standard deviation can now be found using the procedure illustrated above for standard errors.

One-way Analysis of Variance with Three or More Groups. A study design may incorporate more than two experimental conditions or naturally occurring groups. For example, a group differences meta-analysis comparing learning disabled students with low-achieving, but not learning disabled students, may encounter studies that have the two groups of interest plus a group of average achieving students. In intervention meta-analyses, some studies may have multiple treatment groups or multiple control groups. If the individual means and standard deviations are reported, of course, then the standard formula for ES_{sm} can be applied directly to the relevant data. However, studies of this type may report a one-way analysis of variance (F-ratio) testing the differences between all the group means together. The formula presented earlier for computing ES_{sm} from F cannot be used in this situation because a one-way analysis of variance with three or more groups yields an omnibus test between all the means and as such does not directly index the difference for the two groups of interest (e.g., learning disabled students vs. low-achieving students). If means for each group are reported, then the F-ratio can be used to estimate the pooled within groups standard deviation and ES_{sm} can

Table B3

Group	Reading Achievement Test Scores by Group	
	Means	n
Learning disabled students	55.38	13
Low achievers, not learning disabled students	59.40	18
Average achievement students	75.14	37
Advance placement students	88.00	22

then be computed in the usual way. Without the group means, however, an effect size cannot be computed in this case.

F is the ratio of the mean-squares between groups to the mean-squares within groups and the mean-squares within groups is the pooled within groups variance. Therefore, the pooled standard deviation can be calculated by (a) using the group means and sample sizes to compute the mean-squares between groups, and (b) dividing the mean-squares between groups by F and taking the square root. The definition formula for ES_{sm} (Formula 1) can then be applied, using the means for the groups of interest.

Example. Suppose a study reports the data in Table B3. The F-ratio for this data is reported as $F_{(3, 86)} = 7.05$. The meta-analyst wants ES_{sm} for the difference between the first two groups. Unfortunately, the study did not report the standard deviations. An estimate of s_{pooled} nonetheless can be obtained from the mean-squares between $(MS_{between})$ and the F-ratio using Formula 17 in Table B10. $MS_{between}$ can be easily calculated by creating a table with a column for each term of the equation, as shown in Table B4.

Table B4

Group	Calculation of $MS_{between}$				
	$\overline{X}$	$\overline{X}^2$	n	$n\overline{X}$	$n\overline{X}^2$
1	55.38	3066.94	13	719.94	39,870.28
2	59.40	3528.36	18	1069.20	63,510.48
3	75.14	5646.02	37	2780.18	208,902.73
4	88.00	7744.00	22	1936.00	170,368.00
Totals			90	6505.32	482,651.49

Using Formula 17, the MS_{between} is:

$$MS_b = \frac{\Sigma n_j \bar{X}_j^2 - \frac{(\Sigma n_j \bar{X}_j)^2}{\Sigma n_j}}{k - 1}$$

$$= \frac{482651.49 - \frac{6505.32^2}{90}}{4 - 1} = \frac{482651.49 - 470213.20}{3} = 4146.10$$

and s_{pooled} is

$$s_{\text{pooled}} = \sqrt{\frac{MS_b}{F_{\text{oneway}}}} = \sqrt{\frac{4146.10}{7.05}} = 24.25$$

The ES_{sm} effect size can now be calculated using Formula 1 in Table B10 by taking the difference of the two means of interest (learning disabled students and low-achieving students), and dividing by the above pooled standard deviation. Note that s_{pooled} is based on the within group variability for all of the groups, not just the two groups of interest. Under many situations, this will produce a better estimate of the population standard deviation than that based on the smaller sample (two groups only). Only when the within groups standard deviations substantially differ from one another will this produce a biased estimate of the population variance.

Analysis of Variance, Two-way Factorial Designs. The F statistic and associated mean-squares from factorial designs, such as a treatment (two levels) by diagnosis (three levels) design, cannot usually be transformed into a comparable effect size using the prior formulas. This is due to the redefinition of the within-cells variance term for the F. That is, the variability due to the second factor (e.g., that between diagnostic groups) has been removed from the within-cells variance. Thus using the foregoing formulas would produce an underestimate of s_{pooled} and, correspondingly, an overestimate of ES_{sm}. To correct this, the sum-of-squares for the nontreatment factor and the interaction terms are added to the sum-of-squares within cells to obtain the correct sum-of-squares within treatment groups (Formula 18 in Table B10). Dividing the result by the appropriate degrees of freedom and taking the square root produces the pooled standard deviation.

Example. Table B5 is from a 2×2 factorial design with treatment as factor A (treatment vs. control) and subject gender as factor B (males vs. females). The means for the treatment and control groups are 144.09 and 114.86, respectively. The total N is 474.

Table B5

Analysis of Variance Table

Source	SS	df	MS	F
Treatment	78,341.02	1	78,341.02	22.48
Gender	225,853.52	1	225,853.52	64.81
Treatment × Gender	22,915.08	1	22,915.08	2.58
Residual	1,637,885.70	470	3484.86	

Using Formula 18 from Table B10, the pooled standard deviation can be determined for this data (note that $SS = df(MS)$ if it is not reported directly). The effect size ES_{sm} is then calculated using the reported means and pooled standard deviation derived from the analysis of variance table as

$$s_{pooled} = \sqrt{\frac{SS_B + SS_{AB} + SS_w}{df_b + df_{AB} + df_w}}$$

$$= \sqrt{\frac{225853.52 + 22915.08 + 1637885.70}{1 + 1 + 470}} = 63.22$$

$$ES_{sm} = \frac{144.09 - 114.86}{63.22} = 0.46$$

Note that this procedure applies to a two-way factorial design for which both factors are between subjects, that is, no subject is represented in more than one cell of the design. It cannot be applied to a repeated measures design, such as a treatment by testing occasion (pretest vs. posttest) analysis of variance. However, in the simple case of two treatment groups and two measurement occasions (e.g., pretest and posttest), the square root of the residual mean-squares between (denominator of the F-ratio for the treatment factor) is the pooled standard deviation.

One-way Analysis of Covariance. ES_{sm} can be computed from a one-way analysis of covariance if the means for the two relevant groups, the mean-square error or residual from the ANCOVA, and the correlation between the covariate and the dependent variable are reported. Unfortunately, it is rare for all of this information to be available in the written report.

Example. An ANCOVA was performed on a study with two groups (treatment and control) with the pretest scores used as the covariate. The correlation between the pretest and posttest is .88. The treatment group posttest mean is 14.41 and the control group mean is 11.49, with higher scores reflecting better outcomes. The mean-square error or residual in the ANCOVA is reported as 10.49 with $df_{error} = 471$. Using Formulas 19 and 1 in Table B10, the effect size is computed as

$$s_{pooled} = \sqrt{\left(\frac{MS_{error}}{1 - r^2}\right)\left(\frac{df_{error} - 1}{df_{error} - 2}\right)} = \sqrt{\left(\frac{10.49}{1 - 0.88^2}\right)\left(\frac{471 - 1}{471 - 2}\right)} = 6.83$$

$$ES_m = \frac{14.41 - 11.49}{6.83} = 0.43$$

Gain Score Standard Deviation. A situation related to the analysis of covariance is gain score analysis. As discussed earlier regarding estimates of $(\overline{X}_1 - \overline{X}_2)$, the standard deviation of the gain scores indexes the variability in the gain score, rather than in the population variability on the measure of interest. Therefore, to standardize a mean difference between groups on s_{gain} produces an effect size that is based on standardized difference scores rather than on standardized units of the dependent measure. If the correlation coefficient between the pretest and posttest scores is known or can be estimated, then the desired pooled standard deviation can be estimated using Formula 20 in Table B10.

Example. A study reports a gain score analysis for the dependent variable of math achievement contrasting a cooperative learning math tutorial program with a regular instruction comparison group. The gain score standard deviation is reported as 6.34, with a correlation of .65 between the pretest and posttest scores. Using Formula 20, the posttest standard deviation for the dependent measure is estimated as

$$s_{pooled} = \frac{s_{gain}}{\sqrt{2(1 - r)}} = \frac{6.34}{\sqrt{2(1 - 0.65)}} = 7.58$$

Standard Deviation from Another Study. In some situations it may be possible to obtain an estimate of the standard deviation for a specific measure from another study that used that measure with a very similar sample. In other words, the standard deviation for a particular variable in one study could be used to calculate an effect size for another study if the two studies used identical measures and had comparable samples.

Dichotomized Data

A dichotomous measure is one for which there are only two possible values, such as "successful" and "unsuccessful" or "passed" and "failed." Also, a researcher may dichotomize a multi-item scale, grouping subjects into those above and below a certain cut-point. For example, a study on the effectiveness of a treatment for anxiety may group all respondents above a particular score on an anxiety inventory as "anxious" and those below that score as "not anxious." Dichotomized data are often reported descriptively as the number, percent, or proportion in each category. Studies may also present a chi-square test or a phi coefficient (correlation) for such data. Methods for estimating ES_{sm} under varying conditions for dichotomous data are outlined in the following text.

Frequencies, Percentages, and Proportions

It is common to report dichotomized dependent measures as a percent, proportion, or frequency. Examples include the percent of patients improved, the proportion of delinquents who re-offended, or the number of job training clients employed at 12-month follow-up. ES_{sm} can be approximated from such data by differencing the probit or arcsine transformed proportions (Formulas 21 and 22 in Table B10). The probit method always produces a larger absolute value of ES_{sm} relative to the arcsine method and assumes an underlying normal distribution on the construct measured. As an estimate of ES_{sm}, both the probit and the arcsine method may over or underestimate the true value if the construct does not have a normal distributional form. The conditions under which each method performs best are not well known and need further research. We prefer the more conservative arcsine transformation method. For the intervention studies on which we have conducted meta-analyses, the arcsine method has produced effect sizes that are more consistent with the values from similar studies for which direct calculation of ES_{sm} could be made. If probit or arcsine transformed effect sizes are to be combined with effect size values based on means and standard deviations, then a sensitivity analysis should be performed to assess the influence of including the probit or arcsine estimated ES_{sm} values.

Note that only proportions that represent the proportion of *subjects* in each category are suitable for this method of estimating ES_{sm}. Other proportions, such as average proportion of *time* subjects are in treatment, should not be handled in this way. An amount or proportion of time or some other factor for *each* subject is a continuous variable for effect size calculation purposes and *not* a dichotomous one, despite its being called a "proportion." Put another way, eligible proportions are situations in which each subject is categorically assigned to one of two groups according to whatever characteristics define the categories.

Example. A study of a physical rehabilitation program for stroke patients reports the following data on the percentage of clients in the treatment and control conditions rated as "improved" at posttreatment.

	Not Improved	*Improved*
Treatment	*32%*	*68%*
Control	*37%*	*63%*

The success proportion for the treatment groups is 68/100 or .68. Likewise the success proportion for the control group is 63/100 or .63. The arcsine transformed values obtained from Table B14 (at the end of this appendix) that correspond to these proportions are 1.939 and 1.834, respectively. ES_{sm} is the difference between these values, or 0.11, that is:

$$ES_{sm} = arcsine(.68) - arcsine(.63) = 1.939 - 1.834 = 0.11$$

Chi-Square Test

The difference on a dichotomous response variable between two groups is often tested with the chi-square test for 2×2 contingency tables. If a study reports only the chi-square value and not the cell frequencies, then ES_{sm} can be approximated with Formula 23 in Table B10. Note that this formula is *only* appropriate for chi-square values based on a 2×2 contingency table (i.e., a χ^2 with $df = 1$). If the chi-square has more than 1 degree of freedom then the effect size estimate must be based on the frequency table as described earlier. Also note that Formula 23 always returns a positive value. Therefore, the direction of the effect must be determined separately and the appropriate sign given to the ES_{sm}.

Example. You are given a χ^2 value of 4.02, $df = 1$ (i.e., a 2×2 table), in which the control group ($n = 22$) shows more success than the treatment group ($n = 18$). Using Formula 23, the effect size is:

$$|ES_{sm}| = 2\sqrt{\frac{\chi^2}{N - \chi^2}} = 2\sqrt{\frac{4.02}{40 - 4.02}} = 0.67 \therefore ES_{sm} = -0.67$$

Exact Probability of a Chi-Square

A report may provide an exact p-value for a chi-square test without the associated chi-square value. Using Table B16 (at the end of this appendix), the chi-square value associated with the reported p-value can be looked up, interpolating if necessary. Calculation of ES_{sm} then proceeds as above.

Phi-Coefficient (r) for 2 × 2 Contingency Tables

A study may report the correlation between group membership (treatment vs. control or two naturally occurring groups) and a dichotomous dependent variable. This is called the *phi coefficient* and can easily be transformed into an approximate ES_{sm} with the same formula used generally for correlations (Formula 24 in Table B10). This formula is algebraically equivalent to the chi-square method (Formula 23) discussed above. The direction for the effect size (positive or negative sign) can be difficult to determine, since it is depends not only on whether high or low scores are "good" on the dependent measure but also on how group membership was coded. In treatment intervention studies, the treatment group is generally assigned the higher value relative to the control group, such as the value 1 for the treatment and the value 0 for the control. A careful reading of the study report is often needed to ascertain whether or not this convention was followed in a particular study.

Example. You are given the correlation ($r = .15$) between the group variable (treatment $= 1$, control $= 0$) and the dichotomous variable "rehospitalized" (yes $= 1$, no $= 0$), with $N = 50$ ($n = 25$ in each group). Since high scores on the dependent measure are *less* favorable (indicating that the subject was rehospitalized) and the group membership variable is coded with high scores for treatment, the reported *positive* correlation indicates a *negative* treatment effect, i.e., the treatment condition is associated with more rehospitalizations. Using Formula 24, ES_{sm} is calculated as

$$|ES_{sm}| = \frac{2r}{\sqrt{1-r^2}} = \frac{2(.15)}{\sqrt{1-.15^2}} = \frac{.30}{.989} = 0.30 \therefore ES_{sm} = -0.30$$

THE CORRELATION COEFFICIENT EFFECT SIZE

Many eligible studies for a meta-analysis of correlations will report the summary data directly as a correlation coefficient, greatly easing the coding process. However, there may be studies that report the relationship between the constructs of interest in another form, such as a joint frequency table, a chi-square, or as means and standard deviations (i.e., contrasting two groups on a continuous measure). A correlation coefficient can be computed from many of these studies using the formulas in Table B11 at the end of this appendix.

The formulas in Table B11 are organized around the nature of the two measured variables whose association is being represented, starting with formulas for the case of both variables measured on a continuous scale (at least multivalued and ordinal). Next are formulas for ES_r with a dichotomous and a continuous measure. Last are formulas for ES_r based on two dichotomous measures. If the two constructs are both inherently continuous, then the ideal index for ES_r is also based on two variables measured continuously. However, studies investigating the relationship between continuous constructs may nonetheless measure one or both in a dichotomous fashion. For example, in a study of the relationship between the two continuous constructs of drug use in elementary school and involvement in delinquent behavior in junior high school, drug use may be measured dichotomously (using drugs, not using drugs) and so may delinquent behavior (arrest history, no arrest history). Recall from the discussion on effect size adjustments (Chapter 6) that dichotomization of a continuous construct attenuates the strength of the observed correlation (see Chapter 3 for a discussion of combining effect sizes based on constructs measured on both a continuous and dichotomous scale). Therefore, if a study reports the same data in a continuous and dichotomous form, the former is preferable to the latter. In other words, the formulas nearer the top of Table B11 are preferred over those nearer the bottom, other things equal.

Definitional Formula for ES_r

Table B11 presents the standard computational formula for the Pearson product-moment correlation coefficient (Formula 1). This is the typical definition for a correlation coefficient (ES_r) and is presented for reference purposes. It is rare for a study to provide the individual level data needed to apply this formula. Furthermore, as stated previously, many studies of the type collected for a meta-analysis of correlations will report ES_r values based on this or an equivalent formula directly.

It is worth noting that while Formula 1 (Table B11) is designed for continuous data, it can be applied to data where one or both variables are dichotomous, so long as each dichotomous variable has been dummy coded, that is, the categories coded as 0 and 1. The result will be equivalent to what would be obtained from Formulas 2–6 for a dichotomous and continuous variable (the point-biserial coefficient) or from Formulas 8 and 9 for two dichotomous variables (the phi coefficient). Thus, all of these formulas are algebraically equivalent to the definitional formula, although the latter formulas are only appropriate in the specific case of a dichotomous variable or two dichotomous variables.

Joint Frequency Distributions for Discrete or Grouped Continuous Data

The relationship between two variables may be represented via a joint frequency distribution. For example, a study may report the percentage of subjects in each cell of a table that cross-tabulates IQ in the fifth grade (grouped into intervals labeled below normal, normal, and above normal) by involvement in criminal activity in the ninth grade (categorized as none, minor involvement, and serious involvement). The correlation between continuously measured IQ and criminal activity variables would be preferred to the correlation using the grouped data. However, a study may only provide the frequency table. In these situations, ES_r can be estimated by using Formula 2 in Table B11. Note that for a variable with three or more categories to be appropriate for this calculation, it must be at least ordinal in nature; that is, each successive category must represent a higher (or lower) level of the construct than the prior category. In some cases, multiple nominal categories can be collapsed into two meaningful categories, thus creating a dichotomous variable.

Example. A 3 × 5 joint frequency table showing the relationship between conduct disorder and IQ has the data in Table B6. To apply Formula 2 in Table B11, we reorganize the data so that all of the frequencies are in a single column with a separate column indicating row number and column number as shown in Table B7, then compute the indicated products and sums. Inserting the column sums from this table into Formula 2,

Table B6

			Conduct Disorder				
			Low				*High*
			1	2	3	4	5
IQ	*Below normal*	*1*	247	62	33	24	8
	Normal	2	50	44	40	14	6
	Above normal	*3*	18	6	11	4	4

Table B7

r	c	f	$f \times r \times c$	$f \times r$	$f \times c$	$f \times r^2$	$f \times c^2$
1	1	247	247	247	247	247	247
1	2	62	124	62	124	62	248
1	3	33	99	33	99	33	297
1	4	24	96	24	96	24	384
1	5	8	40	8	40	8	200
2	1	50	100	100	50	200	50
2	2	44	176	88	88	176	176
2	3	40	240	80	120	160	360
2	4	14	112	28	56	56	224
2	5	6	60	12	30	24	150
3	1	18	56	54	18	162	18
3	2	6	36	18	12	54	24
3	3	11	99	33	33	99	99
3	4	4	48	12	16	36	64
3	5	4	60	12	20	36	100
Total		571	1591	811	1049	1377	2641

ES_r is calculated as

$$ES_r = \frac{N\Sigma(frc) - \Sigma(fr)\Sigma(fc)}{\sqrt{(N\Sigma fr^2 - (\Sigma fr)^2)(N\Sigma fc^2 - (\Sigma fc)^2)}}$$

$$= \frac{571(1591) - (811)(1049)}{\sqrt{(571(1377) - 811^2)(571(2641) - 1049^2)}} = 0.252.$$

A Dichotomous and a Continuous Measure

A meta-analysis of correlational effect sizes is likely to involve many studies with a dichotomous measure correlated with a continuous measure. If not presented as a correlation, such studies will typically report the data as means and standard deviations for each of the groups represented by the dichotomy or as inferential statistics such as a t-value or F-ratio. For example, the mean and standard deviation in math achievement may be reported for boys and girls. The formulas for computing ES_r in these cases are presented in the following text.

Means and Standard Deviations

The correlation between a dichotomous variable and a continuous variable can be computed from the means and standard deviations for each group of the dichotomous variable using Formulas 3 or 4 from Table B11. For example, suppose a study on gender difference in mathematical ability reports means of 105.2 and 106.5, respectively, on a math aptitude test for a sample of equal numbers of fifth grade boys and girls. The pooled standard deviation is 14.5 (see Formula 1, Table B10). Using Formula 3 in Table B11, the correlation is as follows.

$$ES_r = \frac{(\overline{X}_1 - \overline{X}_2)/s_{pooled}}{\sqrt{((\overline{X}_1 - \overline{X}_2)/s_{pooled})^2 + 1/p(1-p)}}$$

$$= \frac{(105.2 - 106.5)/14.5}{\sqrt{(105.2 - 106.5/14.5)^2 + 1/(.5(1-.5))}} = -0.45$$

If the study reports the full sample standard deviation, rather than individual standard deviations for each group, then use Formula 4.

An Independent t-Test

The t-test for independent groups can be used to test the strength of the relationship between group membership, such as gender, and a dependent measure, such as math performance. If the means and standard deviations are not reported, then an ES_r can be computed from the t-value and the sample sizes of the contrasted groups using Formula 5 in Table B11.

Example. A study of the effect of alcohol and violence reports a t of 0.57 for the contrast of the mean value on the Buss aggression inventory for heavy ($n = 25$) versus light ($n = 52$) users of alcohol. With this data, ES_r, can be computed as

$$ES_r = \frac{t}{\sqrt{t^2 + n_1 + n_2 - 2}} = \frac{0.57}{\sqrt{0.57^2 + 25 + 52 - 2}} = .07$$

An F-ratio from a One-way Analysis of Variance with Only Two Groups

As with the t-value, a correlation can be computed from an F-ratio for the between-groups contrast from a one-way analysis of variance using Formula 6 in Table B11. The F-ratio must represent the contrast between the two groups of interest and not be adjusted for covariates. Since the F-ratio is always positive, Formula 6 always returns a positive value. If the observed relationship between the group membership and the variable of interest is negative, given the desired coding of group membership, then the sign of ES_r must be changed.

Two Dichotomous Measures

The 2 × 2 Contingency Table

The relationship between two dichotomous variables can be represented in a 2 × 2 contingency table and ES_r calculated using the standard formula for phi (Formula 7, Table B11). For example, a study of the relationship between alcoholism and domestic violence for a sample of marital dyads reported the frequency of male partners with a diagnosis of alcoholism by the frequency of marital dyads experiencing abuse perpetrated by the male partner (Table B8). Applying Formula 7 to this data yields ES_r.

$$ES_r = \frac{(ad - bc)}{\sqrt{(a + b)(c + d)(a + c)(b + d)}}$$

$$= \frac{30(105) - 45(20)}{\sqrt{(30 + 45)(20 + 105)(30 + 20)(45 + 105)}} = .268$$

The Chi-Square

Rather than presenting the reader with a 2 × 2 contingency table, some research reports may represent the relationship between two dichotomous variables only as a chi-square value. A chi-square based on a 2 × 2 contingency table can be converted to ES_r using Formula 8 in Table B11. Formulas 8 and 7 are algebraically equivalent, that is, they produce an equivalent ES_r if the chi-square is based on the same data as used in Formula 7. Note that the chi-square used in this formula must have only 1 degree of freedom. Chi-squares based on contingency tables dimensioned greater than 2 × 2, such as a 3 × 2, have more than 1 degree of freedom and cannot be converted to a correlation coefficient. Also note that since chi-square is always positive, this formula will always return a positive value. The coder must determine the direction of the correlation from the text of the study report and apply the appropriate algebraic sign.

Table B8

	Domestic Abuse	No Domestic Abuse
Positive diagnosis for alcoholism	30	45
Negative diagnosis for alcoholism	20	105

Approximations and Probability Values

In rare cases, a study may report the significance level (p) for a correlation and not report the correlation value itself. For correlations between two continuous variables or between a continuous and a dichotomous variable, the probability level for the correlation is based on the t-distribution. To find ES_r from p, look up the t-value associated with the reported p-value and degrees of freedom ($N - 2$) in Table B13 (at the end of this appendix). Compute ES_r using Formula 9 in Table B11. For example, suppose a study reports that drug use among adolescents is not correlated with aggressiveness ($p = .18$) in a sample of $N = 273$. Using Table B13, the t-value for a $p = .18$ with $df = 271$ is interpolated as 1.355. Inserting this value in Formula 9 yields ES_r.

$$ES_r = \frac{t}{\sqrt{t^2 - df}} = \frac{1.355}{\sqrt{1.355^2 + (273 - 2)}} = .08$$

The probability value for an ES_r based on two dichotomous variables is based on the chi-square distribution, not the t-distribution. Therefore, to determine ES_r based on a p-value for the relationship between two dichotomous variables, look up the chi-square value associated with that p-value and $df = 1$ and apply Formula 8 in Table B11. For example, the chi-square value associated with $p = .18$ and $df = 1$ is 1.854. Using Formula 8 and $N = 273$, ES_r is calculated as below.

$$|ES_r| = \sqrt{\frac{\chi^2}{N}} = \sqrt{\frac{1.854}{273}} = 0.08$$

It should not be surprising that ES_r is the same as in the previous example, using the same p-value and sample size. This reflects a basic relationship between all these formulas in general and the relationship between the t- and chi-square distributions in particular.

ODDS-RATIO EFFECT SIZE

Effect size coding for the odds-ratio is straightforward. The odds-ratio is based on the frequencies of a 2×2 contingency table and is thus an index of the relationship between two inherently dichotomous variables. Calculation of an odds-ratio is typically based on the number of persons within each category (cell) of the contingency table. However, the odds-ratio can also be computed from cell or row proportions. If the marginal distributions of the 2×2 contingency table are known, then it is also possible to impute the cell frequencies from a correlation coefficient or a chi-square. The specifics of calculating an odds-ratio in each of these situations are discussed below (see Table B12 at the end of this appendix for a listing of the formulas).

Calculation Based on Cell Frequencies

The simplest formula for the odds-ratio effect size statistic is based on cell frequencies. Suppose a clinical trial for the efficacy of a new infertility drug had two treatment conditions: a group that received the new drug and a group that received a placebo, with 30 subjects in each. The study reported that five women in the treatment condition became pregnant, whereas only two women in the placebo condition became pregnant. These data are presented in a 2 × 2 contingency table in Table B9. Note that the cells have been labeled a, b, c, and d, reading from left to right. Using Formula 1 in Table B12, the odds-ratio is calculated as follows.

$$ES_{OR} = \frac{ad}{bc} = \frac{5(28)}{25(2)} = 2.8$$

Calculation Based on Row Proportions

In the preceding example, the data can also be represented as the proportion within each group (i.e., row) with a successful outcome, that is, p_{G1} and p_{G2}. For the foregoing data, p_{G1} equals 5/30 or 0.167, and p_{G2} equals 2/30 or 0.067. Applying Formula 2 in Table B12 to these proportions yields the same odds-ratio as the formula based on the cell frequencies.

$$ES_{OR} = \frac{p_{G1}(1 - p_{G2})}{p_{G2}(1 - p_{G1})} = \frac{0.167(1 - 0.067)}{0.067(1 - 0.167)} = 2.8$$

Calculation Based on Cell Proportions

The odds-ratio can also be calculated from the proportion of subjects within each cell, p_a, p_b, p_c, and p_d. These proportions are calculated as the cell frequency divided by the total sample size, that is, the sum of all four cell frequencies. With the previous data, for instance, $p(a)$ is 5/60

Table B9

| | Pregnant | | |
	Yes	No	Total
New drug	$a = 5$	$b = 25$	30
Placebo	$c = 2$	$d = 28$	30
Total	7	53	60

or 0.083. Using Formula 3 in Table B12, the odds-ratio for the prior data is once again calculated as 2.8. Note the similarity between this formula and Formula 1.

$$ES_{OR} = \frac{p_a p_d}{p_b p_c} = \frac{0.083(0.467)}{0.417(0.033)} = 2.8$$

Imputation of 2 × 2 Contingency Table from Correlation and Marginal Proportions

Studies of the relationship between two dichotomous variables may report findings as a correlation coefficient and may not report the raw frequencies, proportions, or percentages needed for the preceding formulas. Using the correlation and the marginal proportions, that is, the proportion of subjects in at least one row and one column of the 2 × 2 contingency table, the cell frequency for each cell can be imputed. For example, suppose we know that the correlation coefficient for the data in Table B9 is .156, the proportion of subjects in row one, p_{r1}, is 30/60 or .5, and the proportion of subjects in column one, p_{c1}, is 7/60 or .117. Applying Formula 4 in Table B12 returns the value 5, the frequency of cell a:

$$a = N \left(p_{r1} p_{c1} + r\sqrt{p_{r1} p_{c1}(1 - p_{r1})(1 - p_{c1})} \right)$$

$$a = 60 \left(.5(.117) + .156\sqrt{.5(.117)(1 - .5)(1 - .117)} \right) = 5$$

The remaining cell frequencies can now be found through subtraction. For example, cell b is 30 (.5 of 60) minus 5, or 25. Cells c and d can be found in a similar fashion. After calculating the cell frequencies, apply Formula 1 (Table B12) to calculate the odds-ratio.

Unfortunately, in practice studies that report the marginal frequencies or proportions typically also report the cell frequencies. However, in some situations it may be reasonable to estimate the marginal proportions. The closer the estimates are to .5, the more conservative the calculated odds-ratio.

Imputation of 2 × 2 Contingency Table Based on Chi-Square and Marginal Proportions

With only a slight modification of Formula 4 in Table B12, the preceding procedure for imputing the cell frequencies from a correlation can be applied to a chi-square. Once again the two marginal proportions or reasonable estimates thereof are needed. For the foregoing infertility treatment example, the chi-square equals 1.456. The first cell frequency (a)

can be imputed using Formula 5.

$$a = N \left(p_{r1}p_{c1} + \sqrt{\frac{\chi^2 p_{r1}p_{c1}(1 - p_{r1})(1 - p_{c1})}{N}} \right)$$

$$a = 60 \left(0.5(0.117) + \sqrt{\frac{1.456(0.5)(0.117)(1 - 0.5)(1 - 0.117)}{60}} \right) = 5$$

Imputation of Odds-Ratio from Continuous Data

It may occur that a subset of studies eligible for inclusion in a meta-analysis of odds-ratios use a continuous dependent measure to contrast the groups. For example, many studies of diagnostic tests report data in a dichotomous form as the means on the test for the group with and that without the condition being diagnosed. Hasselblad and Hedges (1995) have shown how the standardized mean difference effect size can be converted into an odds-ratio (and vice versa) for meta-analysis. Using Formula 6 from Table B12, a standardized mean difference effect size computed with any of the formulas from Table B10 can be converted into an odds-ratio (or logged odds-ratio) equivalent. Suppose, for example, that a standardized mean difference effect size computed on means and standard deviations using Formula 1 in Table B10 has a value of .32. Formula 6 in Table B12 then yields the odds-ratio as follows.

$$ES_{OR} = e^{\left(\frac{\pi ES_{sm}}{\sqrt{3}} \right)} = e^{\left(\frac{(3.14)(.32)}{\sqrt{3}} \right)} = e^{.58} = 1.79$$

Table B10
Useful formulas for calculating ES_{sm} from a range of statistical data

Formula	Data needed and definition of terms
Direct calculation formula for ES_{sm}	
(1) $ES_{sm} = \dfrac{\overline{X}_1 - \overline{X}_2}{s_{pooled}}$	Means $(\overline{X})$, standard deviations (s), and sample sizes (n) for each group.
$s_{pooled} = \sqrt{\dfrac{(n_1 - 1)s_1^2 + (n_2 - 1)s_2^2}{n_1 + n_2 - 2}}$	
Algebraically equivalent formulas for ES_{sm}	
(2) $ES_{sm} = t\sqrt{\dfrac{n_1 + n_2}{n_1 n_2}}$	Independent t-test (t) and sample sizes (n) for each group.
(3) $ES_{sm} = \dfrac{2t}{\sqrt{N}}$	Independent t-test (t) and total sample size (N). Assumes $n_1 = n_2$.

Table B10
continued

Formula	Data needed and definition of terms

Direct calculation formula for ES_{sm}

(4) $|ES_{sm}| = \sqrt{\dfrac{F(n_1 + n_2)}{n_1 n_2}}$

F-ratio (F) from a one-way ANOVA and sample sizes (n) for each group.

(5) $|ES_{sm}| = 2\sqrt{\dfrac{F}{N}}$

F-ratio (F) from a one-way ANOVA and total sample size (N). Assumes $n_1 = n_2$.

Exact probabilities levels for a t-value

(6) $t = IDF(p, df)$

Determine the t-value for a p-value and df from Table B13 or an inverse distribution function (IDF) in a spreadsheet or statistical software program. Use result and Formula 3 to obtain effect size. Note: $t^2 = F$.

Calculation of means and standard deviations from a grouped frequency distribution

(7) $\overline{X} = \dfrac{\Sigma x_i f_i}{\Sigma f_i}$

Frequency counts (f) for each level (i) of a variable (x).

(8) $s = \sqrt{\dfrac{(\Sigma f_i)(\Sigma x_i^2 f_i) - (\Sigma x_i f_i)^2}{(\Sigma f_i)^2}}$

Frequency counts (f) for each level (i) of a variable (x).

Approximations based on continuous data

(9) $ES_{sm} = \dfrac{2r}{\sqrt{1 - r^2}}$

Correlation (r) between group membership and dependent variable (assumes equal n in groups).

(10) $ES_{sm} = \dfrac{r}{\sqrt{(1 - r^2)(p(1 - p))}}$

Correlation (r) between group membership and dependent variable, and the proportion (p) of the total sample in one of the two groups.

Estimates $\overline{X}_1 - \overline{X}_2$ of (numerator of ES_{sm})

(11) $\overline{X}_1 - \overline{X}_2 \approx \Delta_1 - \Delta_2$

Mean gain score (Δ) for each group.

(12) $\overline{X}_1 - \overline{X}_2 \approx \overline{X}_{1_{adjusted}} - \overline{X}_{2_{adjusted}}$

Covariate or regression adjusted means $(\overline{X}_{adjusted})$ for each group.

(13) $\overline{X}_1 - \overline{X}_2 \approx B$

Unstandardized regression coefficient (B) for group membership.

Estimates of s_{pooled} (denominator of ES_{sm})

(14) $s_{pooled} = \sqrt{\dfrac{s^2(N - 1) - \dfrac{(\overline{X}_1^2 + \overline{X}_2^2 - 2\overline{X}_1 \overline{X}_2)(n_1 n_2)}{n_1 + n_2}}{N - 1}}$

Full-sample standard deviation (s), group means $(\overline{X})$, group sample sizes (n), and total sample size (N).

Table B10

continued

Formula	Data needed and definition of terms
(15) $s_{pooled} = \dfrac{\overline{X}_1 - \overline{X}_2}{t\sqrt{\dfrac{n_1 + n_2}{n_1 n_2}}}$	Means ($\overline{X}$) and sample sizes (n) for each group, and associated t-value (t).
(16) $s = se\sqrt{n-1}$	Standard error of the mean (se) and sample size (n) for any group.
(17) $s_{pooled} = \sqrt{\dfrac{MS_b}{F_{oneway}}}$ $MS_b = \dfrac{\Sigma n_j \overline{X}_j^2 - \dfrac{(\Sigma n_j \overline{X}_j)^2}{\Sigma n_j}}{k-1}$	F-ratio (F) from a one-way ANOVA with k groups and the mean ($\overline{X}$) and sample size (n) for each group (j).
(18) $s_{pooled} = \sqrt{\dfrac{SS_B + SS_{AB} + SS_w}{df_B + df_{AB} + df_w}}$	The sums-of-squares (SS) and degrees of freedom (df) from a factorial (two-way) ANOVA. Subscripts indicate factors (A and B) and within groups or residual term (w).
(19) $s_{pooled} = \sqrt{\left(\dfrac{MS_{error}}{1-r^2}\right)\left(\dfrac{df_{error}-1}{df_{error}-2}\right)}$	The mean-square error (MS_{error}) and associated degrees of freedom (df), and correlation (r) between covariate and dependent variable from a one-way ANCOVA.
(20) $s_{pooled} = \dfrac{s_{gain}}{\sqrt{2(1-r)}}$	Standard deviation of the gain scores (s_{gain}) and the correlation (r) between time-one and time-two scores.

Approximations based on dichotomous data

Formula	Data needed and definition of terms
(21) $ES_{sm} = probit(p_1) - probit(p_2)$	Probit transformation (Table B15) of the proportion (p) of successes for each group.
(22) $ES_{sm} = arcsine(p_1) - arcsine(p_2)$	Arcsine transformation (Table B14) of the proportion (p) of successes for each group.
(23) $|ES_{sm}| = 2\sqrt{\dfrac{\chi^2}{N-\chi^2}}$	Chi-square (χ^2) with $df = 1$ and total sample size (N).
(24) $ES_{sm} = \dfrac{2r}{\sqrt{1-r^2}}$	Phi-coefficient (r).

Table B11

Useful formulas for calculating ES_r from a range of statistical data

Formula	Data needed and definition of terms
Prototype or definition of the r-type effect size	
(1) $$ES_r = \frac{N\Sigma x_i y_i - \Sigma x_i \Sigma y_i}{\sqrt{(N\Sigma x_i^2 - (\Sigma x_i)^2)(N\Sigma y_i^2 - (\Sigma y_i)^2)}}$$	Individual level data for each variable (x and y) and total sample size (N). This is the standard computational formula for the Pearson product-moment correlation.
Joint frequency or contingency table	
(2) $$ES_r = \frac{N\Sigma(f{\cdot}r{\cdot}c) - \Sigma(f{\cdot}r)\Sigma(f{\cdot}c)}{\sqrt{(N\Sigma f{\cdot}r^2 - (\Sigma f{\cdot}r)^2)(N\Sigma f{\cdot}c^2 - (\Sigma f{\cdot}c)^2)}}$$	Cell frequencies, f, for a k by j table where k or j is greater than 2. N is total sample size, r is table row number, and c is table column number associated with each f.
A dichotomous by a continuous measure (point-biserial r)	
(3) $$ES_r = \frac{(\overline{X}_1 - \overline{X}_2)/s_{\text{pooled}}}{\sqrt{((\overline{X}_1 - \overline{X}_2)/s_{\text{pooled}})^2 + \dfrac{1}{p(1-p)}}}$$	The pooled standard deviation, s_{pooled} for the dependent measure, means ($\overline{X}$) and sample sizes (n) for each group, and the proportion (p) of the total sample in one of the two groups.
(4) $$ES_r = \frac{(\overline{X}_1 - \overline{X}_2)\sqrt{p(1-p)}}{s}$$	Full sample standard deviation (s) for the dependent measure, means ($\overline{X}$) and sample sizes (n) for each group, and the proportion (p) of the total sample in one of the two groups.
(5) $$ES_r = \frac{t}{\sqrt{t^2 + n_1 + n_2 - 2}}$$	Independent t-test (t) and sample sizes (n) for each group.
(6) $$|ES_r| = \frac{\sqrt{F}}{\sqrt{F + n_1 + n_2 - 2}}$$	F-ratio (F) from a one-way ANOVA and sample sizes (n) for each group.
Two dichotomous variables (2×2 contingency table)	
(7) $$ES_r = \frac{(ad - bc)}{\sqrt{(a_b)(c+d)(a+c)(b+d)}}$$	Cell frequencies (a, b, c, and d) of a $2{\times}2$ contingency table.
(8) $$|ES_r| = \sqrt{\frac{\chi^2}{N}}$$	Chi-square (χ^2) with $df = 1$ and total sample size (N).
Significance test for r	
(9) $$ES_r = \frac{t}{\sqrt{t^2 + df}}$$	The t-value (t) testing the statistical significance of r. If exact p reported for r, determine t from Table B13 or inverse distribution function in a spreadsheet.

Table B12
Useful formulas for calculating ES_{OR} from a range of statistical data

Formula	Data needed and definition of terms
Cell frequencies of a 2 × 2 contingency table (1) $ES_{OR} = \dfrac{ad}{bc}$	The cell frequencies, labeled a, b, c, and d, of a 2 × 2 contingency table.
Row or group proportions (2) $ES_{OR} = \dfrac{p_1(1 - p_2)}{p_2(1 - p_1)}$	The proportion (p) of persons in each group or condition with a successful or desirable outcome.
Cell proportions of a 2 × 2 contingency table (3) $ES_{OR} = \dfrac{p_a p_d}{p_b p_c}$	The cell proportions (p) for each cell (a, b, c, d) of a 2 × 2 where the proportion is the cell frequency divided by the total sample size.
Impute cell frequencies from a correlation (4) $a = N\left(p_{r1}p_{c1} + r\sqrt{p_{r1}r_{c1}(1 - p_{r1})(1 - p_{c1})}\right)$ $b = Np_{r1} - a$ $c = Np_{c1} - a$ $d = N - (a + b + c)$	The correlation coefficient for a 2 × 2 contingency table (r), total sample size (N), and the marginal proportion for the first row (p_{r1}) and first column (p_{c1}).
Impute cell frequencies from a chi-square (5) $a = N\left(p_{r1}p_{c1} + \sqrt{\dfrac{\chi^2 p_{r1}p_{c1}(1 - p_{r1})(1 - p_{c1})}{N}}\right)$ $b = Np_{r1} - a$ $c = Np_{c1} - a$ $d = N - (a + b + c)$	The chi-square value for a 2 × 2 contingency table (r), total sample size (N), and the marginal proportion for the first row (p_{r1}) and first column (p_{c1}).
Odds-ratio equivalent from continuous dependent measure (6) $ES_{OR} = e^{\left(\frac{\pi ES_{sm}}{\sqrt{3}}\right)}$	ES_{sm} from any formula in Table B10, $\pi = 3.14$, e = natural logarithm.

Table B13
Two-tailed t-values from the t-distribution by df and p-value

	p-value (Two-tailed)								
df	.80	.50	.20	.10	.05	.02	.01	.002	.001
1	0.325	1.000	3.078	6.314	12.706	31.821	63.657	318.309	636.621
2	0.289	0.816	1.886	2.920	4.303	6.965	9.925	22.327	31.599
3	0.277	0.765	1.638	2.353	3.182	4.541	5.841	10.215	12.924
4	0.271	0.741	1.533	2.132	2.776	3.747	4.604	7.173	8.610
5	0.267	0.727	1.476	2.015	2.571	3.365	4.032	5.893	6.869
6	0.265	0.718	1.440	1.943	2.447	3.143	3.707	5.208	5.959
7	0.263	0.711	1.415	1.895	2.365	2.998	3.499	4.785	5.408
8	0.262	0.706	1.397	1.860	2.306	2.896	3.355	4.501	5.041
9	0.261	0.703	1.383	1.833	2.262	2.821	3.250	4.297	4.781
10	0.260	0.700	1.372	1.812	2.228	2.764	3.169	4.144	4.587
11	0.260	0.697	1.363	1.796	2.201	2.718	3.106	4.025	4.437
12	0.259	0.695	1.356	1.782	2.179	2.681	3.055	3.930	4.318
13	0.259	0.694	1.350	1.771	2.160	2.650	3.012	3.852	4.221
14	0.258	0.692	1.345	1.761	2.145	2.624	2.977	3.787	4.140
15	0.258	0.691	1.341	1.753	2.131	2.602	2.947	3.733	4.073
16	0.258	0.690	1.337	1.746	2.120	2.583	2.921	3.686	4.015
17	0.257	0.689	1.333	1.740	2.110	2.567	2.898	3.646	3.965
18	0.257	0.688	1.330	1.734	2.101	2.552	2.878	3.610	3.922
19	0.257	0.688	1.328	1.729	2.093	2.539	2.861	3.579	3.883
20	0.257	0.687	1.325	1.725	2.086	2.528	2.845	3.552	3.850
21	0.257	0.686	1.323	1.721	2.080	2.518	2.831	3.527	3.819
22	0.256	0.686	1.321	1.717	2.074	2.508	2.819	3.505	3.792
23	0.256	0.685	1.319	1.714	2.069	2.500	2.807	3.485	3.768
24	0.256	0.685	1.318	1.711	2.064	2.492	2.797	3.467	3.745
25	0.256	0.684	1.316	1.708	2.060	2.485	2.787	3.450	3.725
26	0.256	0.684	1.315	1.706	2.056	2.479	2.779	3.435	3.707
27	0.256	0.684	1.314	1.703	2.052	2.473	2.771	3.421	3.690
28	0.256	0.683	1.313	1.701	2.048	2.467	2.763	3.408	3.674
29	0.256	0.683	1.311	1.699	2.045	2.462	2.756	3.396	3.659
30	0.256	0.683	1.310	1.697	2.042	2.457	2.750	3.385	3.646
40	0.255	0.681	1.303	1.684	2.021	2.423	2.704	3.307	3.551
60	0.254	0.679	1.296	1.671	2.000	2.390	2.660	3.232	3.460
120	0.254	0.677	1.289	1.658	1.980	2.358	2.617	3.160	3.373
∞	0.253	0.674	1.282	1.645	1.960	2.326	2.576	3.090	3.291

SOURCE: Computer generated using SPSS 6.0 for Windows.

Table B14
Arcsine transformations (ϕ) for proportions (p)

p	ϕ	p	ϕ	p	ϕ	p	ϕ
0.00	0.000	0.25	1.047	0.50	1.571	0.75	2.094
0.01	0.200	0.26	1.070	0.51	1.591	0.76	2.118
0.02	0.284	0.27	1.093	0.52	1.611	0.77	2.141
0.03	0.348	0.28	1.115	0.53	1.631	0.78	2.165
0.04	0.403	0.29	1.137	0.54	1.651	0.79	2.190
0.05	0.451	0.30	1.159	0.55	1.671	0.80	2.214
0.06	0.495	0.31	1.181	0.56	1.691	0.81	2.240
0.07	0.536	0.32	1.203	0.57	1.711	0.82	2.265
0.08	0.574	0.33	1.224	0.58	1.731	0.83	2.292
0.09	0.609	0.34	1.245	0.59	1.752	0.84	2.319
0.10	0.644	0.35	1.266	0.60	1.772	0.85	2.346
0.11	0.676	0.36	1.287	0.61	1.793	0.86	2.375
0.12	0.707	0.37	1.308	0.62	1.813	0.87	2.404
0.13	0.738	0.38	1.328	0.63	1.834	0.88	2.434
0.14	0.767	0.39	1.349	0.64	1.855	0.89	2.465
0.15	0.795	0.40	1.369	0.65	1.875	0.90	2.498
0.16	0.823	0.41	1.390	0.66	1.897	0.91	2.532
0.17	0.850	0.42	1.410	0.67	1.918	0.92	2.568
0.18	0.876	0.44	1.451	0.68	1.939	0.93	2.606
0.19	0.902	0.43	1.430	0.69	1.961	0.94	2.647
0.20	0.927	0.45	1.471	0.70	1.982	0.95	2.691
0.21	0.952	0.46	1.491	0.71	2.004	0.96	2.739
0.22	0.976	0.47	1.511	0.72	2.026	0.97	2.793
0.23	1.000	0.48	1.531	0.73	2.049	0.98	2.858
0.24	1.024	0.49	1.551	0.74	2.071	0.99	2.941
						1.00	3.142

SOURCE: Computer generated using SPSS 6.0 for Windows.
$\phi = 2 * \text{arcsine}(\sqrt{p})$.

Table B15
Probit transformations (z) for proportions (p)

p	z	p	z	p	z	p	z
0.01	−2.326	0.26	−0.643	0.51	0.025	0.76	0.706
0.02	−2.054	0.27	−0.613	0.52	0.050	0.77	0.739
0.03	−1.881	0.28	−0.583	0.53	0.075	0.78	0.772
0.04	−1.751	0.29	−0.553	0.54	0.100	0.79	0.806
0.05	−1.645	0.30	−0.524	0.55	0.126	0.80	0.842
0.06	−1.555	0.31	−0.496	0.56	0.151	0.81	0.878
0.07	−1.476	0.32	−0.468	0.57	0.176	0.82	0.915
0.08	−1.405	0.33	−0.440	0.58	0.202	0.83	0.954
0.09	−1.341	0.34	−0.412	0.59	0.228	0.84	0.994
0.10	−1.282	0.35	−0.385	0.60	0.253	0.85	1.036
0.11	−1.227	0.36	−0.358	0.61	0.279	0.86	1.080
0.12	−1.175	0.37	−0.332	0.62	0.305	0.87	1.126
0.13	−1.126	0.38	−0.305	0.63	0.332	0.88	1.175
0.14	−1.080	0.39	−0.279	0.64	0.358	0.89	1.227
0.15	−1.036	0.40	−0.253	0.65	0.385	0.90	1.282
0.16	−0.994	0.41	−0.228	0.66	0.412	0.91	1.341
0.17	−0.954	0.42	−0.202	0.67	0.440	0.92	1.405
0.18	−0.915	0.44	−0.176	0.68	0.468	0.93	1.476
0.19	−0.878	0.43	−0.151	0.69	0.496	0.94	1.555
0.20	−0.842	0.45	−0.126	0.70	0.524	0.95	1.645
0.21	−0.806	0.46	−0.100	0.71	0.553	0.96	1.751
0.22	−0.772	0.47	−0.075	0.72	0.583	0.97	1.881
0.23	−0.739	0.48	−0.050	0.73	0.613	0.98	2.054
0.24	−0.706	0.49	−0.025	0.74	0.643	0.99	2.326
0.25	−0.674	0.50	0.000	0.75	0.674		

SOURCE: Computer generated using SPSS 6.0 for Windows.

Table B16

Chi-square critical values for $df = 1$

p-values (Right tail)	χ^2
0.99	0.0002
0.98	0.0006
0.95	0.004
0.90	0.016
0.80	0.06
0.70	0.15
0.50	0.45
0.30	1.07
0.20	1.64
0.10	2.71
0.05	3.84
0.02	5.41
0.01	6.63
0.001	10.83

SOURCE: Computer generated using SPSS 6.0 for Windows.

Appendix C

MS Excel Effect Size Computation Program

An effect size calculation program created in Microsoft's Excel spreadsheet program by David Wilson is available through the Internet. Although this spreadsheet was created using the Windows version of Excel, it can be used by the Macintosh version as well. To download a copy, point your web browser to the following URL address: http://www.wam.umd.edu/~wilsondb/home.html.

This program is useful for computing both standardized mean difference effect sizes and correlation coefficients from a range of statistical data frequently found in published studies (see also Shadish, Robinson, and Lu, 1999). Note, however, that this program does not analyze effect sizes; it is simply a tool to assist in the coding of studies. See Figure C1.

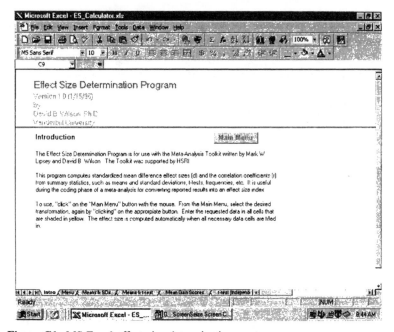

Figure C1. MS Excel effect size determination program.

Appendix D

SPSS Macros for Meta-Analysis

Following are three macros written for SPSS/Win Version 6.1 (will run on newer versions as well). These macros are generic and perform analyses of any type of effect size discussed in Chapter 3. To use, each of these macros needs to be typed into a separate file using a word processor or text editor and saved as an ASCII file (DOS file) with the appropriate name, i.e., MEANES.SPS, METAF.SPS, or METAREG.SPS. Alternatively, they may be obtained via the Internet at the following URL address: "http://www.wam.umd.edu/~wilsondb/home.html." At the web site you will also find variants on each of these macros written specifically for different effect size measures, such as the standardized mean difference, correlation coefficient, and odds-ratio. There are also versions of these three macros available for use with SAS and STATA statistical software packages.

The general procedure for using the macros is to first initialize the macro in SPSS. This is done with the "include" statement. For example, to initialize the macro MEANES, stored in the file named MEANES.SPS, run the following SPSS syntax command:

include 'meanes.sps'.

This assumes that the macro file is in the default directory. If stored elsewhere, such as in a separate subdirectory of the "C" hard drive or on a floppy diskette, simply specify the drive and directory path inside the quotation marks along with the file name, such as

include 'c:\macros\meanes.sps'.

Once a macro has been initialized, it can be used repeatedly and remains in memory until the SPSS program is closed or exited. We have discovered that on some computers only two macros can be in memory at one time. If

208

you have initialized two or more macros and experience numerous errors when running the macro initialized last, you may need to restart SPSS and limit your SPSS sessions to one or two macros. Also, a misspecification of the macro syntax will produce a large number of error and warning messages.

When you exit SPSS, the macro is removed from memory and must be re-initialized the next time you run SPSS. These macros do not have the stability of built-in SPSS commands and it is therefore advisable to save your data file before you use a macro.

SPSS Macro: MEANES.SPS

```
*-----------------------------------------------------------
*' Macro for SPSS/Win Version 6.1 or Higher
*' Written by David B. Wilson (dwilson@crim.umd.edu)
*' Meta-Analyzes Any Type of Effect Size
*' To use, initialize macro with the include statement:
*' INCLUDE "[drive][path]MEANES.SPS" .
*' Syntax for macro:
*' MEANES ES=varname /W=varname /PRINT=option .
*' E.g., MEANES ES = D /W = IVWEIGHT .
*' In this example, D is the name of the effect size variable
*' and IVWEIGHT is the name of the inverse variance weight
*' variable.  Replace D and INVWEIGHT with the appropriate
*' variable names for your data set.
*' /PRINT has the options "EXP" and "IVZR".  The former
*' prints the exponent of the results (odds-ratios) and
*' the latter prints the inverse Zr transform of the
*' results.  If the /PRINT statement is omitted, the
*' results are printed in their raw form.
*-----------------------------------------------------------
preserve
set printback=off
define meanes (es=!charend('/') /w=!charend('/')
  /print = !default('RAW') !charend('/'))
preserve
set printback=off mprint=off


*-----------------------------------------------------------
* Enter matrix mode and get data from active file
*-----------------------------------------------------------
matrix
get x /file * /variables = !es !w /missing omit


*-----------------------------------------------------------
* Compute variables needed to calculate results
*-----------------------------------------------------------
compute k = nrow(x) .
compute es = make(k,1,-99) .
compute es(1:k,1) = x(1:k,1) .
compute w = make(k,1,-99) .
compute w(1:k,1) = x(1:k,2) .
release x .
```

```
*----------------------------------------------------------------
* Compute random effect variance component and new weight
*----------------------------------------------------------------
compute c = ((csum((es&**2)&*w)-csum(es&*w)**2/csum(w))-(k-1))
    /(csum(w)-csum(w&**2)/csum(w)) .
do if (c < 0) .
.compute c = 0 .
end if .
compute w_re = 1/(c + (1/w)) .

*----------------------------------------------------------------
* Calculate summary statistics
*----------------------------------------------------------------
compute df    = k - 1 .
compute mes   = csum(es&*w)   /csum(w) .
compute mes_re = csum(es&*w_re)/csum(w_re) .
compute sem   = sqrt(1/csum(w)) .
compute semre = sqrt(1/csum(w_re)) .
compute les   = mes -   1.95996*sem .
compute ues   = mes +   1.95996*sem .
compute les_re = mes_re - 1.95996*semre .
compute ues_re = mes_re + 1.95996*semre .
compute q     = csum((es&**2)&*w)-csum(es&*w)**2/csum(w) .
do if (df>0) .
. compute p   = 1- chicdf(q,df) .
end if .
compute z = mes/sem .
compute z_re = mes_re/semre .
compute pz    = (1-cdfnorm(abs(z)))*2 .
compute pz_re = (1-cdfnorm(abs(z_re)))*2 .
compute sd = sqrt(q*csum(w)**-1) .

*----------------------------------------------------------------
* Transform Output if Requested
*----------------------------------------------------------------
!IF (!print !eq 'EXP'|!print !eq 'exp'|!print !eq 'Exp') !THEN .
compute mes = exp(mes) .
compute les = exp(les) .
compute ues = exp(ues) .
compute mes_re = exp(mes_re) .
compute les_re = exp(les_re) .
compute ues_re = exp(ues_re) .
compute sem = -9.9999 .
compute semre = -9.9999 .
!IFEND .

!IF (!print !eq 'IVZR'|!print !eq 'ivzr'|!print !eq 'Ivzr'
    |!print !eq 'IvZr') !THEN .
compute mes = (exp(2*mes)-1)/(exp(2*mes)+1) .
compute les = (exp(2*les)-1)/(exp(2*les)+1) .
compute ues = (exp(2*ues)-1)/(exp(2*ues)+1) .
compute mes_re = (exp(2*mes_re)-1)/(exp(2*mes_re)+1) .
compute les_re = (exp(2*les_re)-1)/(exp(2*les_re)+1) .
compute ues_re = (exp(2*ues_re)-1)/(exp(2*ues_re)+1) .
compute sem = -9.9999 .
compute semre = -9.9999 .
!IFEND .

*----------------------------------------------------------------
* Create Output Matrices
*----------------------------------------------------------------
```

```
compute table1 = make(1,4,-99) .
compute table1(1,1) = k .
compute table1(1,2) = mmin(es) .
compute table1(1,3) = mmax(es) .
compute table1(1,4) = sd .

compute table2 = make(2,6,-99) .
compute table2(1,1) = mes .
compute table2(1,2) = les .
compute table2(1,3) = ues .
compute table2(1,4) = sem .
compute table2(1,5) = z .
compute table2(1,6) = pz .
compute table2(2,1) = mes_re .
compute table2(2,2) = les_re .
compute table2(2,3) = ues_re .
compute table2(2,4) = semre .
compute table2(2,5) = z_re .
compute table2(2,6) = pz_re .

compute table3 = make(1,3,-99) .
compute table3(1,1) = q .
compute table3(1,2) = df .
compute table3(1,3) = p .

*--------------------------------------------------------------
* Print summary statistics
*--------------------------------------------------------------
print /title '*****  Meta-Analytic Results  *****'.
print table1
    /title '------- Distribution Description'+
    ' ---------------------------------'
    /clabel "N" "Min ES" "Max ES" "Wghtd SD"
    /format f11.3 .
print table2
    /title '------- Fixed & Random Effects Model'+
    ' -----------------------------'
    /clabel "Mean ES" "-95%CI" "+95%CI" "SE" "Z" "P"
    /rlabel "Fixed" "Random"
    /format f9.4 .
print c
    /title '------- Random Effects Variance Component'+
    ' -----------------------'
    /rlabel 'v    =' /format f10.6 .
print table3
    /title '------- Homogeneity Analysis'+
    ' ------------------------------------'
    /clabel "Q" "df" "p"
    /format f11.4 .
print
    /title 'Random effects v estimated via noniterative'+
    ' method of moments.' .
!IF (!print !eq 'EXP'|!print !eq 'exp'|!print !eq 'Exp') !THEN .
print
    /title 'Mean ES and 95% CI are the exponent of the'+
    ' computed values (Odds-Ratios).' .
!IFEND .
!IF (!print !eq 'IVZR'|!print !eq 'ivzr'|!print !eq 'Ivzr' |
    !print !eq 'IvZr') !THEN .
print
    /title 'Mean ES and 95% CI are the inverse Fisher Zr'+
```

```
' of the computed values (r).' .
!IFEND .
end matrix .

*-----------------------------------------------------------
* Restore settings and exit.
*-----------------------------------------------------------
restore
!enddefine
restore
```

SPSS Macro: METAF.SPS

```
*-----------------------------------------------------------
*' SPSS/Win 6.1 or Higher Macro -- Written by David B. Wilson
*' Meta-Analysis Analog to the Oneway ANOVA for any type of ES
*' To use, initialize macro with the include statement:
*' INCLUDE "[drive][path]METAF.SPS" .
*' Syntax for macro:
*' METAF ES=varname /W=varname /GROUP=varname /MODEL=option .
*' Where ES is the effect size, W is the inverse variance
*' weight, GROUP is the numeric categorical independent variable
*' and MODEL is either FE for a fixed effects model, MM for
*' a random effects model estimated via the method of moments,
*' ML is a random effects model estimated via iterative maximum likelihood,
*' and REML is a random effects model estimated via iterative restricted
*' maximum likelihood. If "/MODEL" is omitted, FE is the default.
*' /PRINT has the options "EXP" and "IVZR". The former
*' prints the exponent of the results (odds-ratios) and
*' the latter prints the inverse Zr transform of the
*' results. If the /PRINT statement is omitted, the
*' results are printed in their raw form.

*' example:
*'
*' metaf es = effct /w = invweght /group = txvar1
*'    /model = fe .
*'
*-----------------------------------------------------------
preserve
set printback=off
define metaf (es=!charend('/')
/w=!charend('/') /group=!charend('/')
/model = !default('FE') !charend('/')
/print = !default('RAW') !charend('/'))
preserve
set printback=off mprint off

*-----------------------------------------------------------
* Enter matrix mode
*-----------------------------------------------------------
sort cases by !group
matrix

*-----------------------------------------------------------
* Get data from active file
*-----------------------------------------------------------
get data /file * /variables = !es !w !group /missing omit
```

```
*----------------------------------------------------------------
* Create vectors and matrices
*----------------------------------------------------------------.
compute es = data(1:nrow(data),1).
compute w = data(1:nrow(data),2).
compute v = (w&**-1) .
compute grp = data(1:nrow(data),3).
compute x = design(grp) .
compute p = make(1,ncol(x),1) .
compute k = make(1,nrow(x),1) .
compute group = inv(T(x)*x)*T(x)*grp .
release data .

*----------------------------------------------------------------
* Recompute weights for random effects models
* Method of moments
*----------------------------------------------------------------.
!IF (!model !eq 'MM'|!model !eq 'mm'|!model !eq 'ML'|
     !model !eq 'ml'|!model !eq 'REML'|!model !eq 'reml') !THEN .
compute xwx = T(x&*(w*p))*x .
compute B  = inv(xwx)*T(x&*(w*p))*es .
compute qw  = csum(es&*w&*es) - T(B)*xwx*B .
compute c = (qw-(nrow(es)-ncol(x)))/
    csum(w - rsum((x&*(w*p)*inv(T(x&*(w*p))*x))&*x&*(w*p))) .
do if c<0 .
+ compute c = 0 .
end if .
compute w  = 1/(v+c) .
!IFEND .

!IF (!model !eq 'ML' | !model !eq 'ml'|!model !eq 'REML'|
     !model !eq 'reml') !THEN .
compute c2 = c .
loop l=1 to 100 .
.compute loops = l .
.compute c = c2 .
.compute w = 1/(v + c) .
.compute xw = x&*(w*p) .
.compute xwx = T(xw)*x .
.compute B = inv(xwx)*T(xw)*es .
.compute r = es -x*B .
.compute c2 = csum(w&**2&*(r&**2 - v))/csum(w&**2) .
.do if c2<0 .
. compute c2 = 0 .
.end if .
end loop if abs(c2 - c)<.0000000001 .
compute c = c2 .
compute w = 1/(v + c) .
compute se_c = sqrt(2/csum(w&**2)) .
!IFEND .

!IF (!model !eq 'REML' | !model !eq 'reml') !THEN .
compute c = c2*(nrow(es)*inv(nrow(es)-ncol(x))) .
compute w = 1/(v + c) .
compute se_c = sqrt(2/csum(w&**2)) .
!IFEND .

*----------------------------------------------------------------
* Compute Statistics
*----------------------------------------------------------------.
compute means = T(T(T(x&*(w*p))*es)*inv(T(x&*(w*p))*x)) .
```

```
compute grpns = diag(T(x)*x) .
compute q = T(x&*(w*p))*(es&**2)-T(T((T(x&*(w*p))*es)&**2)*inv(T(x&*(w*p))*x)) .
compute qt = csum(es&**2&*w) - csum(es&*w)**2/csum(w) .
compute qw = csum(q) .
compute qb = qt - qw .
compute dfb = ncol(x) - 1 .
compute dfw = nrow(es) - ncol(x) .
compute dft = nrow(es) - 1 .
compute se = sqrt(diag(inv(T(x&*(w*p))*x))) .
compute zvalues = means&/se .
compute pz = (1 - cdfnorm(abs(zvalues)))*2 .
compute lmeans = means - se*1.96 .
compute umeans = means + se*1.96 .
compute gmean = csum(es&*w)/csum(w) .
compute segmean = sqrt(1/csum(w)) .
compute pq = make(ncol(x),1,-9) .
loop i = 1 to ncol(x) .
+   compute pq(i,1) = 1 - chicdf(q(i,1),grpns(i,1)-1) .
end loop .


*--------------------------------------------------------------
* Create results matrices
*--------------------------------------------------------------
compute qtable = make(3,3,-999) .
compute qtable(1,1) = qb .
compute qtable(2,1) = qw .
compute qtable(3,1) = qt .
compute qtable(1,2) = dfb .
compute qtable(2,2) = dfw .
compute qtable(3,2) = dft .
compute qtable(1,3) = 1 - chicdf(qb,dfb) .
compute qtable(2,3) = 1 - chicdf(qw,dfw) .
compute qtable(3,3) = 1 - chicdf(qt,dft) .

compute ttable = make(1,7,-9) .
compute ttable(1,1) = gmean .
compute ttable(1,2) = segmean .
compute ttable(1,3) = gmean - segmean*1.96 .
compute ttable(1,4) = gmean + segmean*1.96 .
compute ttable(1,5) = gmean/segmean .
compute ttable(1,6) = (1 - cdfnorm(abs(gmean/segmean)))*2 .
compute ttable(1,7) = nrow(es) .

!IF (!print !eq 'EXP'||!print !eq 'exp'||!print !eq 'Exp') !THEN .
compute ttable(1,1) = exp(gmean) .
compute ttable(1,3) = exp(gmean - segmean*1.96) .
compute ttable(1,4) = exp(gmean + segmean*1.96) .
!IFEND .

!IF (!print !eq 'IVZR'||!print !eq 'ivzr'||!print !eq 'Ivzr' ||!print !eq 'IvZr') !THEN .
compute ttable(1,1) = (exp(2*gmean)-1)/(exp(2*gmean)+1) .
compute ttable(1,2) = -9.9999 .
compute ttable(1,3) = (exp(2*(gmean - segmean*1.96))-1)/(exp(2*(gmean - segmean*1.96))+1) .
compute ttable(1,4) = (exp(2*(gmean + segmean*1.96))-1)/(exp(2*(gmean + segmean*1.96))+1) .
!IFEND .

compute mtable = make(ncol(x),8,-9) .
compute mtable(1:ncol(x),1) = group .
compute mtable(1:ncol(x),2) = means .
compute mtable(1:ncol(x),3) = se .
compute mtable(1:ncol(x),4) = lmeans .
```

```
compute mtable(1:ncol(x),5) = umeans .
compute mtable(1:ncol(x),6) = zvalues .
compute mtable(1:ncol(x),7) = pz .
compute mtable(1:ncol(x),8) = grpns .

!IF (!print !eq 'EXP'|!print !eq 'exp'|!print !eq 'Exp') !THEN .
compute mtable(1:ncol(x),2) = exp(means) .
compute mtable(1:ncol(x),4) = exp(lmeans) .
compute mtable(1:ncol(x),5) = exp(umeans) .
!IFEND .

!IF (!print !eq 'IVZR'|!print !eq 'ivzr'|!print !eq 'Ivzr' |!print !eq 'IvZr') !THEN .
compute mtable(1:ncol(x),2) = (exp(2*means)-1)/(exp(2*means)+1) .
compute mtable(1:ncol(x),3) = -9.9999*T(p) .
compute mtable(1:ncol(x),4) = (exp(2*lmeans)-1)/(exp(2*lmeans)+1) .
compute mtable(1:ncol(x),5) = (exp(2*umeans)-1)/(exp(2*umeans)+1) .
!IFEND .

compute qwtable = make(ncol(x),4,-99) .
compute qwtable(1:ncol(x),1) = group .
compute qwtable(1:ncol(x),2) = q .
compute qwtable(1:ncol(x),3) = grpns - 1 .
compute qwtable(1:ncol(x),4) = pq .


*-----------------------------------------------------------
*  Print Results
*-----------------------------------------------------------.
print
   /title " *****  Inverse Variance Weighted Oneway ANOVA  *****" .
!IF (!model !eq 'ML' | !model !eq 'ml'|!model !eq 'MM'|
  !model !eq 'mm') !THEN .
print /title " *****  Mixed Effects Model  *****" .
!ELSE
print /title " *****  Fixed Effects Model via OLS  *****" .
!IFEND .

print qtable /format f12.4
   /title  "------- Analog ANOVA table (Homogeneity Q)  -------"
   /clabel "Q" "df" "p"
   /rlabel "Between" "Within" "Total" .
print qwtable /format f8.4
   /title  "------- Q by Group -------"
   /clabel "Group" "Q" "df" "p" .
print ttable /format f8.4
   /title  "------- Effect Size Results Total    -------"
   /clabel "Mean ES" "SE" "-95%CI" "+95%CI" "Z" "P" "N"
   /rlabel "  Total" .
print mtable /format f8.4
   /title  "------- Effect Size Results by Group -------"
   /clabel "Group" "Mean ES" "SE" "-95%CI" "+95%CI" "Z" "P" "N" .

!IF (!model !eq 'MM'|!model !eq 'mm') !THEN .
  print c
   /title '------- Method of Moments Random Effects'+
   ' Variance Component ------- '
   /rlabel "v     ="
   /format f8.5 .
!IFEND .
!IF (!model !eq 'ML' | !model !eq 'ml') !THEN .
+ compute mlc     = make(2,1,-999) .
+ compute mlc(1,1) = c .
```

```
+ compute mlc(2,1) = se_c .
+ print mlc
   /title    '------- Maximum Likelihood Random Effects'+
   ' Variance Component ------- '
   /rlabel "v       =" "se(v)  ="
   /format f8.5 .
!IFEND .
!IF (!model !eq 'REML' | !model !eq 'reml') !THEN .
+ compute mlc    = make(2,1,-999) .
+ compute mlc(1,1) = c .
+ compute mlc(2,1) = se_c .
+ print mlc
   /title    "------- Restricted Maximum Likelihood Random"+
   " Effects Variance Component ------- "
   /rlabel "v       =" "se(v)  ="
   /format f8.5 .
!IFEND .

!IF (!print !eq 'EXP'|!print !eq 'exp'|!print !eq 'Exp') !THEN .
print
   /title 'Mean ESs and 95% CIs are the exponent of the'+
   ' computed values (Odds-Ratios).' .
!IFEND .
!IF (!print !eq 'IVZR'|!print !eq 'ivzr'|!print !eq 'Ivzr' |
   !print !eq 'IvZr') !THEN .
print
   /title 'Mean ESs and 95% CIs are the inverse Fisher'+
   ' Zr of the computed values (r).' .
!IFEND .

*-------------------------------------------------------------
* End matrix mode
*-------------------------------------------------------------
end matrix

*-------------------------------------------------------------
* Restore settings and exit
*-------------------------------------------------------------
restore
!enddefine
restore
```

SPSS Macro: METAREG.SPS

```
*-------------------------------------------------------------
*' SPSS/Win 6.1 or Higher Macro -- Written by David B. Wilson
*' Meta-Analysis Modified Weighted Multiple Regression for
*' any type of effect size
*' To use, initialize macro with the include statement:
*' INCLUDE "[drive][path]METAREG.SPS" .
*' Syntax for macro:
*' METAREG ES=varname /W=varname /IVS=varlist
*'    /MODEL=option /PRINT=option .
*' Where ES is the effect size variable, W is the inverse
*' variance weight, IVS is the list of independent variables
*' and MODEL is either FE for a fixed effects model, MM for
*' a random effects model estimated via the method of moments,
```

```
*' ML and REML are random effects models estimated via iterative maximum likelihood,
*' the latter using restricted maximum likelihood. If /MODEL is omitted, FE is the
*' default. The /PRINT subcommand has the option EXP and
*' if specified will print the exponent of the B coefficient
*' (the odds-ratio) rather than beta. If /PRINT is omitted,
*' beta is printed.
*' Example:
*'
*' metareg es = effct /w = invweght /ivs = txvar1 txvar2
*'    /model = fe .
*'

*------------------------------------------------------------
preserve
set printback=off
define metareg (es=!charend('/')
/w=!charend('/') /ivs=!charend('/')
/model = !default('FE') !charend('/')
/print = !default('RAW') !charend('/'))
preserve
set printback=off mprint off

*------------------------------------------------------------
* Enter matrix mode
*------------------------------------------------------------
matrix

*------------------------------------------------------------
*  Get data from active file
*------------------------------------------------------------
get data /file * /variables = !es !w !ivs /missing omit

*------------------------------------------------------------
*  Create vectors and matrices
*------------------------------------------------------------.
compute es = data(1:nrow(data),1) .
compute w = data(1:nrow(data),2) .
compute x = make(nrow(data),ncol(data)-1,1) .
do if ncol(data)>3 .
+ compute x(1:nrow(data),2:(ncol(data)-1))=
                data(1:nrow(data),3:(ncol(data))).
+ else if ncol(data)=3 .
+ compute x(1:nrow(data),2)=data(1:nrow(data),3).
end if .
compute p = make(1,ncol(x),1) .
compute k = make(1,nrow(x),1) .
compute v = (w&**-1) .
release data .

*------------------------------------------------------------
*  Recompute weights for random effects models
*  Method of moments
*------------------------------------------------------------.
!IF (!model !eq 'MM'|!model !eq 'mm'|!model !eq 'ML'|
   !model !eq 'ml'|!model !eq 'REML'|!model !eq 'reml') !THEN .
compute xwx = T(x&*(w*p))*x .
compute B   = inv(xwx)*T(x&*(w*p))*es .
compute qe  = csum(es&*w&*es) - T(B)*xwx*B .
compute c = (qe-(nrow(es)-ncol(x)))/
      csum(w - rsum((x&*(w*p)*inv(T(x&*(w*p))*x))&*x&*(w*p))) .
do if c<0 .
+ compute c = 0 .
```

```
end if .
compute w   = 1/(v+c) .
!IFEND .

!IF (!model !eq 'ML' | !model !eq 'ml'||!model !eq 'REML'|
   !model !eq 'reml') !THEN .
compute c2 = c .
loop I=1 to 200 .
.compute loops = I .
.compute c = c2 .
.compute w = 1/(v + c) .
.compute xw = x&*(w*p) .
.compute xwx = T(xw)*x .
.compute B = inv(xwx)*T(xw)*es .
.compute r = es -x*B .
.compute c2 = csum(w&**2&*(r&**2 - v))/csum(w&**2) .
.do if c2<0 .
. compute c2 = 0 .
.end if .
end loop if abs(c2 - c)<.0000000001 .
compute c = c2 .
compute w = 1/(v + c) .
compute se_c = sqrt(2/csum(w&**2)) .
!IFEND .

!IF (!model !eq 'REML' | !model !eq 'reml') !THEN .
compute c = c2*(nrow(es)*inv(nrow(es)-ncol(x))) .
compute w = 1/(v + c) .
compute se_c = sqrt(2/csum(w&**2)) .
!IFEND .


*-----------------------------------------------------------
*  Compute Final Model
*-----------------------------------------------------------.
compute xw = x&*(w*p) .
compute xwx = T(xw)*x .
compute B = inv(xwx)*T(xw)*es .


*-----------------------------------------------------------
*  Compute Homogeneity Q for each B, for the fit of the
*  regression and for the residuals
*-----------------------------------------------------------.
compute meanes = csum(es&*w)/csum(w) .
compute q =  csum((meanes - es)&*(meanes - es)&*w) .
compute qe = csum(es&*w&*es) - T(B)*xwx*B .
compute qr = q - qe .
compute dfe = nrow(es)-ncol(x) .
compute dfr = ncol(x)-1 .
compute dft = nrow(es)-1 .
compute pe = 1 - chicdf(qe,dfe) .
compute pr = 1 - chicdf(qr,dfr) .
compute se = sqrt(diag(inv(xwx))) .
compute zvalues = B&/se .
compute pvalues = (1 - cdfnorm(abs(zvalues)))*2 .
compute lowerB = B - se*1.96 .
compute upperB = B + se*1.96 .


*-----------------------------------------------------------
*  Compute standardized coefficients (betas)
*-----------------------------------------------------------.
compute d = x - T(T(csum(x&*(w*p)))*k)&/csum(w) .
```

```
compute sx = sqrt(diag(T(d&*(w*p))*d&/csum(w))) .
compute sy = sqrt(q/csum(w)) .
compute beta = (B&*sx)&/sy .
compute r2 = qr/(qr+qe) .
!IF (!print !eq 'EXP'|!print !eq 'exp'|!print !eq 'Exp') !THEN .
compute beta = exp(B) .
!IFEND .

*------------------------------------------------------------
* Create results matrices
*------------------------------------------------------------.
compute homog = make(3,3,-999) .
compute homog(1,1) = qr .
compute homog(1,2) = dfr .
compute homog(1,3) = pr .
compute homog(2,1) = qe .
compute homog(2,2) = dfe .
compute homog(2,3) = pe .
compute homog(3,1) = q .
compute homog(3,2) = dft .
compute homog(3,3) = 1 - chicdf(q,dft) .

compute keep = make(ncol(x),7,-999) .
compute keep(1:ncol(x),1) = B .
compute keep(1:ncol(x),2) = se .
compute keep(1:ncol(x),3) = lowerB .
compute keep(1:ncol(x),4) = upperB .
compute keep(1:ncol(x),5) = zvalues .
compute keep(1:ncol(x),6) = pvalues .
compute keep(1:ncol(x),7) = beta .

compute descrpt = make(1,3,-999) .
compute descrpt(1,1) = meanes .
compute descrpt(1,2) = r2 .
compute descrpt(1,3) = nrow(es) .

*------------------------------------------------------------
* Print Results
*------------------------------------------------------------.
print
 /title " ***** Inverse Variance Weighted Regression *****" .
!IF (!model !eq 'ML' | !model !eq 'ml'|!model !eq 'MM'|
 !model !eq 'mm') !THEN .
 print
 /title " ***** Random Intercept, Fixed Slopes Model *****" .
!ELSE
 print
 /title " ***** Fixed Effects Model via OLS *****" .
!IFEND .

print descrpt /title "------- Descriptives -------"
 /clabel "Mean ES" "R-Squared" "N"
 /format f12.4 .
print homog /title "------- Homogeneity Analysis -------"
 /clabel "Q" "df" "p"
 /rlabel "Model" "Residual" "Total"
 /format f12.4 .
!IF (!print !eq 'EXP'|!print !eq 'exp'|!print !eq 'Exp') !THEN .
print keep /title "------- Regression Coefficients -------"
 /clabel "B" "SE" "-95% CI" "+95% CI" "Z" "P" "EXP(B)"
 /rlabel "Constant" !ivs
```

```
   /format f8.4 .
 !ELSE
 print keep /title "------- Regression Coefficients -------"
    /clabel "B"  "SE" "-95% CI" "+95% CI" "Z" "P" "Beta"
    /rlabel "Constant" !ivs
    /format f8.4 .
 !IFEND .

 !IF (!model !eq 'MM'|!model !eq 'mm') !THEN .
 print c
    /title  "------- Method of Moments Random Effects Variance"+
    " Component ------- "
    /rlabel "v    ="
    /format f8.5 .
 !IFEND .
 !IF (!model !eq 'ML' | !model !eq 'ml') !THEN .
 + compute mlc     = make(2,1,-999) .
 + compute mlc(1,1) = c .
 + compute mlc(2,1) = se_c .
 + print mlc
    /title  "------- Maximum Likelihood Random Effects"+
    " Variance Component ------- "
    /rlabel "v    =" "se(v) ="
    /format f8.5 .
 !IFEND .
 !IF (!model !eq 'REML' | !model !eq 'reml') !THEN .
 + compute mlc     = make(2,1,-999) .
 + compute mlc(1,1) = c .
 + compute mlc(2,1) = se_c .
 + print mlc
    /title  "------- Restricted Maximum Likelihood Random"+
    " Effects Variance Component ------- "
    /rlabel "v    =" "se(v) ="
    /format f8.5 .
 !IFEND .


 *-------------------------------------------------------------
 * End matrix mode
 *-------------------------------------------------------------
 end matrix


 *-------------------------------------------------------------
 * Restore settings and exit
 *-------------------------------------------------------------
 restore
 !enddefine
 restore
```

Appendix E

Coding Manual and Coding Forms for the Example Meta-Analysis of Challenge Programs for Juvenile Delinquents

STUDY-LEVEL CODING MANUAL

Bibliographic reference: Write a complete citation in (approx.) APA form. ˙

1. Study ID Number. Assign a unique identification number to each study. If a report presents two independent studies, i.e., two independent outcome studies with different participants, then add a decimal to the study ID number to distinguish each study within a report and code each independent study separately.

2. What type of publication is the report? If two separate reports are being used to code a single study, code the type of the more formally published report (i.e., book or journal article).

   1 book
   2 journal article or book chapter
   3 thesis or doctoral dissertation

   4 technical report
   5 conference paper
   6 other (specify)

3. What is the publication year (last two digits; 99 if unknown)? If two separate reports are being used to code a single study, code the publication year of the more formally published report.

Sample Descriptors

4. Mean age of sample. Specify the approximate or exact mean age at the beginning of the intervention. Code the best information available; estimate mean age from grade levels if necessary. If mean age cannot be determined, enter "99.99."

5. Predominant race. Select the code that best describes the racial makeup of the sample.

   1 greater than 60% White
   2 greater than 60% Black
   3 greater than 60% Hispanic
   4 greater than 60% other minority

   5 mixed, none more than 60%
   6 mixed, cannot estimate proportion
   9 cannot tell

6. Predominant sex of sample. Select the code that best describes the proportion of males in the sample.

1 less than 5% male
2 between 5% and 50% male
3 50% male

4 between 50% and 95% male
5 greater than 95% male
9 cannot tell

7. Select the code that best describes the predominate level of delinquency risk of the juveniles at onset of treatment.

01 nondelinquent "normal" kids (no evidence of law enforcement contact, juvenile justice contact, or illegal behavior)

02 nondelinquent juveniles with risk factors (no evidence of law enforcement contact, juvenile justice contact, or illegal behavior, but risk factors such as poverty, family problems, school behavior problems, Glueck scale scores, teacher referrals, etc.)

03 predelinquent children, minor police contact (no formal probation or court contact, minor self-reported delinquency, minor drug infractions, traffic and status offenses, etc.)

04 delinquents, probation or adjudication

05 institutionalized, nonjuvenile justice setting

06 institutionalized, juvenile justice setting

07 mixed (nondelinquent and predelinquent)

08 mixed (predelinquent and delinquent)

09 mixed (full range)

99 cannot tell

Research Design Descriptors

8. Unit of assignment to conditions. Select the code that best describes the unit of assignment to treatment and control groups.

1 individual juvenile
2 classroom, facility

3 program area, regions, etc.
9 cannot tell

9. Type of assignment to conditions. Select the code that best describes how subjects were assigned to treatment and control groups.

1 random after matching, stratification, blocking, etc.
2 random, simple (also includes systematic sampling)
3 nonrandom, post hoc matching

4 nonrandom, other
5 other (specify)
9 cannot tell

10. Overall confidence of judgment on how subjects were assigned.

1 very low (little basis)
2 low (guess)
3 moderate (weak inference)

4 high (strong inference)
5 very high (explicitly stated)

11. Was the equivalence of the groups tested at pretest?

    1 yes   2 no

12. Pretest differences, if tested. Note: an "important" difference means a difference on several variables, or on a major variable, or large differences; major variables are those likely to be related to delinquency, e.g., history of delinquency or antisocial behavior, delinquency risk, sex, age, ethnicity, SES. Pretest differences on an outcome variable should be coded as important.

    1 negligible differences, judged unimportant
    2 some difference, judged of uncertain importance
    3 some differences, judged important

13. Total sample size (start of study).

14. Treatment group sample size (start of study).

15. Control group sample size (start of study).

Nature of the Treatment Descriptors

16. Treatment style or orientation. Indicate the dominant therapeutic style of the program. Look for explicit mention of therapeutic technique in the report or infer from description of group therapy sessions. See program description paper for definitions of therapeutic styles. If the program uses more than one style, indicate the one that appears most central to the treatment. If you cannot decide between two types, indicate both in the "other" category. If there is no explicit mention of a therapeutic style, code it as experiential.

    1 experiential therapy   4 punitive therapy
    2 cognitive–behavioral therapy   8 other–combination (specify)
      (inc. reality therapy)
    3 insight therapy

17. Type of activity. Indicate whether the challenge activities were natural (e.g., outdoor rock climbing, river rafting), contrived (e.g., ropes courses, indoor climbing walls), or both.

    1 natural   2 contrived   3 both

18. Is the program primarily a challenge-type treatment? Code as "yes" if the treatment exclusively or mostly involves the challenge activities, including wilderness challenge programs that use individual and group therapeutic techniques. Look for explicit statements of other primary treatments; these programs would be coded as "no." Programs in which participants spend a majority of their time doing nonchallenging activities would also be coded no.

    1 yes   2 no

19. Did the program occur in a wilderness setting? Code as yes if the activities took place outdoors, even if the participants were camping in cabins or other buildings. Code as no if the activities that took place indoors or used man-made contraptions.

    1 yes   2 no

20. Was it a residential program? Code yes if participants resided away from home continuously throughout the program. Code weekend camping and after school programs as no.

    1 yes   2 no

21. Treatment duration in weeks (missing = 999). Approximate (or exact) duration of treatment in weeks from first treatment event to last treatment event, excluding follow-ups designated as such (divide number of days by 7 and round; multiply number of months by 4.3 and round). Estimate, if necessary.

22. Intensity of treatment

    1 low intensity, e.g., low ropes courses, "trust falls"

    2

    3

    4 e.g., high ropes courses, day hikes, indoor

    5 climbing, cabin camping, etc.

    6

    7

    8 high intensity, e.g., white water rafting, backpacking

23. Nature of control group

    01 receives nothing; no evidence of any treatment or attention; may still be in school or on probation, etc., but it is incidental to the treatment strategy or client population as defined

    02 wait list; delayed treatment control, etc.; contact limited to application, screening, pretest, posttest, etc.

    03 minimal contact; instructions, intake interview, etc., but not wait listed

    04 treatment as usual, school setting; control receives the usual treatment in a school setting without the special enhancement that constitutes the treatment of interest; this refers to treatment occurring within a framework common to experimental and control groups with something added for the experimental group

    05 treatment as usual, probation; control receives the usual treatment of probation without the special enhancement that constitutes the treatment of interest; this refers to treatment occurring within a framework common to experimental and control groups with something added for the experimental group

    06 treatment as usual, institutionalization; control receives the usual treatment of institutionalization without the special enhancement that constitutes the treatment of interest; this refers to treatment occurring within a framework common to experimental and control groups with something added for the experimental group

    07 treatment as usual, other (specify)

    08 attention placebo, e.g., control group receives discussion, attention, or deliberately diluted version of treatment

    09 treatment element placebo; control receives target treatment except for defined element presumed to be the crucial ingredient

    10 alternative treatment; control is not really a control but another treatment (other than usual treatment) being compared with the focal treatment; only eligible if the alternative treatment is designed as a contrast and is not expected to work very well (straw man)

    99 cannot tell

24. Overall confidence rating of judgment on the nature of the control group

1 very low (little basis)	4 high (strong inference)
2 low (guess)	5 very high (explicitly stated)
3 moderate (weak inference)	

EFFECT SIZE LEVEL CODING MANUAL

For each effect size, code all of the following items. Note that studies will have different numbers of effect sizes, and hence, different numbers of effect size level data coding forms.

1. Study ID number. Identification number of the study from which the offset size is coded.

2. Effect size number. Assign each effect size within a study a unique number. Number multiple effect sizes within a study sequentially, e.g., 1, 2, 3, 4, etc.

Dependent Measure Descriptors

3. Effect size type. Code an effect size as a pretest comparison if the measures being compared across groups were taken prior to the intervention, including risk factors, such as sex and race. Posttest effect sizes are the first reported comparison between the groups following the intervention. For example, if recidivism at 6 months following the challenge program is the earliest posttreatment recidivism measure, then it should be coded as a posttest comparison. Code any effect sizes measured at future points in time as follow-up comparisons. [*Note: the example database includes only posttest comparison effect sizes.*]

    1 pretest comparison, including risk factors (e.g., sex and race)
    2 posttest comparison
    3 follow-up comparison

4. Approximate (or exact) time period covered by pretest delinquency measure in weeks. This means the period over which counted delinquency occurred. Use number of weeks rounded to nearest whole number (divide days by 7, multiply months by 4.3, code 999 if cannot tell, code 888 if total prior history covered).

5. Category of outcome construct

   1 delinquency–antisocial behavior   4 self-esteem–self-concept
   2 interpersonal skills   5 other psychological measure
   3 locus of control   6 other (specify)

6. Outcome descriptor: Write in a description of the outcome variable.
7. Social desirability response bias. Rate the extent to which this measure seems susceptible to social desirability response bias. At one end of the continuum would be measures based on objective procedures administered by impartial others, e.g., random surprise drug testing. At the other end would be the juvenile's own reports made to someone with authority over him/her.

   1 very low potential
   2
   3
   4
   5
   6
   7 very high potential
   8 not applicable

Effect Size Data

8. Type of data effect size based on

   1 means and standard deviations   5 frequencies or proportions,
   2 t-value or F-value   polychotomous
   3 chi-square ($df = 1$)   6 other (specify)
   4 frequencies or proportions,
     dichotomous

9. Page number where the data for this effect size was found.
10. Raw difference favors (i.e., shows more success for) which group?

    1 treatment group   3 control group
    2 neither (exactly equal)   9 cannot tell or statistically insignificant
                                  report only

When means and standard deviations are reported or can be estimated:

11a. Treatment group sample size (write in appropriate number).
11b. Control group sample size (write in appropriate number).
12a. Treatment group mean (write in the value for the mean, if available).
12b. Control group mean (write in the value for the mean, if available).
13a. Treatment group standard deviation (write in the value for the sd, if available).
13b. Control group standard deviation (write in the value for the sd, if available).

When proportions or frequencies are reported or can be estimated:

14a. *n* of treatment group with a successful outcome (write in appropriate number).

14b. *n* of control group with a successful outcome (write in appropriate number).

15a. Proportion of treatment group with a successful outcome (write in the value, if available).

15b. Proportion of control group with a successful outcome (write in the value, if available).

When significance test information is reported:

16a. *t*-value (write in the value, if available).

16b. *F*-value (*df* for the numerator must equal 1) (write in the value, if available).

16c. Chi-square value (*df* = 1) (write in the value, if available).

Calculated Effect Size

17. Effect size using the Excel effect size determination program (see Appendix C) or calculated by hand using the procedures outlined in Appendix B. Report to two decimals with an algebraic sign in front: plus if difference favors treatment, minus if favors control; +9.99 if NA.

18. Confidence rating in effect size computation.

1 highly estimated (have *N* and crude *p*-value only, such as $p < .10$, and must reconstruct via rough *t*-test equivalence)

2 moderate estimation (have complex but relatively complete statistics, such as multifactor ANOVA, as basis for estimation)

3 some estimation (have unconventional statistics and must convert to equivalent *t*-values or have conventional statistics but incomplete, such as exact *p*-level).

4 slight estimation (must use significance testing statistics rather than descriptive statistics, but have complete statistics of conventional sort)

5 no estimation (have descriptive data such as means, standard deviations, frequencies, proportions, etc. and can calculate the effect size directly)

STUDY-LEVEL CODING FORM
[VARIABLE NAMES IN BRACKETS]

Bibliographic reference: _____

_____

_____

— — — — 1. Study ID number [STUDYID]

—   2. Type of publication [PUBTYPE]

      1 book   4 technical report
      2 journal article   5 conference paper
        or book chapter   6 other (specify):_____
      3 thesis or doctoral

— —   3. Publication year (last two digits; 99 if unknown)?
      [PUBYEAR]

Sample Descriptors

— — . — 4. Mean age [MEANAGE]

—   5. Predominant race [RACE]

      1 >60% White   5 mixed, none more than 60%
      2 >60% Black   6 mixed, cannot estimate
      3 >60% Hispanic   proportion
      4 >60% other   9 cannot tell
        minority

—   6. Predominant sex [SEX]

      1 <5% male
      2 5%–50% male
      3 50% male
      4 50%–95% male
      5 >95% male
      9 cannot tell

— —   7. Delinquency risk of juveniles at onset of treatment
      [RISK]

      01 nondelinquent, normal
      02 nondelinquent with risk factors
      03 predelinquent, minor police contact
      04 delinquents, probation or adjudication
      05 institutionalized, nonjuvenile justice setting
      06 institutionalized, juvenile justice setting
      07 mixed (nondelinquent and predelinquent)
      08 mixed (predelinquent and delinquent)
      09 mixed (full range)
      99 cannot tell

Research Design Descriptors

— 8. Unit of assignment to conditions [UNIT]

    1 individual juvenile
    2 classroom, facility
    3 program area, regions, etc.
    9 cannot tell

— 9. Type of assignment to conditions [ASSIGN]

    1 random after matching, stratification, blocking, etc.
    2 random, simple (also includes systematic sampling)
    3 nonrandom, post hoc matching
    4 nonrandom, other
    5 other_____
    9 cannot tell

— 10. Overall confidence of judgment on how subjects were assigned [CRASSIGN]

    1 very low (little basis)
    2 low (guess)
    3 moderate (weak inference)
    4 high (strong inference)
    5 very high (explicitly stated)

— 11. Was the equivalence of the groups tested at pretest? [PREEQUIV]

    1 yes 2 no

— 12. Pretest differences, if tested. [PREDIFFS]

    1 negligible differences, judged unimportant
    2 some difference, judged of uncertain importance
    3 some differences, judged important

— — — 13. Total sample size (start of study). [TOTALN]

— — — 14. Treatment group sample size (start of study). [ORIG_TXN]

— — — 15. Control group sample size (start of study). [ORIG_CGN]

Nature of the Treatment Descriptors

—   16. Treatment style or orientation [TX_TYPE]

    1 experiential therapy
    2 cognitive–behavioral therapy
    3 insight therapy
    4 punitive therapy
    8 other–combination_____

—   17. Type of activity [ACTIVITY]
    1 natural   2 contrived   3 both

—   18. Primarily a challenge-type treatment? [THRUST]
    1 yes   2 no

—   19. Occur in a wilderness setting? [WILDNESS]
    1 yes   2 no

—   20. Residential program? [RESIDENT]
    1 yes   2 no

— — — 21. Treatment duration in weeks (missing = 999)
       [DURATION]

—   22. Intensity of treatment (1 = low; 8 = high)
       [INTENSTY]

— —   23. Nature of control group [CMP_TYPE]

    01 receives nothing
    02 wait list
    03 minimal contact
    04 treatment as usual, school setting
    05 treatment as usual, probation
    06 treatment as usual, institutionalization
    07 treatment as usual, other
    08 attention placebo
    09 treatment element placebo
    10 alternative treatment
    99 cannot tell

—   24. Overall confidence, rating of the nature of the
       control group [CRCMPTYP]

    1 very low (little basis)
    2 low (guess)
    3 moderate (weak inference)
    4 high (strong inference)
    5 very high (explicitly stated)

EFFECT SIZE LEVEL CODING FORM
[VARIABLE NAMES IN BRACKETS]

_ _ _ _ 1. Study ID number [STUDYID]

_ _   2. Effect size sequence number [ESNUM]

Dependent Measure Descriptors

_   3. Effect size type [ESTYPE]

1 pretest comparison
2 posttest comparison
3 follow-up comparison

_ _ _ 4. Time period covered by pretest delinquency measure in weeks [TIMEDEL]

_ . '   5. Category of outcome construct [OUTCOME]

1 delinquency–antisocial behavior
2 interpersonal skills
3 locus of control
4 self-esteem–self-concept
5 other psychological measure
6 other_____

       6. Outcome descriptor_____

_   7. Social desirability response bias [SOCDESIR]
(1 = very low potential; 7 = very high potential; 8 = na)

Effect Size Data

_   8. Type of data effect size based on [ESTYPE]

1 means and standard deviations
2 t-value or F-value
3 chi-square ($df = 1$)
4 frequencies or proportions, dichotomous
5 frequencies or proportions, polychotomous
6 other_____

_ _ _ _ 9. Page number where effect size data found [PAGENUM]

_   10. Raw difference favors (i.e., shows more success for): [SUCCESS]

1 treatment group
2 neither (exactly equal)
3 control group
9 cannot tell or statistically insignificant report only

Sample Size

— — — 11a. Treatment group sample size [TXN]

— — — 11b. Control group sample size [CGN]

Means and Standard Deviations

— — — — 12a. Treatment group mean [TXMEAN]

— — — — 12b. Control group mean [CGMEAN]

— — — — 13a. Treatment group standard deviation [TXSD]

— — — — 13b. Control group standard deviation [CGSD]

Proportions or Frequencies

— — — — 14a. *n* of treatment group with a successful outcome [TXSUCCES]

— — — — 14b. *n* of control group with successful outcome [CGSUCCES]

— — — — 15a. Proportion of treatment group with a successful outcome [TXPROP]

— — — — 15b. Proportion of control group with a successful outcome [CGPROP]

Significance Tests

— — — — 16a. *t*-value [T_VALUE]

— — — — 16b. *F*-value (*df* for the numerator must = 1) [F_VALUE]

— — — — 16c. Chi-square value (*df* = 1) [CHISQUAR]

Calculated Effect Size

— — . — — 17. Effect size [ES]

—   18. Confidence rating in effect size computation [CR_ES]

    1 highly estimated
    2 moderate estimation
    3 some estimation
    4 slight estimation
    5 no estimation

Bibliography of Recommended Readings

Cook, T. D., Cooper, H., Cordray, D. S., Hartmann, H., Hedges, L. V., Light, R. J., Louis, T. A., & Mosteller F. (1992). *Meta-analysis for explanation: A casebook*. New York: Russell Sage Foundation.

Cooper, H. (1998). *Synthesizing research: A guide for literature reviews* (3d ed.). Thousand Oaks, CA: Sage.

Cooper, H., & Hedges, L. V. (Eds.). (1994). *The handbook of research synthesis*. New York: Russell Sage Foundation.

Durlak, J. A., & Lipsey, M. W. (1991). A practitioner's guide to meta-analysis. *American Journal of Community Psychology, 19*, 291–332.

Glass, G. V. (1976). Primary, secondary and meta-analysis of research. *Educational Researcher, 5*, 3–8.

Hedges, L. V. (1984). Advances in statistical methods for meta-analysis. *New Directions for Program Evaluation, 24*, 25–42.

Hedges, L. V., & Olkin, I. (1985). *Statistical methods for meta-analysis*. Orlando, FL: Academic Press.

Hunter, J. E., & Schmidt, F. L. (1990). *Methods of meta-analysis: Correcting error and bias in research findings*. Newbury Park, CA: Sage.

Overton, R. C. (1998). A comparison of fixed-effects and mixed (random-effects) models for meta-analysis tests of moderator variable effects. *Psychological Methods, 3*, 354–379.

Rosenthal, R. (1991). *Meta-analytic procedures for social research. Applied Social Research Methods Series* (Vol. 6). Thousand Oaks, CA: Sage.

Schmidt, F. L. (1992). What do data really mean? Research findings, meta-analysis, and cumulative knowledge in psychology. *American Psychologist, 47*, 1173–1181.

Sharpe, D. (1997). Of apples and oranges, file drawers and garbage: Why validity issues in meta-analysis will not go away. *Clinical Psychology Review, 17*, 881–901.

Slavin, R. E. (1986). Best-evidence synthesis: An alternative to meta-analytic and traditional reviews. *Educational Researcher, 15*, 5–11.

Wang, M.C., & Bushman, B.J. (1999). *Integrating results through meta-analytic review using SAS software*. Cary, NC: SAS Institute.

References

Alexander, R. A., Scozzaro, M. J., & Borodkin, L. J. (1989). Statistical and empirical examination of the chi-square test for homogeneity of correlations in meta-analysis. *Psychological Bulletin, 106*, 329–331.

Bangert-Drowns, R. L., Wells-Parker, E., & Chevillard, I. (1997). Assessing the methodological quality of research in narrative reviews and meta-analyses. In K. J. Bryant, M. Windle, & S. G. West (Eds.). *The science of prevention: Methodological advances from alcohol and substance abuse research* (pp. 405–429). Washington, DC: American Psychological Association.

Becker, B. J. (1988). Synthesizing standardized mean-change measures. *British Journal of Mathematical and Statistical Psychology, 41*, 257–278.

Becker, B. J. (1992). Models of science achievement: Forces affecting performance in school science. In T. D. Cook, H. Cooper, D. S. Cordray, H. Hartmann, L. V. Hedges, R. J. Light, T. A. Louis, & F. Mosteller (Eds.). *Meta-analysis for explanation: A casebook.* New York: Russell Sage Foundation.

Becker, B. J. (1994). Combining significance levels. In H. Cooper & L. V. Hedges (Eds.), *The handbook of research synthesis* (pp. 215–230). New York: Russell Sage Foundation.

Becker, G. (1996). The meta-analysis of factor analyses: An illustration based on the cumulation of correlation matrices. *Psychological Methods, 1*, 341–353.

Begg, C. B. (1994). Publication bias. In H. Cooper & L. V. Hedges (Eds.), *The handbook of research synthesis* (pp. 399–409). New York: Russell Sage Foundation.

Berlin, J. A., Laird, N. M., Sacks, H. S., & Chalmers, T. C. (1989). A comparison of statistical methods for combining event rates from clinical trials. *Statistics in Medicine, 8*, 141–151.

Borenstein, M. (2000). *Meta-analysis: Study database analyzer.* St. Paul, MN; Assessment Systems Corp. (Information available on the web at www.assess.com and www.meta-analysis.com).

Bozarth, J. D., & Roberts, R. R. (1972). Signifying significant significance. *American Psychologist, 27*, 774–775.

Bradley, M. T., & Gupta, R. D. (1997). Estimating the effect of the file drawer problem in meta-analysis. *Perceptual and Motor Skills, 85*, 719-722.

Bushman, B. J. (1994). Vote-counting procedures in meta-analysis. In H. Cooper & L. V. Hedges (Eds.). (1994). *The handbook of research synthesis* (pp. 193–213). New York: Russell Sage Foundation.

Bushman, B. J. & Wang, M. C. (1995). A procedure for combining sample correlation coefficients and vote counts to obtain an estimate and a confidence interval for the population correlation coefficient. *Psychological Bulletin, 117*, 530–546.

Bushman, B. J., & Wang, M. C. (1996). A procedure for combining sample standardized mean differences and vote counts to estimate the population standardized mean difference in fixed effects models. *Psychological Methods, 1*, 66–80.

Cedar, B., & Levant, R. F. (1990). A meta-analysis of the effects of parent effectiveness training. *American Journal of Family Therapy, 47*, 373–384.

Chalmers, T. C., Berrier, J., Sack, H. S., Levin, H., Reitman, D., & Nagalingam, R. (1987). Meta-analysis of clinical trials as a scientific discipline. *Statistics in Medicine, 6*, 733–744.

Chalmers, T. C., Smith, H., Jr., Blackburn, B., Silverman, B., Schroeder, B., Reitman, D., & Ambroz, A. (1981). A method for assessing the quality of a randomized control trial. *Controlled Clinical Trials, 2*, 31–49.

Cleary, R. J., & Casella, G. (1997). An application of Gibbs sampling to estimation in meta-analysis: Accounting for publication bias. *Journal of Educational and Behavioral Statistics, 22*, 141–154.

Cochrane Collaboration (2000). Review Manager (RevMan). Information available on the web at www.cochrane.org.

Cohen, J. (1977). *Statistical power analysis for the behavioral sciences* (Rev. ed.). New York: Academic Press.

Cohen, J. (1988). *Statistical power analysis for the behavioral sciences* (2nd ed.). Hillsdale, NJ: Erlbaum.

Cohen, J., & Cohen, P. (1975). *Applied multiple regression/correlation analysis for the behavioral sciences*. Hillsdale, NJ: Lawrence Erlbaum.

Cook, T. D., Cooper, H., Cordray, D. S., Hartmann, H., Hedges, L. V., Light, R. J., Louis, T. A., & Mosteller, F. (1992). *Meta-analysis for explanation: A casebook*. New York: Russell Sage Foundation.

Cooper, H. M. (1989). *Integrating research: A guide for literature reviews* (2nd ed.). Newbury Park, CA: Sage.

Cooper, H., & Hedges, L. V. (Eds.). (1994). *The handbook of research synthesis*. New York: Russell Sage Foundation.

DerSimonian, R., & Laird, N. (1986). Meta-analysis in clinical trials. *Controlled Clinical Trials, 7*, 177–188.

Dobson, K. S. (1989). A meta-analysis of the efficacy of cognitive therapy for depression. *Journal of Consulting and Clinical Psychology, 57*, 414–419.

Durlak, J. A., Fuhrman, T., & Lampman, C. (1991). Effectiveness of cognitive behavior therapy for maladapting children: A meta-analysis. *Psychological Bulletin, 110*, 204–214.

Elvik, R. (1998). Evaluating the statistical conclusion validity of weighted mean results in meta-analysis by analyzing funnel graph diagrams. *Accident Analysis and Prevention, 30*, 255–266.

Eysenck, H. J. (1952). The effects of psychotherapy: An evaluation. *Journal of Consulting Psychology, 16*, 319–324.

Eysenck, H. J. (1978). An exercise in mega-silliness. *American Psychologist, 33*, 517.

Fleiss, J. L. (1994). Measures of effect size for categorical data. In H. Cooper & L. V. Hedges (Eds.), *The handbook of research synthesis* (pp. 245–260). New York: Russell Sage Foundation.

Garrett, C. J. (1985). Effects of residential treatment on adjudicated delinquents: A meta-analysis. *Journal of Research in Crime and Delinquency, 45*, 287–308.

Gibbs, L. E. (1989). Quality of study rating form: An instrument for synthesizing evaluation studies. *Journal of Social Work Education, 25*, 55–67.

Glass, G. V. (1976). Primary, secondary and meta-analysis of research. *Educational Researcher, 5*, 3–8.

Glass, G. V., McGaw, B., & Smith, M. L. (1981). *Meta-analysis in social research*. Beverly Hills, CA: Sage.

Gleser, L. J., & Olkin, I. (1994). Stochastically dependent effect sizes. In H. Cooper & L. V. Hedges (Eds.). (1994). *The handbook of research synthesis* (pp. 339–355). New York: Russell Sage Foundation.

Greenland, S. (1994). Invited commentary: A critical look at some popular meta-analytic methods. *American Journal of Epidemiology, 140,* 290–296.

Greenwald, R., Hedges, L. V., & Laine, R. D. (1994). When reinventing the wheel is not necessary: A case study in the use of meta-analysis in education finance. *Journal of Education Finance, 20,* 1–20.

Guilford, J. P. (1965). *Fundamental statistics in psychology and education* (4th ed.). New York, McGraw-Hill.

Haddock, C. K., Rindskopf, D., & Shadish, W. R. (1998). Using odds ratios as effect sizes for meta-analysis of dichotomous data: A primer on methods and issues. *Psychological Methods, 3,* 339–353.

Hall, J. A., & Rosenthal, R. (1995). Interpreting and evaluating meta-analysis. *Evaluation and the Health Professions, 18,* 393–407.

Hasselblad, V., & Hedges, L. V. (1995). Meta-analysis of screening and diagnostic tests. *Psychological Bulletin, 117,* 167–178.

Hauck, W. W. (1989). Odds ratio inference from stratified samples. *Communications in Statistics, 18A,* 767–800.

Hays, W. L. (1988). *Statistics* (4th ed.). Fort Worth, TX: Holt, Rinehart and Winston.

Hedges, L. V. (1981). Distribution theory for Glass's estimator of effect size and related estimators. *Journal of Educational Statistics, 6,* 107–128.

Hedges, L. V. (1982a). Fitting categorical models to effect sizes from a series of experiments. *Journal of Educational Statistics, 7,* 119–137.

Hedges, L. V. (1982b). Estimating effect size from a series of independent experiments. *Psychological Bulletin, 92,* 490–499.

Hedges, L. V. (1994). Statistical considerations. In H. Cooper & L. V. Hedges (Eds.), *The handbook of research synthesis* (pp. 29–38). New York: Russell Sage Foundation.

Hedges, L. V., & Olkin, I. (1985). *Statistical methods for meta-analysis.* Orlando, FL: Academic Press.

Hedges, L. V., & Vevea, J. L. (1996). Estimating effect size under publication bias: Small sample properties and robustness of a random effects selection model. *Journal of Educational and Behavioral Statistics, 21,* 299–332.

Hedges, L. V., & Vevea, J. L. (1998). Fixed- and random-effects models in meta-analysis. *Psychological Methods, 3,* 486–504.

Heinsman, D. T., & Shadish, W. R. (1996). Assignment methods in experimentation: When do nonrandomized experiments approximate the answers from randomized experiments? *Psychological Methods, 1,* 154–169.

Huffcutt, A. I., & Arthur, W. (1995). Development of a new outlier statistic for meta-analytic data. *Journal of Applied Psychology, 80,* 327–334.

Hunter, J. E., & Schmidt, F. L. (1990a). Dichotomization of continuous variables: The implications for meta-analysis. *Journal of Applied Psychology, 75,* 334–349.

Hunter, J. E., & Schmidt, F. L. (1990b). *Methods of meta-analysis: Correcting error and bias in research findings.* Newbury Park, CA: Sage.

Hunter, J. E., & Schmidt, F. L. (1994). Correcting for sources of artificial variation across studies. In H. Cooper & L. V. Hedges (Eds.), *The handbook of research synthesis* (pp. 323–336). New York: Russell Sage Foundation.

Hunter, J. E., Schmidt, F. L., & Jackson, G. B. (1982). *Meta-analysis: Cumulating research findings across studies.* Beverly Hills, CA: Sage.

Jacobson, N. S., & Truax, P. (1991). Clinical significance: A statistical approach to defining meaningful change in psychotherapy research. *Journal of Consulting and Clinical Psychology, 59,* 12–19.

Johnson, B. T. (1989). *DSTAT: Software for the meta-analytic review of research literatures.* Hillsdale, NJ: Erlbaum.

Kalaian, H. A., & Raudenbush, S. W. (1996). A multivariate mixed linear model for meta-analysis. *Psychological Methods, 1,* 227–235.

Kraemer, H. C., Gardner, C., Brooks, J. O., III, & Yesavage, J. A.(1998). Advantages of excluding underpowered studies in meta-analysis: Inclusionist versus exclusionist viewpoints. *Psychological Methods, 3,* 23–31.

Landman, J. T., & Dawes, R. M. (1982). Psychotherapy outcome: Smith and Glass conclusions stand up under scrutiny. *American Psychologist, 37,* 504–516.

Lehman, A. F. and Cordray, D. S. (1993) Prevalence of alcohol, drug and mental disorders among the homeless: One more time. *Contemporary Drug Problems: An Interdisciplinary Quarterly, 20,* 355–384.

Light, R. J., & Pillemer, D. B. (1984). *Summing up: The science of reviewing research.* Cambridge, MA: Harvard University Press.

Light, R. J., Singer, J. D., & Willett, J. B. (1994). The visual presentation and interpretation of meta-analyses. In H. Cooper & L. V. Hedges (Eds.), *The handbook of research synthesis* (pp. 439–453). New York: Russell Sage Foundation.

Lipsey, M. W. (1990). *Design sensitivity: Statistical power for experimental research.* Newbury Park, CA: Sage.

Lipsey, M. W. (1992). Juvenile delinquency treatment: A meta-analytic inquiry into the variability of effects. In T. D. Cook, H. Cooper, D. S. Cordray, H. Hartmann, L. V. Hedges, R. J. Light, T. A. Louis, & F. Mosteller (Eds.), *Meta-analysis for explanation: A casebook* (pp. 83–127). New York: Russell Sage Foundation.

Lipsey, M. W., & Derzon, J. H. (1998). Predictors of violent or serious delinquency in adolescence and early adulthood: A synthesis of longitudinal research. In R. Loeber & D. P. Farrington (Eds.). *Serious and violent juvenile offenders: Risk factors and successful interventions.* Thousand Oaks, CA: Sage, 1998.

Lipsey, M. W., & Wilson, D. B. (1993). The efficacy of psychological, educational, and behavioral treatment: Confirmation from meta-analysis. *American Psychologist, 48,* 1181–1209.

Lipsey, M. W., Wilson, D. B., Cohen, M. A., & Derzon, J. D. (1996). Is there a causal relationship between alcohol use and violence? A synthesis of evidence. In M. Galanter (Ed.). *Recent developments in alcoholism, Volume 13: Alcoholism and violence* (pp. 245–282). New York: Plenum.

Little, R. J. A., & Rubin, D. B. (1987). *Statistical analysis with missing data.* New York: Wiley.

Matt, G. E. (1989). Decision rules for selecting effect sizes in meta-analysis: A review and reanalysis of psychotherapy outcome studies. *Psychological Bulletin, 105,* 106–115.

McGuire, J., Bates, G. W., Dretzke, B. J., McGivern, E., Rembold, K. L., Seabold, D. R., Turpin, B. M., & Levin, J. R. (1985). Methodological quality as a component of meta-analysis. *Educational Psychologist, 20,* 1–5.

McNemar, Q. (1960). At random: Sense and nonsense. *American Psychologist, 15,* 295–300.

McNemar, Q. (1966). *Psychological statistics* (3rd ed.). New York: John Wiley and Sons.

Mosteller, F., & Colditz, G. A. (1996). Understanding research synthesis (meta-analysis). *Annual Review of Public Health, 17,* 1–23.

Mullen, B. (1989). *Advanced BASIC meta-analysis.* Hillsdale, NJ: Erlbaum.

Mullen, B., & Rosenthal, R. (1985). *BASIC meta-analysis: Procedures and programs.* Hillsdale, NJ: Erlbaum.

Olkin, I. (1992). Meta-analysis: Methods for combining independent studies. *Statistical Science*, *7*, 226.

Orwin, R. G. (1983). A fail-safe *N* for effect size in meta-analysis. *Journal of Educational Statistics*, *8*, 157–159.

Orwin, R. G. (1994). Evaluating coding decisions. In H. Cooper & L. V. Hedges (Eds.), *The handbook of research synthesis* (pp. 139–162). New York: Russell Sage Foundation.

Orwin, R. G., & Cordray, D. S. (1985). Effects of deficient reporting on meta-analysis: A conceptual framework and reanalysis. *Psychological Bulletin*, *97*, 134–147.

Overton, R. C. (1998). A comparison of fixed-effects and mixed (random-effects) models for meta-analysis tests of moderator variable effects. *Psychological Methods*, *3*, 354–379.

Premack, S. L., & Hunter, J. E. (1988). Individual unionization decisions. *Psychological Bulletin*, *103*, 223–34.

Pigott, T. D. (1994). Methods for handling missing data in research synthesis. In H. Cooper & L. V. Hedges (Eds.), *The handbook of research synthesis* (pp. 163–175). New York: Russell Sage Foundation.

Raudenbush, S. W. (1994). Random effects models. In H. Cooper & L. V. Hedges (Eds.), *The handbook of research synthesis* (pp. 301–321). New York: Russell Sage Foundation.

Rosenberg, M. S., Adams, D. C., & Gurevitch, J. (1997). *Metawin: Statistical software for meta-analysis with resampling tests.* Sunderland, MA: Sinauer Associates.

Rosenthal, R. (1979). The "file drawer problem" and tolerance for null results. *Psychological Bulletin*, *86*, 638–641.

Rosenthal, R. (1984). *Meta-analytic procedures for social research.* Beverly Hills, CA: Sage.

Rosenthal, R. (1991). *Meta-analytic procedures for social research. Applied Social Research Methods Series* (Vol. 6). Thousand Oaks, CA: Sage.

Rosenthal, R. (1994). Statistically describing and combing studies. In H. Cooper & L. V. Hedges (Eds.), *The handbook of research synthesis* (pp. 231–244). New York: Russell Sage Foundation.

Rosenthal, R., & Rubin, D. B. (1978). Interpersonal expectancy effects: The first 345 studies. *The Behavioral and Brain Sciences*, *3*, 377–415.

Rosenthal, R., & Rubin, D. B. (1982). Comparing effect sizes of independent studies. *Psychological Bulletin*, *92*, 500–504.

Rosenthal, R., & Rubin, D. B. (1983). A simple, general purpose display of magnitude of experimental effect. *Journal of Educational Psychology*, *74*(2), 166–169.

Rubin, D. B. (1987). *Multiple imputation for nonresponse in surveys.* New York: Wiley.

Sacks, H. S., Berrier, J., Reitman, D., Axcona-Berk, V. A., & Chalmers, T. C. (1987). Meta-analyses of randomized controlled trials. *New England Journal of Medicine*, *316*, 450–455.

Schmidt, F. L. (1992). What do data really mean? Research findings, meta-analysis, and cumulative knowledge in psychology. *American Psychologist*, *47*, 1173–1181.

Schmidt, F. L. (1996). Statistical significance testing and cumulative knowledge in psychology: Implications for training of researchers. *Psychological Methods*, *1*, 115–129.

Schmidt, F. L., & Hunter, J. E. (1977). Development of a general solution to the problem of validity generalization. *Journal of Applied Psychology*, *62*, 529–540.

Schulz, K. F., Chalmers, I., Hayes, R. J., & Altman, D. G. (1995). Empirical evidence of bias: Dimensions of methodological quality associated with estimates of treatment effects in controlled trials. *Journal of the American Medical Association*, *273*, 408–412.

Schwarzer, R. (1996). *Meta-analysis programs.* Unpublished manuscript, Göttingen: Hogrefe. (Available on the web at www.yorku.ca/faculty/academic/schwarze/meta_e.htm).

Sechrest, L., McKnight, P., & McKnight, K. (1996). Calibration of measures for psychotherapy outcome studies. *American Psychologist, 51*, 1065–1071.

Sellers, D. E., Crawford, S. L., Bullock, K., & McKinlay, J. B. (1997). Understanding the variability in the effectiveness of community heart health programs: A meta-analysis. *Social Science & Medicine, 44*, 1325–1339.

Shadish, W. R., Jr. (1992). Do family and marital psychotherapies change what people do? A meta-analysis of behavioral outcomes. In T. D. Cook, H. Cooper, D. S. Cordray, H. Hartmann, L. V. Hedges, R. J. Light, T. A. Louis, & F. Mosteller (Eds.), *Meta-analysis for explanation: A casebook* (pp. 129–208). New York: Russell Sage Foundation.

Shadish, W. R., & Haddock, C. K. (1994). Combining estimates of effect size. In H. Cooper & L. V. Hedges (Eds.), *The handbook of research synthesis* (pp. 261–281). New York: Russell Sage Foundation.

Shadish, W. R., Robinson, L., & Lu, C. (1999). *ES: Effect size calculator.* St. Paul, MN: Assessment Systems Corp. (Information available on the web at www.assess.com).

Shapiro, D. A., & Shapiro, D. (1982). Meta-analysis of comparative therapy outcome studies: A replication and refinement. *Psychological Bulletin, 92*, 581–604.

Sharpe, D. (1997). Of apples and oranges, file drawers and garbage: Why validity issues in meta-analysis will not go away. *Clinical Psychology Review, 17*, 881–901.

Sindhu, F., Carpenter, L., & Seers, K. (1997). Development of a tool to rate the quality assessment of randomized controlled trials using a Delphi technique. *Journal of Advanced Nursing, 25*, 1262–1268.

Slavin, R. E. (1986). Best-evidence synthesis: An alternative to meta-analytic and traditional reviews. *Educational Researcher, 15*, 5–11.

Slavin, R. E. (1995). Best evidence synthesis: An intelligent alternative to meta-analysis. *Journal of Clinical Epidemiology, 48*, 9–18.

Smith, M. L. (1980). Publication bias and meta-analysis. *Evaluation in Education, 4*, 22–24.

Smith, M. L., & Glass, G. V. (1977). Meta-analysis of psychotherapy outcome studies. *American Psychologist, 32*, 752–760.

Smith, M. L., Glass, G. V., & Miller, T. I. (1980). *The benefits of psychotherapy.* Baltimore, MD: John Hopkins.

Stauffer, J. M. (1996). A graphical user interface psychometric meta-analysis program for DOS. *Educational and Psychological Measurement, 56*, 675–677.

Stock, W. A. (1994). Systematic coding for research synthesis. In H. Cooper & L. V. Hedges (Eds.), *The handbook of research synthesis* (pp. 125–138). New York: Russell Sage Foundation.

Stock, W. A., Benito, J. G., & Lasa, N. B. (1996). Research synthesis: Coding and conjectures. *Evaluation and the Health Professions, 19*, 104–117.

Vevea, J. L., & Hedges, L. V. (1995). A general linear model for estimating effect size in the presence of publication bias. *Psychometrika, 60*, 419–435.

Wang, M. C., & Bushman, B. J. (1998). *Integrating results through meta-analytic review using SAS software.* Cary, NC: SAS Institute, Inc.

Weisz, J. R., Donenberg, G. R., Han, S. S., & Weiss, B. (1995). Bridging the gap between laboratory and clinic in child and adolescent psychotherapy. *Journal of Consulting and Clinical Psychology, 63*, 688–701.

Weiss, B., & Weisz, J. R. (1990). The impact of methodological factors on child psychotherapy outcome research: A meta-analysis for researchers. *Journal of Abnormal Child Psychology, 18*, 639–670.

Weisz, J. R., Weiss, B. D., & Donenberg, G. R. (1992). The lab versus the clinic: Effects of child and adolescent psychotherapy. *American Psychologist, 47*, 1578–1585.

Wilson, D. B. (1995). *The role of method in treatment effect estimates: Evidence from psychological, behavioral, and educational treatment intervention meta-analyses.* Doctoral dissertation, Claremont Graduate School, Claremont, CA.

Wilson, D. B., Gallagher, C. A., Coggeshall, M. B., & MacKenzie, D. L. (1999). A quantitative review and description of corrections-based education, vocation, and work programs. *Corrections Management Quarterly, 3*, 8–18.

Wolf, F. M. (1986). *Meta-analysis: Quantitative methods for research synthesis.* Beverly Hills, CA: Sage.

Wolf, I. M., (1990). Methodological observations on bias. In K. W. Wachter & M. L. Straf (Eds.). *The future of meta-analysis* (pp. 139–151). New York: Russell Sage Foundation.

Wortman, P. M. (1994). Judging research quality. In H. Cooper & L. V. Hedges (Eds.), *The handbook of research synthesis* (pp. 97–109). New York: Russell Sage Foundation.

Yeaton, W. H., & Wortman, P. M. (1993). On the reliability of meta-analytic reviews: The role of intercoder agreement. *Evaluation Review, 17*, 292–309.

Index

About the Authors

Mark W. Lipsey is Professor of Public Policy at Vanderbilt University's Peabody College where he also serves as Co-director of the Center for Evaluation Research and Methodology at the Vanderbilt Institute for Public Policy Studies. His professional interests are in the areas of program evaluation, social intervention, field research methodology, and research synthesis. The foci of his recent meta-analytic research are risk and intervention for juvenile delinquency and issues of methodological quality in program evaluation research. His other books include *Design Sensitivity: Statistical Power for Experimental Research* and (with Peter Rossi and Howard Freeman) *Evaluation: A Systematic Approach* (6th ed.). Professor Lipsey is a former Editor-in-Chief of *New Directions for Evaluation* and serves on the editorial boards of *The American Journal of Evaluation, New Directions in Evaluation, Evaluation and Program Planning*, and *The American Journal of Community Psychology*. He is a recipient of the American Evaluation Association's Paul Lazarsfeld Award and a Fellow of the American Psychological Society.

David B. Wilson received his doctorate in applied social psychology from Claremont Graduate University in 1995. He has conducted meta-analyses on a range of topics, including the effectiveness of juvenile delinquency interventions, the effects of sugar on children's behavior, the effects of alcohol on violent behavior, and the effectiveness of school-based prevention programs. In his current position as Jerry Lee Assistant Research Professor in the Department of Criminology and Criminal Justice at the University of Maryland, he is engaged in meta-analytic projects examining effective strategies for the prevention of crime and violence and the rehabilitation of criminal offenders. In 1999, the American Evaluation Association honored him with the Marcia Guttentag Award for Early Promise as an Evaluator.

APPLIED SOCIAL RESEARCH
METHODS SERIES

Series Editors
LEONARD BICKMAN, Peabody College, Vanderbilt University, Nashville
DEBRA J. ROG, Vanderbilt University, Washington, DC

Other volumes in this series are listed on the series page